A Psychologist Looks at Marriage

SAMUEL TENENBAUM, Ph.D.

Long Island University

SOUTH BRUNSWICK AND NEW YORK:
A. S. BARNES AND COMPANY
LONDON: THOMAS YOSELOFF LTD

A. S. Barnes and Co., Inc.
Cranbury, New Jersey 08512

Thomas Yoseloff Ltd
18 Charing Cross Road
London, W.C. 2, England

6648

Printed in the United States of America

A PSYCHOLOGIST LOOKS AT
MARRIAGE

PREFACE

I have tried to present here what insights I have learned about the marital relationship in my practice as a psychologist. They were learned while listening to two human beings in agony and grief trying to come to grips with a relationship that was and is so crucial to them. You would think that two persons who give each other so much misery, whose very proximity arouses violent rages, where hatreds may mount until one may wish the other's death —you would think that such a relationship would be easy to sever. If there are those who think so, they suffer from a grievous error. What impresses me as a therapist is how, even in a bad marriage, each strives to preserve the marriage: how appalling, frightening, and traumatic is the prospect of its termination.

Nearly always both want the marriage preserved—not on the old basis, which they cannot endure, but on a changed basis. One wants the other altered, changed, remade, redone, refusing to understand or accommodate to the other as he is. Hence, instead of giving each other regard, admiration, acceptance, each transmits to the other a sense of his being selfish, stupid, inadequate. Yet this very relationship which appears and is so destructive they desperately seek to maintain. Unspoken is the belief that if the spouse's undesirable traits could be eliminated,

5

then the marriage would be extricated from its morass and the marriage could proceed happily. Implied is this feeling: "My husband, my wife, is a good person, a fine person—if he or she only would do this, that, or the other thing; or if he or she would not do this, that or the other thing."

I should say that only persons strongly middle class figure in the marriages discussed here. I know lower class persons only faintly. As a psychotherapist, I do not see them as patients; socially, I do not mix with them; as a teacher in a university, I do not find them in my classes. Equally, I know the upper classes only faintly. Occasionally from the road while driving, I catch a glimpse of their magnificent homes hidden deep behind walls, without ever an occupant in view. Occasionally, I get a peep-hole view of their lives when one of their number writes a revealing book of this closed circle, or when one figures in a newspaper scandal.

A great deal, however, is known of the middle class. They are the solid foundation and strength of our society, as they are of every society. Our middle class culture stresses hard work, ambition, achievement. This class is my concern; and it is for this class that the book is aimed. My fear is that our middle class has become so driving, so ambitious, so competitive—obsessively and compulsively so—that they may be doing irreparable harm to themselves and their offspring. I ask: Is this competitive, achieving culture destroying our capacity for good, warm, loving relationships—traits crucial to the good marriage? Are our ambitions devouring us? Are middle class parents with their insatiable demands for ever-higher achievement casting a blight on their offspring, so that they become driving and hard, not the soft and warm human beings so crucially essential if they are to become good husbands and wives.

Each marriage is unique, takes its own course, establishes its own laws and creates its own demands. As there are no two human beings alike, so there are no two marriages alike. Benjamin Franklin wisely observed that after a three-day visit, even one's own mother begins to smell like three-day old fish. Each marriage develops its own day-to-day rhythm. This rhythm, formed and created by the couple, becomes after awhile fixed and inexplicably satisfying. An outsider is an intruder.

I sometimes think of marriage as operating in a vault-like chamber, encapsulated, a world within itself. The quality of the relationship, that which binds the two, has in it elements of the inscrutable, not only to an outsider but often to the participants themselves. The only outsider who can somewhat comprehend the meaning of the relationship is the therapist and that is only when the therapy proceeds well and there is free flowing articulation of feelings.

To preserve the anonymity of the person, drastic changes have been made in the cases cited. It should also be said that only fragments of a marriage have been recorded. To present the full marriage, with its interplay of forces, the demands, wants and hopes that are in a marriage, would require unlimited space and skill of the highest literary quality.

Marriage represents to me the closest relationship known to man; but that does not make it a matter of small moment. It is my belief that there is nothing so powerful, so moving, so healing as a good relationship and that there is nothing so debilitating and so destructive of the person as a bad relationship. When Winston Churchill was asked what was the most important moment in his life, he answered with rare wisdom: "When I met Clementine" (his wife).

I want to acknowledge my debt to Dr. Carl R. Rogers. What the relationship means, how healing it can be, I learned from him. As a teacher, he opened an entire new world to me. From him I learned how a relationship can make man better, kindlier, more compassionate. I know of no other person who has explored the relationship with the genius that he has, and I know no one who has written more wisely in this area.

SAMUEL TENENBAUM

ACKNOWLEDGMENTS

I am grateful to the following persons and publishers who have permitted me to include copyright material. I have omitted listing passages which have been adequately acknowledged in the text. My gratitude to those concerned is none the less.

McGraw-Hill Book Company for passage from *The World of the Formerly Married* by Morton M. Hunt.

Ernest Haveman for passage from *Men, Women and Marriage*, published by Doubleday & Co.

International Universities Press, Inc., for passages from *Life Is With People* by Mark Zborowski and Elizabeth Herzog.

Harcourt, Brace and World for passage from *Love Against Hate* by Karl Menninger.

Harper & Row for passage from *Man in the Modern World* by Julian Huxley.

George Allen and Unwin, Ltd., for passage from *The Conquest of Happiness* by Bertrand Russell.

Mrs. Ellen C. Masters for poem *William and Emily* from the *Spoon River Anthology* by Edgar Lee Masters, published by the MacMillan Co.

David McKay for passages from *My Darling Clementine* by Jack Fishman and *Lust for Life* by Irving Stone.

Beacon Press for passages from *Man's Search for Mean-*

ing by Viktor E. Frankl, © 1959, 1962 by Viktor E. Frankl; and *The Organism* by Kurt Goldstein.

William Heinemann for passages from *The Integrity of the Personality* by Anthony Storr.

Charles Scribner's Sons for passage from *The Light and the Dark* by C. P. Snow.

Random House for passage from *The Days Between* by Robert Anderson.

Viking Press for permission to quote two letters from *The Collected Letters of D. H. Lawrence,* edited with an introduction by Harry T. Moore, © 1932 by the estate of D. H. Lawrence; © 1960 by Angelo Ravagli and C. Montague Weekley.

For permission to quote the two D. H. Lawrence letters outside the United States, my thanks to Laurence Pollinger, Ltd., and the estate of the late Mrs. Frieda Lawrence.

CONTENTS

A PSYCHOLOGIST LOOKS AT
MARRIAGE

PART I

A Psychologist Looks at Marriage

1

MAN'S NEED FOR MARRIAGE

HAVELOCK ELLIS, SPEAKING OF PROF. EDWARD WESTERMARCK, whose *The History of Human Marriage* is a classic in the field, said that for one lifetime Westermarck contributed much to the subject; but what, said Ellis, is one lifetime when dealing with a subject so vast and intricate. Havelock Ellis was quite right.

What is one lifetime when we come to a subject so profound, so unfathomable, one that touches every aspect of man, his deepest inner core, the crux of his being, his social, physical, spiritual, erotic, and neurotic self? Marriage is the subject of science and of art—of poetry, fiction, song, and music; and despite all the centuries of dissection, analysis, and probing we have not come to the bottom of this profoundly pervasive relationship.

The Greeks had a beautiful myth and it tells more about marriage, more of its profundity and deeper meaning, than any I know. The legend goes as follows: Once upon a time man and woman were united and they were one; together, as one, they were whole and complete; neither had to seek; they were content and they were happy. In their contentment and completeness, they angered Zeus, and he tore them asunder, separating the man from the woman. Since then each has been seeking his other half; and the seeking goes on to this day.

In the Torah, there are two somewhat similar stories. The Bible says: "Man and woman created He them." Elaborating on this, the Talmud says that originally man and woman were together and then God separated them and they have been apart since; and from then on, each has been looking for the other part to become one and whole again. "Just as truth is made up of positive and negative elements, so reality is composed of contrasting parts, each of which is indispensable."[1]

Another Talmud version of marriage, says: "The complete Jew is an adult with a mate and offspring. No man is complete without a wife; no woman is complete without a husband. For each individual the ideal center of gravity is not himself, but in the whole of which he is an essential part."

Man and woman seek to be whole. Only the need is now more intense because our civilization has become more atomistic, more alienated, so that it has become ever more crucial for the incomplete half to find his other half to achieve completeness. All one need do is to examine the anatomy of the male and female bodies to understand in what a remarkable way each fits into the other, how they complement each other. If one never finds the other, we know that terrible harm is done.

The bachelor is in all ways inferior to the married male. He does not live as long or as well; he is not as healthy; he suffers from a higher incidence of psychosis and commitment to mental hospitals. He has a higher crime rate;

[1] Mark Zborowski and Elizabeth Herzog, "Life is with People; the Culture of the Shtetl," New York: Schocken Books, 1965, p. 124.

he is not as stable emotionally; he is not nearly as adequate a person. In scarcely any measure can the bachelor stack up against his counterpart, the married male.

Marriage seeks to break down man's loneliness. Man is born with a skin, with an outer impenetrable wall. His dreaming, hoping, wishing, striving, frustrated self is confined mostly within these walls. For the most part man lives alone, he suffers alone, he dies alone.

Anatole France tells the story of a Caliph, who at the beginning of his reign called together the great scholars of his land and said: "I have a vast dominion. I have power and I want to rule wisely. Bring me wisdom so I can rule wisely." The story goes that they went forth in search of wisdom, and after many years they came back with a mound of books. "In these books," they said, "is the wisdom of the ages." The Caliph said: "I am an old man. I haven't the time to read these books. You must condense and make it briefer." They departed and later they came back with a smaller number of books. "I am now," said the Caliph, "too old to read even these fewer books. You must condense further." Finally, they came back with one volume. "You find me on my death bed," said the Caliph. "I cannot even read one volume. You must condense further." And the scholars did and as the Caliph lay on his death bed, they condensed the wisdom they had found in one sentence: "They lived. They suffered. They died."

In marriage, man can find some allayment of his suffering, of his loneliness. "Love consists in this," said Rainer Maria Rilke, "that two solitudes protect each other." Marriage provides the best prospect of penetrating the skin with which man is born. By himself alone he cannot pierce this skin. Marriage permits him to share his innermost self. It is these rare moments of sharing—when one touches another in warmth, sympathy, and understanding—that we now realize are healthy and therapeutic and good. Further, I have come to believe that it is only such rare moments—when two human beings touch one another warmly—that stay with us and comfort us and make this life liveable and good.

Ideally, what can a good marriage do? It can give to each from the other strength, support, warmth, understanding, sympathy, comradeship; it can build up the person, giving each in the marriage self-esteem, self-regard, admiration from a beloved partner.

We shall use these words or synonyms of these words again and again, for the more abundantly the qualities expressed by these words enter the relationship the better the marriage; the more judgmental, the more critical, the more hostile, the more demanding, the more attacking the relationship the worse the marriage.

In a good marriage, each partner builds up the other, makes the other feel nobler, wiser, kindlier, more lovable. In a bad marriage, each makes the other feel inferior, more stupid, ignoble, smaller, weaker, unlovable. We will repeat this again and again; these qualities are the key to the good marriage. In the good marriage, each gives the other warmth, sympathy, praise, support, love, admiration, regard, respect; each is able and willing to sacrifice for the other. In the vicissitudes that characterize any relationship involving anything as complex as two human beings, there is also the need for each to have the capacity for patience, fortitude, stamina, courage, the qualities that we have come to call emotional maturity.

Only recently have we begun to perceive the need of

man, if he is to be emotionally healthy, to throw in his lot with man. As John Dewey said in effect: Even the hermit has to commune with God. Said Eric Fromm: "To feel completely alone and isolated leads to mental deterioration just as physical starvation leads to death."

Wrote William Heard Kilpatrick: "It was said in early times that 'no man liveth to himself,' that 'we are all members of one another,' and later that 'no man is an Iland, intire of it selfe.' In fact, it is only with others that one truly lives—in the family, in the community, in the nation, in humanity. Also, only in and through a socially built and socially transmitted culture do any of us live civilized lives."

Man is a product of man; he is a social organism; his very speech is man-made; his very being came about because adults protected and sheltered him in the many years of his helplessness. As a social organism, man can function healthily only as he intertwines his lot with his fellow men.

The first sign of emotional illness, I have come to believe, is the withdrawal from other human beings. An essential of good mental health, I believe, is the capacity to love and to be loved, to give affection and receive affection, to sacrifice for and to be sacrificed for. The inability to love, to give affection and warmth, I believe, is the sign of emotional illness. In our society, we have so many who want to be loved but cannot love.

Once man lived and died as part of a larger group. An entire city comprised one family, and members of a city felt drawn to one another, tied together in the closest bounds. To be a Greek or a Roman meant not merely being an inhabitant of the city, but being involved in and

with the city in a deeply mystical and spiritual way. You
were tied religiously to your city; the gods that you worshipped were your city gods, who protected you, your
family, your city and all the other inhabitants of your city.
In all this there was a sense of community and personal
involvement. Your city, the whole city, was your family.
You may have been poverty-stricken, lived in alleys and
in basements; but the gay pageantry of the street, what
went on there, gave you a sense of family; they were your
people, and you were witness and part of what went on.
The religious ceremonies and festivals that the city throngs
celebrated were your ceremonies and your festivals in a
very personal sense.

But here in America, our society, our culture, has taken
another turn. For the most part in our urban society we
live in cubicles called apartments, and for many this separation and isolation is built-in, deeply-rooted, the fact of
their existence. They remain in their dark and dreary
apartments, their doors shut since no person enters. The
main aspect of our society today is this sense of isolation.
Ask the mass of workers, "Is this corporation where you
work your corporation? Is it truly yours? Do you feel
part of it? Are you deeply involved with your full self
in what goes on?" Hear their replies; how distant they
feel from an activity that engages most of their energy
and time.

Once during World War II, so as to build up good will,
a corporation making airplanes invited the families of the
workers to see the finished product; and the families gathered and they saw the finished airplanes and they touched
them and walked inside them; and proudly, the workers
accompanying their families told of their contribution to
the whole. Not only did the families see the airplanes for

the first time, but so did most of the workers. When the workers actually saw what their work meant—how it fitted into the whole—production zoomed, for now their screwing of bolts had some meaning when hitherto it hadn't. Ask college students, representing I suppose the elite of our culture: "Is this, the university you are attending, your university? Do you actually feel that this campus and these buildings are yours?" Invariably, the great majority will say no; it belongs to the big shots, a few. Even more strange, ask the faculty of a university the same question, and they, too, for the most part express a sense of alienation; that there are some big shot members of the faculty who run things, but in essence, what they do is to go to class and then go home, leaving the great structure behind them as some amorphous mass, not really a vivid, integral part of their lives.

Our very culture is sick and creates sickness. It is so highly competitive that for some it becomes almost impossible to live. With increasing frequency parents look at their newly-born child and view him as an entry in a lifelong race. Brothers and sisters become rivals; friends become rivals; and even parents and their own children have been known to become rivals. By adulthood, the once-child has introjected strivings for achievement, success, fame, material opulence, which by their very nature are never-ending and insatiable. In the process, he has frequently not only alienated himself from himself but has come out of the struggle feeling inadequate, inferior, shamed by his own being.

Isolated, suffering, alone, he cannot resort even to his nearest kin for succor; for his competitiveness, his living for success and achievement, result all too often in brother

vying with brother, friend with friend, family members
with other family members, children with parents. In his
travail, he cannot obtain what little comfort there comes
from acknowledging fear, guilt, weakness; for by our conventions he is expected to be strong and brave, so that
often he hides behind a façade of fake bravado the small,
suffering, little human being he is and we all are. And
in truth, one does not go in weakness to a rival for help.

Man's tragedy is further compounded in that the mighty
things he creates and builds further alienates him from
himself and society. His mighty machines and his never-
ceasing industry in the end dominate and enslave him.
Our giant industries have become too big for man. His
government, created to serve him, has in its vastness become so remote that he, the little man, is lost and engulfed. Even his social life has become complex, organized like a business and even worse—competitive.

We have known millionaires who have died in big
mansions in their massive beds, surrounded by five nurses
and three doctors, but without a soul present to touch
their hand in human kindness. The struggle to achieve
and to amass has created, not human warmth, but an
empire of things, remote and cold, and of no comfort,
in the deepest sense, outside of the ease of dying.

Man has become isolated and alienated and been made
small.

The existential reality is this: We—all of us—are on a
sinking vessel. Every day we are dying a little. Every
day we are a step nearer to the cemetery. As Jean-Paul
Sartre has told us: "Man can count on no one but himself; he is alone, abandoned on earth in the midst of his
infinite responsibilities without help . . . " and Hobbes
has warned us that the solitary life is "poor, nasty, brut-

ish and short." And life has become solitary, certainly spiritually solitary.

This loneliness, this horrible loneliness, this fear of the night! In large cities, we know there exist all-night establishments, and there the wandering souls of the night gather, hoping to overcome the blackness of the night, the fear of the night, the fear of entering their empty homes alone. Dag Hammarskjold in *Markings* described it well:

> Too tired for company
> You seek a solitude
> You are too tired to fill.[1]

In our culture, individualistic and atomistic, marriage becomes an island where two persons can give the other significance; they can make the other feel big and important. You as well as I have seen a dull, unprepossessing person ignite and become attractive when with his beloved. In each other's presence, by their mutual involvement and sensitivity, the dull, colorless person becomes animated, alive, significant. As isolation leads to mental distintegration so relatedness leads to health and growth of the person. In the presence of a beloved, the very stance of the person changes; he becomes more of a person; before your eyes he becomes transformed. This once lacklustre person becomes vital, significant.

The word "cure" comes from the word "care." What a wise insight! One who truly cares for another person touches him with healing power. What better "caring" can there exist than in a good marriage. "One might add that . . . to be completely related," wrote Anthony Storr,

[1] Dag Hammarskjold, *Markings*, trans. Lief Sjoberg and W. H. Auden, N.Y.: Alfred A. Knopf.

"to another person is to be most oneself, to affirm one's personality in its totality." Says Alfred Adler: "If you can get one person to think of one other person in a social and helpful way you can save him from neurosis."

Man's crucial task in life, says Martin Buber, is to fulfill himself, to realize his uniqueness, to become the person he was meant to be. He tells of Rabbi Zusya, who on his deathbed, said: "In the world to come they will not ask me, 'Why were you not Moses?' They will ask, 'Why were you not Zusya?'"

Said Nietzche: "Only from love springs profound insight."

Where better than in marriage can one become his true self, develop the courage to be and to live, to become what one was meant to be? What better way to escape the horrible isolation and atomization that characterizes modern man?

2

GOOD AND BAD MARRIAGES

WE SEEK OUT PEOPLE WHO MAKE US FEEL GOOD, UNSELFISH, noble, wise, kind. We avoid people who make us feel stupid, selfish, inferior, worthless. In a good marriage, you have a built-in partner who through her admiration and love can make you feel good and noble—for a lifetime. You need not seek and search. The marriage is made permanent by society, custom, and law. The husband and wife are there for each other—as long as each lives. By years of common sharing and experiencing, both can develop in a good marriage the capacity to reach out to the other in the most profound way.

Even when the highest regard exists, the non-marital relationship is necessarily restricted by the limited mutual experience and knowledge of each other. It can never be as deep or as varied or as profound or as continuous or as permeating as in marriage. In marriage, common experiences include maintaining a home together, sleeping together, having sex together, having and rearing children together, entertaining family and friends together, participating jointly as a family in the community, and withal, jointly sharing the joys and the agonies, the triumphs and the failures of living.

How can any other relationship duplicate the quality and the depth of these common experiences and living? What a capacious reservoir from which to draw for understanding and solace! In a good marriage, the partner becomes like an alter ego, all knowing, intimately knowing, reinforcing in moments of despair and doubt all the weak strands in the other, giving him strength and courage. Also, since each is a repository of the experiences of the other, what added pleasure to share in retrospect, in calmer moments, the pageant of one's life, the bright luminous colors, the grey and the devastatingly depressing blacks that willy-nilly enter, no matter what.

Likewise, in a bad marriage, the horror when each spouse reinforces in the other all that is painful and sick and destructive in the other, making the other feel ugly, stupid, selfish, ignoble, guilty, at that very moment when he needs beyond all else someone to lessen the present pain, the self-doubts, the guilt, the anxiety, the self hate. Further, since the spouse through the years of living together knows the partner so well, how much more effective can he be at his job of destroying the other. What powerful ammunition can he hurl against the other, since by practice in a bad marriage, both have learned how to aim sharp, penetrating darts of irritation, dislike and even hate, penetrating the weakest and most defenseless areas. Both in the marriage can and often do play at this frightening game, frightening in the sense that it is so destructive of the person. In this kind of relationship, which so frequently characterizes the bad marriage, each is destroying the other.

Let me cite a concrete illustration of what I mean. They were patients of mine. Mr. A had come home from work

and had told his wife that he had had a terrible day. And
then he proceeded to explain why. Lately he had noticed
that his superior had become critical of him; and of late
whatever he did seemed wrong. It had bothered him a
great deal, but he hadn't spoken of it to his wife, who,
to put it mildly, was not sympathetic. But today something had happened to really unnerve him. His superior
had hired a young man, and Mr. A felt threatened by what
was happening. Mr. A was middle-aged and had worked
for this firm for the major part of his life.

"That young man is smart," he told his wife. "Believe
me, he's smart! What will happen to me? Who'll hire
me at my age?"

In his face, there appeared fear, despair, misery.

How did his wife respond? How did she come to his
aid? What comfort did she offer him?

First she began to bemoan her own lot. "There were
others; and I had to choose you—get stuck with you. I
thought Mr. Goddard [his superior] was smart and it's
taken all this time to find you out."

And thus it went on in the same vein. Full of self-pity,
she didn't bother to hide her disgust and disapproval of
her husband.

No, there is no comfort from such a wife and such a
marriage.

Miserable, unhappy he was made to feel more miserable, more insecure and inadequate by a wife who demeaned him, made him feel small, stupid, incompetent.

Instead of getting support, strength, regard from his
wife, he was made to feel inferior, inept, stupid. Already
whittled down to a small size at the office, his wife reduced him further. From his wife, his marriage, Mr. A
received no strength, no courage, no sense of self worth;

no sense of a partner who is there by his side, loyal to him, understanding him, empathizing with him, having faith in him.

If it were a good marriage, how vastly different would be the interaction of the two. Let us duplicate the scene. Let us call him Mr. B, so as to differentiate this marriage from the foregoing. Mr. B comes home from work. He is sad and depressed. His wife is immediately sensitive to his mood. She knows and understands him as no other person possibly can. She shows her concern and solici- tude. Mr. B explains that of late his superior has shown his disapproval of him and that whatever he, Mr. B, does seems wrong; and it's been bothering him. And now he saw a new man come into the office, and it looks as if some bad things may be happening to Mr. B.

As his wife listens, she shows more and more concern and sympathy. He senses this concern and sympathy: senses her sadness that he feels so depressed. And then, as she listens further, she gets more and more furious that her husband, so wise, so good, so able, should be subjected to such indignity. "That schmo boss of yours! That fool! What can one do with an idiot! After all these years suffering with that numbskull, covering up for his mistakes! What have you to worry about? You can get a job anywhere. It's that boss numbskull of yours who has to worry. Who would hire him?"

Mrs. B can scarcely contain herself. "I'm going to call up that numbskull right now. What's his number?"

It's now the husband's job to calm his wife. "I may be imagining things. It may blow over."

In this intimacy, in their affection for each other, they both talk—he pouring out his heart, she listening with empathy and understanding. She reminds him of previous crises in their life of a similar nature, and what they were most worried about did not happen; and if it did, how well it turned out in the end, better than if things went smoothly. By her faith in him, Mrs. B makes her husband feel that *no man like him* has anything to worry about. He could get a job in a minute. She reminds him of business associates, of offers, of all the triumphant incidents in the past to reassure him about the present and the now.

What is Mr. B's wife doing? She is giving her husband support, pride, courage, regard, devotion, love. She is bolstering his ego.

Is she doing this deliberately, as a task? If so, she could not fool anyone, least of all her husband. One can't fake an emotion; it is there for anyone to see, even more sharply apparent for false words. She actually feels this way about her husband. *If she didn't feel this way—truly feel this way—she couldn't be of help.* And she communicates these feelings, and like a health-giving drug, it is therapeutic, making him stronger.

How often have we heard husbands and wives making snide remarks, derogatory and denigrating remarks, about their spouses in social situations, or equally bad, to each other. If they think of such interchanges as idle badinage, I myself would be fearful of the outcome; not only are they, it seems to me, in bad taste but they may have unfortunate outcomes. Of course, if they are expressions of genuine hostility, it is indeed unfortunate if it goes beyond the two. There are some individuals who out of frustration, without meaning to attack, may choose the spouse as a scapegoat for fear of confronting the real source of the grievance. How often has a husband come home from work and made himself ugly and mean to wife and children because of abuse by his superior whom he fears to attack?

In company you have heard such or similar outbursts:

"She has a hairbrain." And the husband giggles and giggles and giggles.

"Leave it to him. He knows how to ball up things so that after he is through no one can ever straighten it out."

"As usual, you don't know what you are talking about." He shakes his head in disgust.

"You're just like that family of yours." And the spouse proceeds in great detail to deride mother, father, brother, sister, aunt, and uncle.

"You must be nuts."

"Don't be so stupid."

And thus it goes on.

I cannot imagine anything more damaging to a marriage.

All of it boils down to this: Here is a stupid, silly, idiotic, untrustworthy, ignoble, selfish, greedy, unlovable horrible person. In bad marriages, the couple carry on an underhand war, each sniping at the other, making each other feel small.

"You think you know everything. How do you explain that dumb deal you entered and lost that money?"

"And you think you're such a great highbrow and know everything. The last book you read was by Micky Spillane. And, then, I don't believe you understood what you read. I had to explain it to you. And you call yourself sensitive, artistic, refined. It's to laugh! Look at that ugly picture you bought and how much you paid for it! And when Harry Levien, who really knows art, looked at it he said one word, 'Junk.' And I'm supposed to be the ignorant one in the family."

And thus it goes, each destroying the other, each making the other feel small and ignorant. Since each learns through years of living together the sensitive areas, each acquires the ability to put with fiendish cleverness salt at the end of the dart and with diabolical accuracy to aim at the other's weak spots, delighting in hurting the other. This underhand warfare goes on and on.

In such a marriage, one never knows when and from where the attack will come and what will be its nature. Of a sudden, when one least expects it, the spouse lashes out. The attack may occur while the two are in bed, while they are talking about some apparently neutral subject, while in company—anywhere. One cannot predict the time or the place when a pitched battle will start. How effective are the blows in this war, since they are based on intimate knowledge, on knowing what is painful to the other!

As a good marriage can uplift the person, bring out the best in him, so a bad marriage can crush a person, prevent the development of his talents and his fulfillment as a person. There comes to mind the woman who married a brilliant man of great promise who needed further education to realize himself but she flatly opposed such a course. "I didn't marry a school boy," she said. It would have meant some material sacrifice; and she didn't want to make it. Even worse is the jealous, rivalrous wife who doesn't want to have her husband get ahead for fear he may outpace her. Or a talented wife who needs to be encouraged but marries a man who insists that a wife's place is "kitchen, children, and church." Or those who

come into a marriage holding high ideals; but soon it
becomes plain that the only way they can continue to
hold the affection and regard of their spouses is to settle
down and try to pile up sufficient material goods to move
into a big suburban home and acquire an automobile
bigger than the home. And on a baser level, we find drug
addicts, alcoholics, cheats, thieves, and gamblers making
of their spouses drug addicts, alcoholics, cheats, thieves
and gamblers.

We do not know exactly how much one partner may influence another, but I am sure it is considerable. From
our own experience we know how some one human being
has been the means of changing our whole lives, our outlook, our wants, our ambitions; how some one human
being has stirred us, and exhilarated us, and filled us
with new purposes, new objectives and has given us the
courage and the strength to achieve. How much more so
does this hold true in the intimate relationship of husband
and wife. I am quite sure that many a man has been
destroyed by the evil influence of a wife, and many a
woman has been destroyed by the evil influence of a
husband.

It is said that when foreign ambassadors wanted something from King Louis XV of France, they did not parley
with the king. Rather they sought out Madame de Pompa-
dour, his mistress; if she said it could be managed, it
was; if she said no, then it did not come to pass. These
diplomats showed rare discernment in adopting such wise
strategy; they were aware of the facts of life.

As the bad marriage can weaken and destroy, the good
marriage can uplift and give strength and courage, so
that both can do what either alone cannot or dare not do.
Those who have experienced a good marriage know this.
If you have not been that lucky, you probably have ex-

perienced some episode—perhaps temporary and fleeting
—when because of a friend or an acquaintance, you were
made to see and feel everything with heightened awareness, or led into experiences which you would not venture
or dare alone, or you were introduced to a circle of people
through whom you made friendships which you alone
could not manage. These episodes in one's life come and
go. But marriage stays and is permanent.

Whatever a friend can do a spouse can do better, and
by his faith and admiration, he can give his marital
partner the courage to venture, when alone he or she
would not dare.

In a good marriage, to repeat, each gives the other comfort, support, strength, admiration, warmth, and love.
Because of their sensitivity to each other, they are aware,
as no other human being can possible be, of each other's
needs and wants. In the good marriage, each builds up
the other, makes him big and strong. As Nietzche says:
"One really knows only what one loves." In the bad marriage, each attacks the other, throwing salt-edged darts
at the other, cutting the other down, in an effort to make
her feel inferior.

The Talmud tells us: "Make yourself a slave to your
husband and he will make himself a slave to you." How
true that is! Conceive a relationship where a wife is
devoting herself to pleasing her husband, sensitive to his
needs and wants; and through her loyalty and devotion
she becomes like a therapist, serving him in his trials and
tribulations. If the husband does not respond with equal
loyalty and love, what is there to say—except that this
person is a sick person, an immature person, an infantile
person, unfit for any deep and profound relationship.

In counseling husband and wife to give each other
devotion and admiration, to make a slave of themselves

to each other, I do not advocate that anyone debase him-
selt or become a subservient or a "faceless person." I do
mean that one should give from inner strength, from
deliberate choice; for each is a person and a *person* has
his own wants and desires and has need for dignity and
respect. There can be no relationship of any worth unless
there is mutual respect. One chooses to give to the marital
partner out of one's self-respect and strength, not out of
fear and cowardice, for the latter would destroy what is
best in any relationship—the sincerity and the integrity
of the person. Only two equal, independent persons can
maintain the deep, satisfying relationship envisioned in
marriage.

It is in the following sense, as explained by Walker
and Fletcher, that the counsel is meant:

"The need for love is a need, not for strength in the
self but for strength in the bond between selves. It is a
need to discover our personal reality in the only possible
way, by discovering the personal reality of another being
of our own kind in a relationship that is reciprocal. We
could not know that we possessed material bodies if we
were not living in a world of matter with which we are
in sensitive contact, a world that is at once responsive
and resistant to our touch and so 'makes its presence felt.'
Love is at bottom the desire for contact or communication with another being like ourselves who 'makes his
presence felt' in a manner that reveals his essential nature
to us and by so doing reveals our essential nature to ourselves. So the search for love is a search for recognition
and our desire to be loved is a desire to be recognized,
not for what we do but for what we are."[1]

[1] Kenneth Walker and Peter Fletcher, "Sex and Society," pp. 31–32,
Pelican Books, 1958.

It is indeed suspicious when two persons think and feel so alike that they scarcely differ. If this rare and *suspicious* event does occur, then of course, it becomes simple for each to do exactly what the other wants with integrity and probity.

It is true that frequently in a marriage one can without sacrificing strong convictions say: "Yes, I'm glad to do this. You like it and I like it." More often there is a continuum of feelings, starting with the foregoing and ending with strong negative feelings. One will have to say to the spouse: "I myself would not do it on my own, but yet to please you—since I have no particularly strong convictions in the matter—I'll do it. But remember I'm doing it to please you." At times one will have to say: "I know how much this means to you. And I know how it will hurt you if I didn't go along with you; and you know how it hurts me to hurt you. But I must refuse to do this. I'd be ashamed of myself if I did. It would violate my person."

If there is generosity and good-will on both sides, such differences can be absorbed. If the issues are fundamental, involving the very crux of the person, then they can become the source of bickering, attack, and hostility—and even hate.

In marriage, two people are involved, their whole persons, in the most profound and deepest possible relationship known to man. Hence, as we shall state again and again, it is best when two people come to the marriage as nearly alike as possible—in values, outlook, and beliefs; or if there are differences, then it is best that these differences beget from the partner respect and admiration.

3

LOVERS AND CLOSENESS

WHEN TWO PEOPLE ARE IN LOVE, THEY WANT TO BE CLOSE. They will seek every opportunity for contact. They will hold each other's hand while walking; they will kiss and hug each other; in the theatre they will hold hands; in sleeping, they will remain embraced all night. They will seek out situations where they can be together—at a picnic, at play, reading to one another. They are attracted by carnival rides that thrust their bodies together. When separated, they will see their beloved in each strange face in the crowd. It would appear as if they want to get inside each other, become one, as they were before Zeus, according to legend, cast them asunder.

We assume this closeness; we take it for granted. In truth, this desire for closeness is extraordinarily rare and unique. Few realize how unnatural it is. Watch people. See how they keep their distance. When one brushes against another by accident, he apologizes as they quickly draw apart. It is not by chance that seats in theatres and public places have arms attached to them to assure the privacy of the person. Separation, distance, walls between persons are the normal and the natural. Try to

38

visualize yourself living with the intimacy and the closeness of lovers; how repulsive and abhorrent the thought
if there is no love present.

I have seen couples in my office—there for marital
counseling—when their feelings softened to one another,
draw their bodies closer, visibly drawn to one another
like steel to a magnet, their hands reaching out to each
other. As soon as disagreement or anger set in, the position, the stance of their whole body changed and they
withdrew from one another, their hands retreating to
their own isolated bodies. Again they went back to what
is normal; they were alone and isolated.

In rare moments of universal good will, a sense of closeness can prevail on a wider base, namely during celebra-
tions, at festivals, or at some special event which elicits
the good feelings in man. At such moments, the walls of
separation may come tumbling down. People will embrace
and hug one another; they will feel very close; they will
show enormous good will and loving. Such rare episodes,
so unique and special, stay with us, and later, even in
recall, they give us comfort and a feeling of goodness. I
want to emphasize that such occurrences are not the general and the expected; they are the rare, wonderful moments of living. Normally, man is separated from others
by high fences and frightening barriers.

Only in love can these walls, these barriers, most ef-
fectively be broken down.[1] Lovers do penetrate the walls

[1] Here is a woman talking of her first marriage, a bad one, and her
second marriage, a good one:

It was a very smooth organization that we ran and called a marriage.
We didn't have fights—that wasn't the trouble—it was just that there was
nothing between us. Even when he finally came from his many activities for the weekend, he wanted to sleep and rest, and read in bed and
be left alone. There was no companionship, no communication, little

and bridge the barriers; and they do touch each other in oneness as cannot be achieved in any other kind of relationship. When lovers quarrel and develop antagonisms, they revert back to the norm. Each goes back to his own isolated self. Walls and the barriers spring up again. And they withdraw from each other, physically as well as spiritually. Their skin, with which they were born, acts as a barrier, a shield from the other. Once seeking out the other, finding completion when their bodies were like one, they now find each other's touch repulsive. The magic and the wonder that love creates between two separate human beings are gone; they become again like ordinary mortals. Each returns to his own painful isolation. As long as this antagonism and hostility last, they cannot come close. Like ordinary human beings, they have to suffer the lot of man—apartness, distance, isolation.

Said Hegel: "Only through love one becomes one with the object."

---

sex. I felt unimportant and purposeless—but I thought all marriages were like that after the honeymoon period.

But in contrast, my present husband, though he is a whirlwind and a hard worker—he's a gynecologist—is warm and intense, and I come first in his life and he in mine. It is more beautiful and exciting after four years than I could have imagined. We spend every possible moment together, because we want to. We have traveled to Asia and Australia together, lectured together, cleaned the barn and hunted, fished and skied together; *we sleep rolled in one tight ball together.* [Italics mine.] Each of us wants to make the other feel secure in our love. Ours is a genuine union." (Morton M. Hunt, "The Rocky Road to Remarriage," McCall, October, 1966, from book "The World of the Formerly Married," N.Y.: McGraw Hill, 1966.)

4

MARRIAGE AND MATURITY

AT THE END OF FABLE AND STORY, THE HERO MARRIES THE heroine and "they live happily forever after." This is a simple and childish way to look at a marital relationship—or any relationship. If it is a good relationship, it is an unfolding one, with its ups and its downs, with its vicissitudes, with its moments of despair, and its moment of beauty and wonder. It is anything but a smooth, straight path.

That is why marriage involves character, why the base of it is emotional maturity, the ability to suffer and to sacrifice self. The child is full of "I's." "I want this." "I like this." "What have you for me?" If the parcel you bring home is not a gift for the child, he will walk off, disinterested. In a store, his eyes will be attracted to an object, and he will cry out: "Buy me that." His day begins with "I" and ends with "I." If a stranger holds up a colorful balloon and beckons to him, he will leave his parents without a backward glance and run toward the balloon. A child cannot enter into so mature and so difficult a relationship as marriage.

But one need not worry. That is the nature of the child;

41

and that is how he ought to be. As parents pour love and
affection into him, the day will come when he will be
grown up, mature, and he will be able to give love and
affection, as it was given him.

But some never grow up; they do not develop normally.
These remain children at twenty, at thirty, at forty, at
fifty, forever. Their sole concern remains their "I," they
live by and for their "I." You see such infantile adults,
self-engrossed, strutting before the mirror, admiring their
image and in love with themselves. In this condition, they
are unable to love anything or anyone outside of themselves.

Such are not fit for marriage, and when they do marry,
they cause only grief.

Marriage has been aptly described as a test of character.
In marriage, a spouse does not come to the relationship
with a clean slate, a blank mind, and an unformed self.
He comes with a long background of living, with a philosophy of life, with an ethical outlook, with fairly fixed
character traits. Before the altar stands the prisoner of
his past—the fully formed person and his character. And
this—his person and his character—are the sole and the
crucial ingredients in any marriage.

We are beginning to realize that the basis for a good
marriage are two mature people, grown-ups who can work
together, suffer together, sacrifice for common causes.
That is why Alfred Adler says that the only child is a
poorer marital risk than the one coming from a large
family. The only child, he says, is more likely to be pampered, catered to, and little is demanded of him. The
result is that he learns to demand and want. Of course,
what Adler says applies to any pampered child; he need
not necessarily be an only child. When such a pampered

child grows up, wanting and demanding, but not able or wanting to give of himself or to sacrifice for anyone, he is indeed a poor marital risk.

In the struggle and the tribulations that come in the normal course of living, the young couple, if they are emotionally mature, develop a way of living unique to themselves. It is in the give and the take of daily vicissitudes that the couple develop generosity, kindliness, helpfulness, stick-to-it-iveness. These common experiences make for unity and common need. Emotionally immature couples seldom develop strength in vicissitudes; instead they lead only to bickerings and irritations. This couple finds it hard to compromise or develop a give-and-take relationship. Successful marriages are not the result of miraculous chance. They come about as a result of "blood, toil, tears and sweat." The emotionally immature husband and wife crack up before these inevitable trials and tribulations.

Count Hermann Keyserling goes so far as to say that only in the assumption of responsibilities, only in the capacity to suffer, can man and woman find themselves in marriage and, withal, find their truest happiness; only in the sharing of woes and joys, in the rearing of children, can man and woman develop their personalities to the fullest and thereby achieve simultaneously real and lasting happiness.

"The supreme aim of marriage," said Felix Adler, "is to contribute to the growth of character, of the mind, and of the feelings." He who has the romantic notion that by being lucky in marriage—by which is meant finding an ideal partner—he can attain eternal happiness is headed for tragic disappointment. Life is not that way. The concept of static, eternal happiness is a false and misleading ideal;

one attains happiness by growing as a person, by adjusting ever better to the realities of living. Happiness is acquired by struggling with the trials and vicissitudes of life; it cannot be obtained ready-made and complete, like buying a pair of shoes. Happiness is a concomitant of living a good, rich, useful life.

It is for this reason that the neurotic generally experiences such unsuccessful marriages; he expects and wants it to resolve all his difficulties and problems.

It is for this reason that good, wholesome, kindly families—families in which there is great warmth and affection, which are social-minded in outlook, in which there is cooperation and sympathy—provide the best breeding grounds for good husbands and wives. And conversely, broken and divorced families, or families where the parents are neurotic and maladjusted, in which there is quarreling and bickering, and discord, produce offspring that are the poorest marital risks. Children reared in such families have never seen by example how parents have learned to adjust differences amicably, and neither have they seen by example this kindly, self-sacrificing living, which is the *sine qua non* of a successful marriage. In his study of marriage, Professor Terman came to this conclusion: "Happiness of parents rates highest. . . . This item is more predictive of success or failure in marriage than any composite of half a dozen items such as income, age of marriage, religious training, amount of adolescent 'petting,' or spouse differences in years of schooling." At another point, he says that "hardly less important is the rated happiness of respondent's childhood."[1]

Perhaps the wisest observations on marriage have been made by Dr. Alfred Adler, who organized a pioneer marital clinic in Vienna. The writer had occasion to inter-

---

[1] Terman, Psychology Factors in Marital Happiness, p. 372.

view Dr. Adler at length on his views. The adolescent,
Dr. Adler said, is not ready for marriage, and he *will not
fall in love*. While in this state, the young man feels that
he is a Napoleon; that he is not part of the commonalty
of man, that he is apart and unique; that the laws of this
earth do not apply to him. The adolescent girl dreams of
a knight on a white horse who will come and sweep her
off her feet. The adolescent, hence, is not fit for marriage
and will not fall in love.

Life has a way of dealing blows to all of us. Eventually,
the young man and the young woman through bitter experience learn that they are made of the same stuff that
all mankind is. As failures pile up and as reality begins to
tarnish adolescent dreams, both the young man and the
young woman become more ready to accept marriage. As
soon as they are ready for marriage, they fall in love. They
do not fall in love, says Dr. Adler, and then marry; they
first become ready for marriage; and then they fall in
love.

From this point on, the success of the marriage will depend on how social-minded, how cooperative, how unselfish the mates are. "The majority of unsuccessful marriages," said Dr. Adler, "are caused by pampered children.
They grow up with the habit of dominating. They demand
and they demand and they demand. They give little of
themselves, if anything. At the beginning of the marriage,
one of the mates may play up to the selfish partner, but
with chronic coddling, particularly when there is no re-
ciprocation, the other spouse will eventually find the relationship unsatisfactory and begin to object and protest,
for his or her own personality is being disregarded or perhaps worse, being destroyed." Resistance to the will of the
pampered mate leads to the divorce court.

The most important concept to be remembered about

the successful marriage is that each of the partners should feel worthwhile and adequate. They should feel, said Dr. Adler, that they are engaging in worthwhile and important activities; that they are doing the things they want to do, and that they are expressing their individuality in a manner pleasing to them. If one dominates and overrides the other, then to that extent the self and the personality of the other is being minimized. There must be cooperation of two equal parties; they both must feel that one is indispensable to the other.

"Marriage is a task with its own laws and its own rules," said Dr. Adler. "It is a task for two, never for one alone. It is a task for all mankind, for monogamy with its concomitants, the equality of the sexes, furnishes the goal and the ideal of modern civilization. A marriage begins with nothing. It contains only that which two individuals, as a result of their creative living, manage to evolve and develop. The basic law of marriage is the ability to give of oneself, unselfishly and unasked, and in the giving complete happiness is found. The only thing that should concern the other is how and in what way he can give. When one partner awaits and expects, there will be great disappointment and unfulfillment. If it did not have such tragic import, it would be indeed a comedy to watch the antics of two pampered children carrying on in marriage. Both are expecting and neither is giving. One or both are annoyed, disappointed, bitter. They seek to get away, either in divorce or in some flirtation with another person."

Dr. Adler opposed any arrangement that lessened the sense of permanency and the sense of eternity in any marital decision. "When man makes a decision to marry, it should be a final decision, without loopholes. It is a projection of man into the future; and it includes, as all marriages made for eternity should include, the having of children. Monogamy is the highest form of the sexual relationship, as it permits equality. It cannot be limited to a definite number of years; that is a bad start. When you come to analyze them, most extra-marital liaisons have this 'fire-escape' idea in the mind of one of the parties." On entering marriage, all doubts should be cast out, such as: Are we really in love? Is the other person worthy of my love? Was I right in making this choice? Such doubts are disturbing and distracting, and they make for lessened cooperation, fundamental to a successful marriage. As Mlle. Scuderi said: "Men should keep their eyes wide open before marriage, and half shut afterwards."

Sometimes the marital relationship becomes so crucially meaningful that when one dies, the other does not want to live.

Says an old epitaph:

He first deceased, she for a little tried
To live without him, lik'd it not, and died.

There is a great deal of evidence to indicate that a person can will his own death. The wish of the living spouse to vanish from the living and join another in death can and at times does become so strong that death is welcomed and comes. The anthropoid or manlike apes are known to be able to will their death and die when their mate dies.

I have been witness to a marriage where a wife chose to die when her husband died. She deliberately chose not to live without her husband. Both had met while university students and married while students. Their relationship from the very beginning was so close that outsiders seemed intruders. He became a physician, but before he achieved financial success, they both struggled. While he interned, she worked and they lived in a hall bedroom. Later, while he laboriously built up his own practice, she was by his side as his nurse, his mistress, his beloved, his wife, the mother of his children.

When he came home from a call, he would shout "Rachel!" And if she wasn't there, he told me the home seemed empty and bereft and scarcely livable. They took vacations together; I never remember them apart. They read together, they discussed the husband's cases together, they were active in many movements together. When you thought of them, it was not as two separate persons, but as a unit. I have never encountered two human beings who were so close. When they differed, there was a gentleness in the discussion of these differences; each would look at the other, tenderly and kindly, fearful of hurting the other, sorry that they had to differ. Of all the marriages I have seen, I do not believe there was another that so exemplified the "oneness" of the Greek myth. One seemed to be the complement of the other.

When the husband died, I would visit the wife, for they were good friends of mine and I had liked both enormously. What I saw happen to her grieved me greatly. Before my eyes she seemed to wither away. She lost interest in food; she removed herself from society; she dropped the activities in the many organizations with which she and her husband were associated.

Concerned and troubled about her, I said: "It seems to me as if you have not buried David."

She said: "No, I don't know whether I want to bury him."

As she continued to decline perceptibly, I said: "You have to bury David."

"I don't know whether I want to. I have not decided yet."

Still later I said to her: "It seems to me as if you want to die, to be buried with him."

"That's true," she said. "I still don't know whether I want to live without him."

And then when I saw her continue to decline, I said: "It seems to me as if you want to die."

"I believe I don't want to live without David."

It was not long afterwards that she, too, went where her David was.

When a relationship is so close, the loss of it can make life bereft and unendurable.

5

THE LADY LORELEI AND MARRIAGE

IT IS QUITE TRUE THAT EVEN IN GOOD MARRIAGES THERE ARE periods of boredom and dullness. Unfortunately, too much is expected of marriage. There is the notion that it ought to make one happy. What is there in life that can make one continuously happy?

In life we have disagreements, we experience sorrow, triumph, disappointments. In life, the best of friends have disagreements and even lose one another. Yet from marriage, these very same people expect perpetual happiness. There is probably no marriage where at some time one of the two did not contemplate divorce or hope for freedom. That, too, is natural. Marriage, like life, has its vicissitudes. For this reason marriage has rightly been called a test of character and why it demands the highest kind of emotional maturity.

Even animals, it is believed, are excited by variety. The Lorelei is in man's heart and is always beckoning. This insatiable yearning has been the theme of song, literature, and poetry. Almost invariably such Walter Mittyish dreams end in misadventure and disappointment. The fair lady is not there, and if a Lorelei does seem to appear, in the end it turns out to be an irritating and frustrating experience. It is much better to have troubadours sing of the dream; it is not meant for reality.

Kinsey reports that when the wife leaves home for several days, the husband begins to dream of adventure. Such dreams invariably end up with a forlorn meal in a restaurant with the wrong food in the stomach, doubly disappointing, for with that meal went such visions of what might be. Then follows a dreary night at home, with no one there to intrude on one's loneliness. Even if the fantasy materialized; even if there were the lovely damsel, sweet and gentle, could she compete with a reality based on a relationship of years of duration? I doubt it.

Poetry, fiction, the cinema, and the mind can conjure up better, but the marital relationship is real and durable and the fact of life and the stuff of life. It is this, the reality, with which one lives and forges a life. The romantic notion of love existed and exists not in reality, but in the insatiable cry of the heart; the yearning with which men seek perfection, beauty, everlasting happiness. The truth is that man strives and is imperfect and fallible but he grapples with the stuff of life and in the process he attains fortitude, character, and wisdom.

The romantic troubadours sang of hapless love: the young man who pined his heart away for the fragile maiden high up in the inaccessible tower or dedicated his heart to Her Royal Highness, the Queen, more beautiful and virtuous than in a fairy tale. This is the stuff of troubadours. It is a theme to sing about, dream about, and on which to peg a yearning heart. It is a rule of fiction that no live person can compete with a dead one, for you never have disillusioning reality to intrude on what your imagination can conjure up. But all this has nothing to do with marriage. It is destructive of marriage, since it is adolescent in nature. I should like to quote a passage that has enormous meaning for me. It presents marriage in an intelligent manner. It is written by Ernest Haveman and appeared in his book, *Men, Women and Marriage.*

Love is not a constant round of candy, flowers and birthday presents. It is more likely to be a long series of sacrifices in which the fishing trip gives way to a down payment on a washer and the new party dress gives way to an appendectomy, and where even the weekly night out at the movies may have to give way to new shoes for the kids. It is not a guarantee of living happily ever after, for every marriage involves struggle, boredom, illness, financial problems and worry over the children. Perhaps true love can best be recognized by the fact that it thrives under circumstances which would blast anything else into small pieces.

The groom, seen in a bathrobe, turns out to have legs like pipestems. The love nest in the suburbs has a leaky roof, crabgrass, a mortgage that burns up every second paycheck, and mice which the bride has to catch and dispose of single-handed because the husband has an annoying way of being on a business trip during every crisis.

The groom, alas, is not quite so brilliant as promised. His job prospects fade. He never earns that million dollars. He loses his hair and his teeth. His wife loses her figure. The babies are not the dimpled darlings of the ads but imperious tyrants who have to be bottled, burped, bathed and changed—and later agonized over when they start getting into fights in elementary school and staying out too late in high school. There are moments when the husband is fed to the teeth and would like to run off to Australia. There are moments when the wife wishes she had entered a nunnery. And still . . . . and still. . . .

You can see them alongside the shuffleboard courts in Florida or on the porches of the old folks' homes up north:

an old man with snow-white hair, a little hard of hearing, reading the newspaper through a magnifying glass; an old woman in a shapeless dress, her knuckles gnarled by arthritis, wearing sandals to ease her aching arches. They are holding hands, and in a little while they will totter off to take a nap, and then she will cook supper, not a very good supper, and they will watch television, each knowing exactly what the other is thinking, until it is time for bed. They may even have a good, soul-stirring argument, just to prove that they still really care. And through the night they will snore unabashedly, each resting content because the other is there. They are in love. They have always been in love, although sometimes they would have denied it. And because they have been in love they have survived everything that life could throw at them, even their own failures.[1]

This is marriage, good in the living, in the reality.

---

[1] Ernest Haveman, *"The Intricate Balance of a Happy Marriage,* pp. 215–6, New York: Doubleday, 1962.

6

MARRYING TO REFORM

WHEN SOMEONE MARRIES TO CHANGE A SPOUSE, IT CAN BE predicted with a high degree of confidence that he will have lots of trouble. Such marriages, it has been my experience, do not work out well; and if they continue, the grief generally is more than a human being ought to bear. The reason for this, it seems to me, is simple and obvious.

What in essence prompts a person to merge his life with another? Stated rather simply, it centers around these feelings: "I like him. I admire him. I feel complete and whole when in his presence, and when the time for parting comes, it is hard and unpleasant. I wish to bind my life to his so that law and society and convention will make it difficult for either of us to separate. The thought of living apart from him is depressing distressing, unbearable." In terms of probability, the best base for a match is this mutual admiration and regard and need.

Once you start from another base, once you marry with the intention—consciously or unconsciously—to reform your spouse, what are you in effect implying? You are saying: "I do not like you the way you are. You, my spouse, may be all right—once you are fixed up, changed, altered, modified. You would never do as you are." You are saying: "I would like you, my spouse, if . . . if you were this, that or the other thing." The "if" is the part which says: "You are wrong as you are. You are an impossible person as you are."

Even though you may not use these words, they are there—implied. Once you start from this base—"You are wrong as you are"—you remove the cement that binds a relationship and makes it good in the living. It means that one marital partner has reservations about the other, refusing to accept him the way he is, disliking him the way he is. In such a relationship, there exists no admiration and affection of the person before you as he is. Such an attitude violates the elementary needs of a good marriage. The prognosis for such a marriage, it seems to me, can be nothing but grief.

Even if you should not put these feelings into words, you cannot help but communicate them, no matter how you tried. How often have you met persons who used the most endearing words, "sweet," "lovely," "wonderful," and these words fell on unlistening ears and had no meaning? You knew they were hypocritical words, lying words.

Emotions are communicated in every movement of the body, in the shake of the head, in the inflection of the voice. You know, without being told, whether this person is reacting to you with warmth and affection or the reverse. Early in my practice, I had a patient, a young man, a college student. The session was over, and as he was leaving my office, as is my custom, I held out my hand to him. He took my hand and I felt his body stiffen in anger. I was taken aback. "You know that I touched you in kindliness and friendship," I said. His face contorted. "It's that bitch of a mother. She never liked me. She speaks sweet words, but every time she touched me and touches me, I feel like taking my foot and pushing it against that face of hers."

We pretty well know whether we're liked, tolerated, or disliked. You can't fool even a child. The mother who uses sweet words and physical caresses for her child, only to rush off to her true interests—that child knows he is being rejected by his mother. You can't fool anyone regarding an emotion; every gesture of your body—the look in your eyes, the tone of voice—will reveal it as surely as if you spoke these feelings.

Since I am convinced that the best relationships are based on acceptance and unconditional regard, I myself can see nothing but bleak prospects for the marriage motivated by reform of the other. When you marry someone to change and alter him, you have, as I see it, the worst possible foundation on which to build a good creative relationship.

How foolhardy it is to marry the alcoholic, the drug addict, the gambler, the irresponsible no-account to reform him! From such a relationship one can expect only failure and grief. In the relationship itself there is built-in criticism and demand.

You may ask: Isn't discord, criticism, demand, disagreement built into every relationship, no matter how idyllic, because human beings are what they are? The answer is yes. When, however, a relationship is suffused with respect and admiration, it is essentially sound and will absorb the disagreements that will inevitably arise. As I have pointed out, there are no two living things in the universe exactly alike, not even two blades of grass. Hence, differences are inevitable, even in good relationships, some quite bitter and disillusioning. If in the relationship there is this essential quality of admiration and affection, it will survive these differences. In fact, these differences—if they are not so wide that the two cannot accommodate to them—will further strengthen the relationship, for they will provide increased insight. If both are emotionally mature and have mutual regard, each disagreement, if wisely handled, will lead to increased understanding, so that each becomes more sensitive to the other's needs and wishes. If resolution is impossible, even this becomes understanding. As a wife said to me, speaking of her husband: "We disagree on this point and see differently, but I know how he feels and he knows how I feel. Fortunately, we respect each other's view and we manage."

More and better love making takes place after an argument than at any other time, for each feels the sense of having inflicted hurt and subsequent guilt and there is the desire to expiate guilt and to be kind and loving.[1]

As a prerequisite to a relationship as close and pervasive as marriage, it is essential that the two like one another. When there is non-acceptance, dislike for the person as he is, there is no desire to please—only to part, to maintain distance; or if the two are engaged in battle, to inflict hurt and pain.

To marry to reform another person is to take on a thankless and ugly job from which can come little good, neither to the one who feels superior to the marital partner or to the luckless victim.

This lesson, so plain and obvious, often has to be learned with much travail.

---

[1] Speaking at the convention of The American Psychological Society, George B. Bach said that 90 per cent of the married couples make up their quarrels by sex. He added that unfortunately the differences remain; the couples do not try to resolve them. ("Most Murders Found Committed in Families Among Friends," The New York Times, September 3, 1967.)

7

MARRYING FOR THE WRONG REASONS

IT IS AMAZING WHAT PEOPLE WILL EXPECT FROM MARRIAGE. Many regard it as some sort of medicinal prescription, a cure to heal and clear up personal trouble. A marital relationship is difficult enough, but when it is burdened with extras that do not belong to it, it only adds to its inherent difficulties.

The only thing that one has a right to expect in a marriage is another person to make and share a life, solely that and nothing more. No one has a right to expect marriage to supply him with a nurse, a provider, a mother, a father, a servant, or an admirer who will slavishly feed his vanity; one has no right to expect from marriage a remedy for boredom nor a social life to shield him from loneliness.

Yet so many come to marriage with insatiable expectations. There is no limit to what they demand from marriage. Some adults, still adolescents in emotional development, expect marriage to be a panacea to rid them of all problems and woes. It is, I suppose, because romance has in our society been so exalted that persons look to it as the answer to whatever ails them. They begin to regard romance as some sort of Nirvana representing perpetual and eternal happiness. It is probably for this reason that marriages have proved for many so egregiously disappointing.

Writes Karen Horney:

"Because it corresponds to a vital need, love is overvalued in our culture. It becomes a phantom—like success—carrying with it the illusion that it is a solution to all problems. Love itself is not an illusion—although in our culture it is more often a screen for satisfying wishes that have nothing to do with it—but it is made an illusion by our expecting much more of it than it can possibly fulfill. And the ideological emphasis that we place on love serves to cover up the factors which create our exaggerated need for it. Hence the individual—and I still mean the normal individual—is in the dilemma of needing a great deal of affection but finding difficulty in obtaining it."[1]

Marriage can provide only a relationship. For two mature persons, that ought to be sufficient; they should be able to make something of it—something good and lasting. What form and shape their marriage will take will depend on the two and their uniqueness. Marriage is not a static thing; it is a living, growing venture, the unfolding and the outcome depending on the capacity for growth and creativity of the partners. The course of each marriage will be unique; it will not be similar to any other marriage.

What do I mean by saying marriage is not to be used as a medicine, a cure for anything?

There is the young man with bad habits—be it alcohol-

[1] Karen Horney, "The Neurotic Personality of Our Time," New York, Norton, 1937, pp. 286–287.

ism, drug addiction, gambling, criminality. There is the hope ever present—held by him or his family—that the right marriage will change him.

There is the unstable person who gets into all kinds of unfortunate escapades. There is the hope that a right marriage will change him.

There is the social climber who wants to get into a society which he cannot achieve by his own efforts. There is the hope that a right marriage will do it.

There is the ne'er-do-well, lazy, not wanting to work. There is the hope that the right marriage will provide a meal ticket.

There is the adolescent who never grew up, who has job after job, affair after affair. There is the hope that a right marriage will fix him up.

There is the ambitious one who wants to get ahead vocationally. There is the hope that the right marriage will push him ahead of others.

There is the person who is alone, who has no friends and cannot relate to others. There is the hope that the right marriage will save him.

There is no right marriage for people with problems. They enter marriage only as cripples, placing burdens and handicaps on it. Marriage is not a medication; it is not a cure for anything. It is a relationship, good in itself, an end in itself. It is of enormous help to the person in enhancing him, in developing him. It cannot change him, remake him, cure him. For that purpose, the best we know at present is psychotherapy. Marriage is anything but that; it is too demanding a relationship.

Does it happen that one attains business success through marriage? It does.

Does it happen that marriage may make one more stable and more mature? It does.

Does it happen that through marriage one advances oneself socially? It does.

It happens when there is a mutuality of needs and common purposes. The two in the marriage make a life serving each other in these needs. It sometimes happens that the individual who is well-placed socially needs a partner with financial means to maintain his position; the ambitious young woman who seeks a husband to carry on the family enterprise, the older, maternal woman who wants as a husband a child to nurse; the man who fears an adult woman for a wife and out of low self-esteem seeks an obedient child—these combinations, because of the complexity of man, sometimes function well.

Havelock Ellis said the neurotic marries another neurotic. The neurotic finds the normal and healthy person too bland, placid, saltless, and of no interest. Always in a stew, tempestuous, constantly in disturbance, the neurotic appears to another neurotic interesting and complex. Sometimes they function well with one another.

I have seen one such marriage. I have in mind a patient who had many elusions and delusions and a wife who reinforced him in these beliefs and gave him vast comfort. He would tell of how his boss put wires in him in order to eavesdrop on his thoughts.

His wife would become alarmed, excited, sympathetic, and indignant. "Oh, you poor dear, how that horrible man makes you suffer! And to have wires in you all the time, way inside, so that no one can see them. How awful!" And she would caress him and take him to her bosom, running her hands through his hair for comfort. At times he could not reach his work, for he would have to emerge from the subway before the train reached his destination. "People were pushing me, wanting to hurt me," he would explain to his wife. She would console him. "How can people be so mean! How awful! And how you suffer!" There are couples like that who give each other a great deal of help.

These are the rare exceptions. As Emerson told us, "Consistency is the hobgoblin of little minds." Such marriages are the exception that proves the rule.[2]

It sometimes happens that one who jumps out of the fortieth story window of a skyscraper is caught by the shirt tail on a flagpole protruding from the third floor and lives. We can say, nevertheless, with some certainty that one who makes such a leap is destined for destruction.

Marriage entered with the notion of exploiting another person, of using the marital partner selfishly for one's own purposes, cannot unfold with richness and beauty, unless in the course of the marriage there develop mutual needs and desires, so that the relationship enhances and fulfills both.

---

2 Although I do not like to stretch a point, even this may not violate our thesis too much. We shall discuss the subject of mutual need in marriage; and in the achieving of this *mutual* needs there develops regard, affection and devotion, which, I believe, is the base of a good relationship.

8

AMBITION, BEAUTY, AND MARRIAGE

A NOTION PREVAILS THAT THERE IS SOME CONNECTION, SOME
correlation between physical beauty and a good marriage.
I believe this notion is altogether erroneous. A handsome,
able, very ambitious, aggressive, successful man may make
a bad husband; a glamorous, ravishingly beautiful woman
may make a bad wife. The crux, the gravamen, the center
resides, it cannot be reiterated often enough, in the capacity to give love, affection, empathy, and to sacrifice
for another. And good-looking men and women, successful and ambitious, may be bereft of these qualities.

I had a patient who met all the foregoing requirements,
and yet he would make the worst possible husband. Robert was in his late thirties: very successful, a stalwart,
bronzed, powerful man, head of his own business, very
able and aggressive; and he was headed for even higher
and better. Robert was a bed-hopper. That was a passion with him, his hobby and avocation. As he said, "My
campaign is to see how soon I can get their panties down."
When he did, he had made it, achieved, and lost interest.

He went away on week-ends, and if there wasn't a
woman accompanying him, it was a lost week-end. Espe-

63

cially did he like a new woman. Seldom did he talk of
these women with affection or regard. Mostly he termed
them "penis wipers."

What prompted him to go to all the pains and expense
and work—for he did work at it and hard—to get a woman's "panties down?" "I like women to like me," he said.
"I feel good and powerful when they do. I enjoy sex.
When women don't like me, I feel depressed and unhappy."

Typical of so many in our culture, he liked to be loved
but he seemed to be unable to love.

What brought him into therapy? There were nights
when he would call up a woman from his address book
and she would not be available; and then he would call
up a second and then a third and then a fourth; and they
would not be available; and then he would have to live
with himself, alone, deserted, rejected; and he was approaching forty; and great fears set in that life was leaving him and he would become old. And he couldn't sleep,
and frightened, distraught, he'd call up at two a.m. a
"reliable." But even this "reliable" had become fed up
with him; she had eaten enough gall; and she threatened
him with the police if he dared come. In desperation, he
came anyhow; and managed to have sex with her, and
afterwards, he felt low and ashamed and debased. So
life was not easy for him; and he was often depressed.

Pity any woman who gets involved with Robert. He
is a well-built, powerful man; he is an able, successful
man, and vocationally there is no limit to how high he
may reach; and any woman would feel most attractive
and most feminine as he walks her into a drawing room
or a theatre or a restaurant. But in this man, there is no

constancy, no affection, no concept of a deep, sharing relationship. And these are the criteria for a good marriage, and he flunks in all of them.

Pity any woman who gets involved with Robert.

For some reason, in our culture there are more males who act and feel this promiscuous way. At times, you find a woman who also cannot develop a deep, sharing relationship. Evelyn was in her early twenties. She was a doctoral candidate at a large university. She was beautiful, brilliant, a scholarship student, apparently all a young man would want in a woman. Although she had many young men vying for her favor, she could not get involved with any. "I don't feel," she said. What bothered her was that so many young men liked her, and they meant nothing to her. In therapy, her constant refrain was: "I have no feelings for anyone. I never think of anyone after I leave him."

She was having some sort of a relationship with a fellow student. She was very happy about this. "I believe I have some feelings for him." Evelyn was smart and had read the literature and intellectually knew the importance of being related to another. Coldly, intellectually, as an experiment, she asked the man to sleep with her.

In a session with me afterwards, she said: "I called him up and we had sex. I tried to see if sex could arouse any feelings in me. It was nothing, plain nothing. I thought I liked him." This was the first and the last of the experiment. The affair was over. The young man sought her out and pleaded with her for her friendship, but she'd have naught of him. "I thought I liked him, but he's nothing."

Pity the young man who gets involved with Evelyn.

In her he would find a hard wall and he would never be able to penetrate into soft, warm, giving flesh; it would be all hard and surface.

Beautiful women and handsome men may be total flops and failures as lovers and mates.

Physically small, unattractive, even ugly persons can develop deep, stirring, creative relationships that bring forth from the person his best and loftiest self. Isadora Duncan, the dancer, relates what made D'Annunzio, the Italian poet, whose mistress was the actress Eleanora Duse, the great lover he was. Physically, D'Annunzio was not prepossessing; he was small, tiny, well under five feet.

In her book, *My Life,* Isadora Duncan wrote: "When D'Annunzio loves a woman, he lifts her spirit from this earth to the divine region where Beatrice moves and shines. In turn he transforms each woman to a part of the divine essence, he carries her aloft until she believes herself really Beatrice. . . . He flung over each favorite in turn a shining veil. She rose above the heads of ordinary mortals and walked surrounded by a strange radiance. But when the caprice of the poet ended, this veil vanished, the radiance was eclipsed, and the woman turned again to common clay. . . . To hear oneself praised with that magic peculiar to D'Annunzio is, I imagine, something like the experience of Eve when she heard the voice of the serpent of Paradise. D'Annunzio can make any woman feel she is the center of the universe."

Ideally, it seems to me the aim is for both to make each other "the center of the universe." That is the secret that cements two human beings together. The inconstancy of D'Annunzio is not to my mind desirable. How much better, how much more satisfying it would be—and is—if such passionate attachments were durable and lifetime lasting.

How much more could each give the other with the increased knowledge and insights gained by years of learning about each other? If you say such intensity cannot last, then I would say that the closer it approaches this relationship in a durable, lasting way the happier for the two.

9

AS THE THERAPIST SEES THE SPOUSE

I HAVE HAD FREQUENT OCCASION TO SAY TO A PATIENT: "I wish there was a peephole so that your spouse can see you, hear you as I hear you; see how intelligent and reasonable you are, how sensitive and kind you are. He could not help but be moved."

How true this is!

When I tell them this individually in a private session, they both become filled with hope that this could be; for that is how they want it to be.

Why don't they perceive their spouses as I do?

When they are with me, their therapist, they are at their best, their least defensive self, for I try to give each of them regard, acceptance, and understanding. And for me, each becomes lovely and good and kind; and they are.

It is an unfortunate tragedy that so many husbands and wives will never see each other as I see and come to know them individually. I am indeed fortunate. I see them at their best.

In a bad marriage, each is guarded, watchful, suspicious, angry, defensive, hostile. If one makes a suggestion or criticism, the other feels attacked and they both imme-

diately lash out. "So you think you're smart!" And thus
the counter offensive starts. They then proceed with a
recital of the past and the future—and you may be sure
never in a complimentary way—so that the two emerge
not uplifted from the exchange, but each dragged down,
besmirched with mud. There is no talking or understanding, only in-fighting.

How tragic the fact that both—deep-down filled with
the greatest desire and need to live with each other in
amity and good will, deep-down seeing in their spouse a
special, unique person who has vital meaning for them—
cannot see the other in this open, non-defensive sympathetic way that the therapist does. Often, I wish the spouse
could see his partner the way he is when at ease, secure
from attack; and how warmly and affectionately he can
relate to another person.

In marital counseling, I have had occasion to explain to
a patient why his spouse got angry, what prompted what
appeared to be a hysterical outburst beyond forgiving.
After listening, he would be surprised and contrite. And
then, when I would explain to the spouse what prompted
the other's anger, she would be equally surprised and
contrite.

To understand all is to forgive a great deal.

Why do spouses appear so loving and lovable to me
and not to their mates? For one, with me, they need not
be defensive; they are not in battle; they need not be on
guard; they can be themselves. They know I will not
attack them; that they will be understood and listened
to with generosity and kindliness, with every effort made
to understand and be sympathetic; and because of this,
their very best, loveliest self comes forth. When with
their spouse, each is defensive, argumentative, quarrel-

some, not listening, using everything that is said in the exchange against the person, as if what each is saying becomes evidence for self-incrimination. Under such situations, human beings are at their worst, their most disagreeable and loathsome selves.

Can you imagine two persons on warring sides in battle developing affection for each other? Under such circumstances, the worst in the person comes forth, his insecurity, his fears, his hostility, his hate, his sadism, his paranoia, all his unhealthy and destructive qualities. Man, then, acts, feels, and thinks as his most hateful self. No, he is not a lovable object.

How tragic that so many married persons never see each other at their best, their kindest and most lovable selves, but only as caricatures of themselves, twisted, distorted, fearful, insecure!

In therapy, when I am able to bring the two together in joint sessions, I ask them to "listen to your spouse in the same way I listen to you." Some at first cannot. They become offensive, attacking or defensive, defending.

"Try to understand," I ask them. "Don't agree; don't disagree. Try to understand. Just listen."

Often what appears to be something akin to a miracle takes place. This especially holds true when the spouse perceives that despite appearances, the partner bears a vast reservoir of good will and affection toward him; and this comes as a surprise. If I have learned anything, it is this: the driving desire of married couples—at least those who consult me—is to find a *modus vivendi*, a way of life, to live well in the marriage; and if at all possible, to maintain and preserve it. This is all the more astonishing when you think of how much tugging and tearing and searing had gone on and is going on between the two.

Hitherto, before they started to talk and listen to each

other, they nursed their grievances. These grievances were for the most part unspoken. Under such circumstances, walls develop between a couple and the grievances lay in the stomach unresolved, and they stew there, poisoning the person, getting worse, contaminating the body all the more, as the concoction boils within, not cast out. When it gets beyond what a person can endure, some slight disagreement occurs, and there erupts a volcanic outburst in amount and in fury altogether disproportionate to the incident. The spouse suffers through this outburst, so unexpected, so unwarranted, so out of proportion to the situation; and the spouse is more convinced than ever that he was justified in his feelings about his partner, convinced the other was even more evil than he even thought. Neither partner has ever learned how to vent, cope, and accommodate himself to small differences.

In many instances we meet unpleasantness by fight or flight. In flight, the thought is that if you run away from the unpleasantness it will disappear. Facing the unpleasantness may be disagreeable, but there is the hope that you might learn how to cope with it; at least you may develop some workable arrangement. But in flight, that possibility does not exist. True it is an escape, but it leaves the situation as bad as when you left it; it is a sort of surrender, really a defeat. At any rate, when couples do not resolve disagreements and differences as they arise (and in any relationship such differences are inevitable), then pressures are being built up, and then, when they become uncontainable, the vessel breaks, sometimes with catastrophic consequences. A frequent kind of flight is to build walls around certain subjects. They become too ticklish to handle, too charged with emotions, and then there is silence, with hostility and hatred mounting.

On a battlefield, there can be little good will between

two enemies, only wariness, fear, suspicion, hate. When one is under attack and in danger, one is not apt to be at his best; one is not apt to be lovable, kind, and generous. And these are the ingredients of the good marriage; and these qualities are destroyed in the bad marriage.

It is the therapist—if he is sympathetic and accepting—who sees the person at his best, at his most lovable self.

And for this reason, I frequently wish there were a peephole into my office so that the spouse can see his partner. I am certain he would be agreeably surprised and amazed.

10

CASTING OUT ALL OTHERS

IF WE ACCEPT THE PREMISE THAT THE TWO IN THE MARRIAGE have to be dedicated and devoted to each other, they should both come to the marriage emotionally free of all others in priority of commitment. It also becomes a necessity for both to be psychologically weaned, to have cut the umbilical cord to parents. The spouses should have their emotional insides free, clear for each other exclusively, without reservations. No other should take precedence, not father, mother, brother, sister, friends.

Why should there be this urgent need for a clear, free emotional inside? In my experience where there are even vistigial remains of a prior commitment, there is not full and exclusive spouse-centered emotional involvement and concern.

Unless a fairly substantial measure of parental emancipation has taken place, there is little likelihood of a marriage in any event. There generally isn't sufficient urgency and need for a marital relationship and the implied exclusive commitment. If such a person does develop some sort of heterosexual relationship, he still remains psychologically oriented to parents; and hence cannot give himself to the other exclusively and with full devotion. Generally such relationships peter out. Unless the person has gained psychological independence from his parents, emotionally, he remains essentially a child who regards his parents, not his own person, as the center of his life. When an infantile person does succeed in marrying, the burden on the marriage is great and the prognosis for its success is bleak.[1]

In some instances, children are deliberately kept in bondage by parents who will not give them up; they want them to remain children. This is especially true of daughters, although it may happen to either sex. As one mother said to her son: "You have everything you need here. Who will love you as much? Who will take care of you as well? Who will do for you as much?" The parents keep these offspring close, will not give them freedom, and the result is that they have no room emotionally for outsiders of a central nature. Even should these meet a proper partner, the relationship comes to nothing.

The family may decide, consciously or unconsciously,

[1] Apparently, it need not be only parents that clutter up the emotional insides of a person, so he has no room for a marital partner to join his life in a pivotal, fundamental way. Dr. Alfred Adler records in *The Problem of Neurosis* the story of a man who lived with two sisters who doted on him, spoiled him, and served his every need. He had become engaged several times, and always he had broken off the relationship before its final termination in marriage. He himself was advancing in years, and his sisters were in their sixties. If he ever were to marry, he realized that now was the time. He was fond of a woman and he became engaged to her, this time meaning to carry through. When the time for the marriage arrived, he said that he could not consummate the marriage. He wore a dental plate, he explained, and he was certain that eventually he would contract cancer of the mouth, and he said it wasn't fair to mess up a woman's life with a man whose life was to end so disastrously. Although he himself was a physician and although no doctor could find any evidence of this disease, nothing would persuade him to the contrary. Again, he broke off the engagement. (Alfred Adler, "Problems of Neurosis," p. 166.)

that it would be a nice thing to have a daughter forever, until she dies. Such children become household orna- ments or household drudges, depending on economic well- being. Because they are held so closely to household tasks and household loyalties, they have no room for a private, independent emotional involvement. Even when by some miracle, these engage in some faint, weak heterosexual relationship, it is quickly squelched.[2]

When such child-women become old, they are pathetic. Sometimes you see them with their mothers, close, like little girls, or even worse, with their fathers, also close, like wives. The inappropriateness of the relationship is so apparent as almost to embarrass any witness to it. Watch an old mother who has an old son for a husband or an old father with an old daughter as a wife. In truth, a mother

---

[2] Upper class girls, the very rich, have unusual difficulties in this regard. They are expected to marry men in their own class, and upper class men frequently exploit lower class women sexually. Also, at times they marry outside their class; and some choose not to marry.

Hence, the lot of the upper class girl maritally is difficult. Kept shel- tered, many do not engage or engage little in adolescent heterosexual mingling and dating relationships. Such "puppy" loves are learning loves, learning experiences about the opposite sex and the nature of one's own personality. Denied this free experience, this probably ac- counts for the impossible marriages made by upper class girls—heiresses marrying a cowboy, a policeman, the family chauffeur, and the like. It is knowledge acquired in the course of heterosexual experience that serves as a base for an intelligent choice of a permanent, life-long part- ner. The ignorant have nothing to go by, and it has been my experience that couples who marry with little or no adolescent heterosexual experi- ences have more difficulty with their marriages than those who do.

An interesting sidelight is provided to these observations by Cleveland Amory, who writes in *The Last Resorts* (page 28):

"Of the new 'naughty millionaires,' dominated as they were by New Yorkers like Sloanes, Schermerhorns and Parsons, the most puritanical was Lenox's late Grenville Winthrop. His wife having died after the birth of his second child, Winthrop brought up his two daughters so severely that they never were allowed to speak to a boy unless a chaperone was present. In September, 1924, the two girls engineered a clandestine dou- ble-elopement, marrying, respectively, an electrician and a chauffeur."

is an inappropriate wife to a son; and a father an inappropriate husband to a daughter.

When a child is caught up in this kind of situation, unable or unwilling or without the courage to extricate himself or herself, I wish they could see the final denouement: what happens as one gets older living this relationship. Even more pathetic, what happens when the parents die leaving the aged son or daughter still a child in thought and in feeling; and like a child, living their remaining years bereft and forsaken.

I had a patient, as admirable a woman as you would wish. She was in her sixties; and she was going through a personal hell. When sixteen, Ruth's mother died. Her father, who owned a grocery store, made Ruth the mother of his four children, all younger than she.

It is remarkable how she carried on. A brilliant high school student, specializing in Greek, she was compelled to give up her schooling. She cooked, sewed, took care of the house, her father, her brothers and sisters. Every thought was concentrated on her father, (whom she thought of as her husband), and her brothers and sisters. The father felt no need to educate his daughters, but it was Ruth who insisted that the girls, her sisters, go to school. Ruth's next older sister became a teacher. Her two older brothers also were graduated from college because Ruth fought their fight with her father, who was most unsympathetic to education. He wanted them to work as he had worked as a boy. Ruth loved books. Her hope was some day to own a book store.

Her emancipation from her father came late in life, but it wasn't a total or full emancipation. She rebelled like a mother on behalf of a child.

Her youngest sister showed great talent as a singer.

She appeared at local churches and entertainments. Old fashioned, the father would not have any of it; while Ruth—regarding Faye, her sister, as her child—could not stand having Faye's obvious talent go undeveloped. And here began her struggle—the first in her life—with her father; the agony and the horror with which she left the household (besides Faye only the father now comprised it; all the others had married); and went to New York so as to provide opportunity for Faye, her sister. For the first time Ruth experienced a new world. She found work so as to obtain the wherewithal to give Faye singing and dramatic lessons. And Faye became all that Ruth hoped for. She became a star in musicals, with her name on Broadway marquees in big lights. This was a great adventure for Ruth, as life became for the first time exciting. True enough she lived vicariously, but Ruth and Faye were close, and whatever adventure happened to Faye, Ruth knew and lived out in detail. And this might have been satisfactory for Ruth, for it was more than she ever had in her life. But again, a sister is not a husband, and this comprises the terrible, irretrievable mistake so often made in all such twisted, inappropriate relationships.

Travelling with a company in which she starred, Faye went off alone, and in the course of the tour, she married. For a time she kept this secret from Ruth. But such secrets cannot keep and when it was disclosed, Ruth was emotionally distraught, very sick, very lonely, and very miserable—especially since Faye's husband would not have her around.

Ruth was still in contact with all her other children— no, my mistake, *sisters and brothers*—and their children; and she was always available whenever they wanted her in whatever way—as a baby sitter or as a confidante or as

a kitchen helper. She was not proud. When they entertained, she would be quite willing to efface herself by
acting as the maid. She had no real choice at this point.
She had no life of her own; she did not know how to make
a friend or be one. She was the wife to her father and the
mother to her sisters and brothers; and this, since she was
neither, is a queer, sick role.

What brought her to therapy was her discovery that
none of the sisters nor the brothers wanted her around.
The nephews and nieces, for whom she always had room
in her New York apartment and enough money for theatre
tickets and restaurants, which she frugally saved from her
meager salary, did not care to visit with her. They had
their own friends and their own life, while Ruth had no
life and sponged on the life of these others. This heart-
breaking insight developed when she discovered that one
of her sisters was to undergo an operation, and she carried on in a hysterical manner. It was then that one of
her sisters said to Ruth: "I wish you would stay out of
my affairs and my home life. Let me have my own operation. It is mine and not yours. Please stay away."

It was from Ruth that I learned that one has no right
to take away anyone else's problems; and it does no good,
only harm. And her sister was quite right in demanding
that since it was her operation, it was she who should have
the right to the pain, the concern, the worry in connection with it; and as a companion to support and console
her she had her husband. An outsider was an interloper.

In therapy, I shared the pain, the grief and travail of
a woman, in her sixties, highly intelligent, highly literate
(she still hoped to find work in or to own a rare book
shop), good and self-sacrificing in all ways, who at this
late age was deserted by all who were dear to her—in
the only world she ever knew.

Willy nilly, she now had to make a new life for herself; it was strange and hard, and she did not know how to go about it. I remember the first trip she took out of the city. With what trepidations she went! I remember her first joining a walking tour of the city, later a museum tour. I remember how first she made a conscious effort to talk to a neighbor. How hard it was! I remember how first she tried to entertain a person she had come to know on her first venture into the world—that holiday trip she made. She had to learn what she should have as a child, when she first stepped out of her home and went to school. Her fright, her terror, her fears! She had to learn how to live in her middle sixties as a full, complete person.

When it got too much, more than she could bear, she would revert back to her isolation, so deep and impenetrable that for days and weeks she did not speak to a human being. Even in her work—she had held the job for years—she was isolated. When sick, the prospect of walking up to her superior and asking for the day off so terrified her that she, rather than undergo this, would work with high temperature. One time she collapsed at the end of a day's work outside her office building and had to be taken to a hospital. She was back at work in four days, against doctors' orders. A poor, horrible, sick, wasted life! And such a lovely woman and such a beautiful person!

Sometimes children may rebel from parents and save themselves for healthy living. An illustration follows:

Emily was a school teacher in her forties. She lived with her mother who was widowed when she was a child. As a girl, whenever Emily brought a young man to her home, after he was gone the mother spent the rest of the evening mimicking him to his discredit, making small of him. Thus it continued till Emily was in her twenties, and in her thirties, and now she was in her early forties. In her mother's eyes there was no man good enough for her.

Emily was now engrossed in a very close relationship with a man of her own years, and no matter how her mother ridiculed him, how she stormed against him, Emily persisted in maintaining the relationship. When her mother perceived that her old strategy was of no avail, her campaign took another track. She had more frequent heart attacks and they appeared to be of a more serious nature. Even while Emily was at the theatre with her fiance, her mother paged her, and when Emily reached the phone, her mother said that she was very sick and needed her immediately. She would excuse herself from her fiance and would leave the theatre in panic. And thus this behavior continued until Emily's suitor stopped calling.

Emily realized this was her last chance for marriage. But her fiance was firm. He had gone through this business of heart attacks and the ups and the downs of the relationship. He was adamant. She would have to decide here and now, firmly and definitely, whether she would marry him. If not, he would seek elsewhere. Pressed by him, her decision was yes.

The mother now really carried on. Her heart attacks became worse than ever. One evening before her daughter went out with her fiance, she had her most severe heart attack ever; this one would kill her. The daughter did not break with her fiance. When the mother saw that all this was of no avail, she spoke frankly and harshly. "I have worked and slaved for you all my life. I brought you up without a father. I gave up my life for you. And this is the gratitude I get. This is how you intend to pay me back. Have you no pity on your poor, old mother? No shame!"

And thus the struggle continued.

Emily held out and won out; she finally married her suitor. In a last effort to break up the proposed marriage, just before the wedding, the mother put on one of her worst heart attacks. On returning home one night, Emily found her mother on the floor, saying that she was dying and talked of her will. Emily immediately called the doctor, and when he came, the doctor, after examination, told Emily that it wasn't necessary to hospitalize her mother. Her mother's heart, he said, was not too good, but for a woman of her years, it was as good as one would expect.

Throughout her courtship, her mother had made Emily feel guilty. The mother was never reconciled to the marriage, and refused to attend the ceremony. The night of the wedding the mother was at home having the "worst dying heart attack." She survived that. If the mother succeeds in keeping Emily guilty and concerned about her, so that the husband assumes a subsidiary emotional place in her being, the prognosis I would say for the marriage is poor.

Some children, kept infantile by parents, never succeed in entering upon a marriage. I had a patient, Elizabeth, who was excited by her forthcoming marriage. She was a student, in her early twenties, and her fiance was a dentist in his middle thirties. Once she came to me weeping copiously, in a misery such as I haven't witnessed. The marriage was off.

This was the story she told me. Her fiance, Herbert,

had become sick, and Elizabeth, sympathetic, tried to nurse him. Her fiance's mother stepped in, took over with great authority, and brushed Elizabeth aside. The mother cooed and billed over her son, and ignored the girl. "The two were so close I couldn't wedge myself between them," Elizabeth said. "You should have seen how she fed Herbert, as if he were a little child of two. And Herbert loved it. Between the two, I was completely ignored." Miffed, miserable, apparently unwanted, she was not as assiduous in attending Herbert as she should have been if she had felt needed. The mother now convinced Herbert that Elizabeth was not at all the proper wife for him; that she was cruel and unfeeling and cared nothing about him.

After her classes were over, Elizabeth would rush to her fiance. This time she was greeted with more than usual coldness and formality. Elizabeth felt that there was something amiss, and she was not mistaken. During the course of the evening both mother and son together told her that the engagement was off; the whole thing was impossible. Elizabeth took it very badly and she was in misery for a long time.

The sequel to the story came about half year later. She learned that this was Herbert's third broken engagement; and what happened to her was a pattern. In the previous instances, Herbert also got ill and both mother and son concluded that his fiance was cruel and heartless; and the good kind mother was there ready to rescue him from the horrible fate that might have befallen him.

As I listened to the story, even from the first, my own thoughts were "Good riddance." Chronologically, by age, this man, this dentist, was a grown man, but emotionally, he was still a child, not ready for marriage.

Both the man and the woman in a marriage need to be free, completely free, inside and outside, all around, if they want to start rightly on this most complex relationship known to man. Even if this condition holds, it does not mean that the marriage will necessarily be successful. It only means that they start out with a fighting chance. Before his marriage Sigmund Freud made his wife promise to hate her parents.[3] I thought it was a cruel demand. That Freud was a genius I am sure. What he demanded still seems harsh. That he had a point—the amount and the extent I do not know—I am also sure.

---

[3] "But Freud's jealousy was by no means restricted to other young men; it equally applied to Martha's affectionate feelings for her family. He demanded from her 'that she should not simply be able to criticize her mother and brother objectively and abandon their foolish superstitions,' all of which she did, but she had also to withdraw all affection from them—this on the grounds that they were his enemies, so that she should share his hatred of them." (Erich Fromm, *Sigmund Freud's Mission*, p. 20. N.Y.: Harper & Brother's, 1959.)

11

PARENTS, HUSBANDS AND WIVES

IN OUR CULTURE, GIRLS ARE HELD MORE TIGHTLY TO THE family; they are given less freedom than their brothers, who are expected to go out into the world and make their own way. Further, it is the girl who gestates the child and has the responsibility for its rearing, while her brother sows his seed and goes off. Held tighter and closer by family, the girls are more frequently emotionally committed to family even after marriage than the boys. It is the girls who are more apt to call up their home every hour on the hour. And in young marriages, when things go bad, it is more apt to be the wife who rushes off to mother and father for solace and comfort. But it need not necessarily be confined to the wife. The husband can likewise be tied to family in a detrimental way. The following will illustrate the foregoing.

It was a bad marriage, the kind where each nurses grievances in silence. One inappropriate word triggers off violent outbursts.

In therapy, the situation was beginning to improve. The walls of separation were becoming thinner and in some areas dents were made and communication opened. Hitherto full of distrust and suspicion, the couple had begun to perceive what it means to accept one another, and to learn to speak, not in hostility, not to hurt and wound, but to understand. And best of all, they were beginning to acquire a sense of generosity and softness to each other. In the process of counseling, they experienced an episode that set them back considerably and that started both thinking anew of a divorce.

It came about as a result of the couple's routine visit to the husband's mother on a Friday night. Before we can fully appreciate what happened, we should know the background of the marriage. The mother had an unhappy marriage. Her husband was a shadowy figure in the household, but the son more than filled the household vacuum with prominence and importance. "My darling, darling son," his mother called him. Martin disappointed her in only one way: she had set her heart on his becoming a doctor, but his grades weren't good enough and he became a teacher instead. "He is very, very bright, I'd say a genius, but his teachers are very, very bad. So what can you do? And my Martin has to suffer. Poor boy."

When he started dating girls, Mrs. A didn't mind too much at first. It titillated and excited her. She waited up for him. While sitting on his bed, he told of his evening's experiences in great detail.

"Such a boy like Martin. Who wouldn't want him?" She said she wanted him to get married. But there was one trouble: there was no girl good enough. No girl born to woman could be good enough for her Martin; it was as simple as that. He was seriously involved heterosexually several times, but each such involvement came to nothing. He was now in his middle thirties and he was lonely, unhappy, depressed. He taught in a school in a low socio-economic neighborhood, and he was miserable at his job. During this period he became friendly with another teacher, who was of great help to him professionally in enabling him better to meet the problems he was facing in the classroom and also helping him emotionally.

Mrs. A, the mother, again tried to interfere, but Carolyn, herself a strong, independent woman, was able to stand up to her; and despite the mother's opposition, Martin married Carolyn. The mother attended the wedding looking pale and worn out. From the day of the marriage, the mother had competed with the wife for her son. It was nip and tuck as to who would end up the most important figure in Martin's life. At the beginning of the marriage, it was definitely Carolyn who was winning out. Martin was greatly dependent on her; Carolyn gave him comfort and support in his teaching, which was giving him great tension and anxiety. At the beginning of the marriage, Martin's wife served both as a mother and as a professional colleague.

Soon Carolyn tired of the role of mother and wife. She got fed up with being married to a child and demanded that Martin assume more responsibility. Through the disagreements that ensued, the mother wedged her way into the marriage to protect her "poor darling boy," and the marriage became very bad, and it looked as if it would end disastrously.

At this point, the couple entered counseling—which proved from the start unusually effective in their case. Walls had broken down, and they had learned to talk to each other. Carolyn was by nature a dominant, aggressive woman, and Martin was passive and dependent—a person who needed someone to lean on for support. Carolyn was also in her middle thirties and she was glad to escape a lonely life. I would say there was enough in the two, if let alone, to build some kind of a marriage.

Now we come to that Friday evening when Martin and Carolyn, in all innocence and good will, went to her mother-in-law's for supper.

The first word with which his mother greeted Martin was "You don't look well. Are you sure you're resting enough? I got up a meal just for you, exactly what you like. After a hard week's work, you ought to have good food. Your health should come first. Guess what I made for you. Come into the kitchen and smell. Good, eh? I remember when you were a little boy. You remember what a sickly little boy you were and how I would stay up with you all night? Oh, those terrible days, how I suffered. You remember, Martin. I don't expect you to think of me. Now that you have your wife, forget about me. But look after your health. Eat good food. Yes, yes, what can you expect of children? When they are grown up and strong and healthy, they ought to forget their mothers. As long as you are enjoying yourself. What else matters? What does a mother count?"

"Ma, there's no one who can cook like you," Martin reassured his mother. "No one, Ma. This meal is going to set me up for the week."

Mrs. A beamed. "Maybe you can drop in for lunch once or twice a week. I don't care how much work it is, as long as it will help my little boy."

They both embraced; and then Martin turned to his wife, Carolyn, and said proudly: "Isn't she wonderful!"

Mrs. A looked at her son admiringly. "A mother feels for her child. When he's sick, she's sick. She doesn't have to be told. She knows. Oh, the many nights I stayed up with you. You remember, Martin?" And here she pro-

ceeded to catalog all the diseases Martin had. "You remember when you had influenza and had such a high
temperature? God forbid, we thought you were about
to . . . better not to talk."

As Mrs. A talked, the years slipped away from Martin
and he was a little boy again, ready to sit on his mother's
lap and snuggle his head against her breast and even take
his mother's warm milk. Looking at Carolyn somewhat
guiltily, Martin reluctantly admitted he was both tired
and feeling sickish. Mrs. A solicitously took off his jacket,
settled him down in his favorite, comfortable chair and
wanted right there and then to tuck him into bed.

By this time Carolyn was annoyed and upset and ventured that Martin was perfectly all right when he came
home from work, and he did not complain till he came
to Mrs. A's house.

Mrs. A looked at her son in sympathy, as if some unfeeling person was talking about him, and Martin looked
at his wife afresh, as if he were seeing her with his mother's eyes; he felt misunderstood and unfairly treated.

"It takes a mother to understand her son," Mrs. A said
reassuringly to Martin.

By now Carolyn could scarcely contain herself. "Why
don't you let him alone; why do you make a baby out of
him?"

One word led to another.

Mrs. A began to weep. "My child, my poor child!"
Harsh words came from her in a stream: "selfish," "caring for no one but herself," "all she knows for my Martin
is to teach in that terrible school," and "all she knows is
how to spend."

It was a highly traumatic experience for both, and they
spoke of it at great length at the time it occurred and

afterwards. I am setting it down in detail because there are so many elements in it that run to pattern.

Martin is talking in a therapy session: "I know my mother can be trying. She loves me, and she wants the best for me. What's so horrible about that? Why should Carolyn get angry? It is true that my mother worked hard all her life, and that she sacrificed her life for me. Carolyn ought to be glad. If my mother didn't stay up nursing me, wearing herself out for me, I would be dead. It is true I was a sickly child. Why should Carolyn be so nasty? My mother is an old, sick woman. Why can't Carolyn be kind? She's unfeeling and she's cruel. She's not a real wife and doesn't care about me."

Carolyn is now talking in a therapy session: "When I visit his mother, it invariably happens. The woman is a witch. While with her, my husband appears to me to be so ugly that I can't stand looking at him. His mother turns her little finger and he eagerly rushes into her arms and becomes a child. His mother makes my husband feel that I treat him badly. After a visit with her, when we return home, I feel as if he has deserted me; that he wants to run back home to his mother. And I feel I have no husband.

"His first thoughts are of her. He is filled with her. He calls her up every day, and if he followed his own wishes, he'd go back to live with her; that's what he really wants. He would like his mama—fussing over him like a child. I'm his wife and not his mother, and I don't want to play a mother's role. I want him to be a husband, a man; and as a grown-up man, he has to learn to withstand pain and disappointment, and in return he might have the pleasure of amounting to something. As it is he feels like a child and thinks like a child; and who could respect a child with Martin's façade—big, overgrown, and aging? If he did grow up, I believe there's a great deal in him. He has a brain, you know. If only he used it he could amount to something and be respected.

"That possessive mother of his would, if she had her way, put him back in a baby carriage. She wants a child and she's always fighting to keep him a child. After he left his mother's house that night, he was cold and distant to me and whatever I did was wrong. Of course, I cannot compete with his mother. One time I could. But now I don't want to. I'm fed up with having a child for a husband, who puts all the household responsibility and burdens on me; and then, to boot, I have to take care of him. I don't want a child for a husband. It's no good and it won't work. After being with that mother of his, my cooking is no good—not like his mother's—and I'm no good —I don't worry about him as his mother does."

At this point, Carolyn, strong, powerful, broke down and tears came to her eyes. She became sad and pensive. "If that mother would stay out, we could manage to have a good life and our marriage would be all right. Martin is a kind, sweet boy."

As I have said, I am constantly astonished by the strong wish and need to preserve a marriage, even one that seems to an outsider so bad.

"How can Martin ever become a man with a mother like that, with all her pampering, with her sickening, cloying attention? It's not healthy attention; it's debilitating; it's the kind that makes a person weak."

Now she gave way and wept.

What is the prognosis for this marriage? One never knows. It depends on the maturity of the principals—how much they can stand—and also on their fears and insecurities; for they may not have the courage to do what they know is best and wise for themselves. The variables are so many—and that holds true for nearly anything that concerns human beings—that there can be no prediction. That there is and will be a lot of grief and despair in the marriage—of that I feel fairly sure.

12

PRIORITIES OF COMMITMENT IN MARRIAGE

IN MARRIAGE, I HAVE BECOME CONVINCED THAT AS A WORK-ing hypothesis it is desirable to observe the following priorities of commitment. This is not to be regarded as a hard and fast formula. I find it helpful, though.

First and foremost come the husband and wife, the two united as one. The two are the primary persons who matter in the marital relationship. They should come before all else. Each should be committed to the other fully and without reservations. In the good marriage, there is and should be room for no one else. "Therefore shall a man leave his father and mother," says the Bible, "and shall cleave unto his wife." They should feel and think as a unit, each involved in the other with his full self, until death. No one should take precedence over a spouse, not mother, not father, not children, no one. Their commitment and dedication should be of an unconditional nature; each to the other; and the two as a unit facing the world, until death.

Second comes the work. Without work, there can be no home, no children, no family unit. The work provides the wherewithal to maintain a functioning family. In our culture, there is no substitute for money; and work provides the money.

Said Carlyle: "Blessed is he who has found his work." In our society, work is necessary for the money it brings into the home; also, through work, a person acquires a sense of achievement, of feeling worthwhile, of purpose, of community respect and regard. Without some task that has meaning for the person, life is empty. Without work, I myself cannot see how a person can fill the long day, and even worse, the long, long years. William Burnham, in his great book, *The Normal Mind,* talks of the blessed rhythm of work, fatigue, rest, and sleep. Without work, he says, you cannot have fatigue, and without fatigue, you cannot have good, contented, satisfying rest. And without work and fatigue, you cannot experience good, sound, satisfying sleep. Thus, said Burnham, there is the blessed rhythm of work, fatigue, rest and sleep.

In our culture work is therapeutic. As a therapist, I know, that the prognosis of helping a person with an emotional problem who has no work is bleak. Nothing makes me rejoice more than a patient who has developed the need and the desire for work and the strength and the courage to seek work, to find it, and to engage in it.

One earns a holiday.

You cannot have a holiday every day; you must work first, and then you can have a holiday. Work is so allied to social position that those denied work, the old and the discards of industry, find it hard to maintain self respect and the sense of feeling worthwhile. Since work is so important to the person in our society, it should loom large in the marital relationship. For a spouse to slight or to be indifferent to the partner's work is to shut off from the relationship an area that engages a person's deepest and most profound self. The sinews and the gut of the relationship are eliminated. It is like leaving out the beef and concentrating on the mustard in the sandwich. It is hard to imagine a really deep and binding marital relationship unless the work becomes the concern, the interest of both. It is hard to imagine a really good and satisfying relationship unless the spouse, understanding the work, is able to share the vicissitudes, the doubts and the challenges that go with one's work. The work is not only important in maintaining the home, but it is also an essential for the emotional well-being of the spouse. Since it is so vital and crucial to the spouse, it should become, as a matter of course, vital and crucial in the marriage.

Third, come children. Normally, the two in the marriage would want to combine their seed and create brand new life together. How essential this is to a happily functioning marriage is still a matter of dispute. But once children are there, they become the solemn obligation of the parents. *But children come third, never first.* Those who disturb the order and place the children first are doing a grave injury to their marriage. The husband and wife come first; not the children. If once the children take a prior position in emotional involvement, in commitment, you have a disturbed and bad marital arrangement. Only your spouse should be your beloved, joined together till death. The two parents love their children, the two as a unit. Both father and mother love their children. Once children come between them you have a disturbed relationship.

The child's task is to fulfill himself, to become a person. And this is no mean or easy task. It will require all the courage a person can muster; and the parents should be by the child's side while he struggles. From the moment the child walks out of the home to go to school, he should be walking away from his home with increasing independence, so that ultimately, growing in maturity, he will be able to assume his own marital responsibilities and establish his own home with his own spouse and his own children.[1]

This is a difficult and frightening task, and some never succeed. The task of the parents is to encourage the child as he seeks to actualize himself, to fulfill himself; this means giving the child increasing independence and freedom from home and parents. It is an anxiety-provoking task both for parents and children; but unless this is achieved, the offspring will not fully develop as he should or become the person he should. Hence, the task of the home and the parents is to give the child the strength and the courage to emancipate himself from the home and the parents; to develop his talents and become the person he was meant to be. For that he needs courage and freedom and two understanding, sympathetic parents.

How twisted and distorted becomes the relationship when a child becomes a substitute for husband or wife! When this occurs woe to the child and the parent! A child cannot substitute for a husband or a wife.

If parents have achieved their task, done it well, they will have the satisfaction of seeing their offspring established in their own homes with their own husbands and their own wives. This brand new life, brought to the par-

---

[1] In the nineteenth century, much less so now, it was common to keep offspring, especially daughters, tied to the home. Elizabeth Browning, kept an invalid by her father, managed to escape with the help of Robert Browning, and as we know she lived a full and rich life. The Brontes, sheltered and kept to the home, at least managed to find an outlet in writing. But what about those who did not have a Browning or great talent to help them? What lives did they eke out?

ental home, will revive the old parental home, give it new importance and significance, and will enrich the lives of the aging parents.

Whatever good there is in marriage flows from the marital pair, husband and wife, even for the children. We are now beginning to realize how essential it is for a child to be reared in a home where he can witness a good marriage; and that means one in which the heads of a household live happily together, exemplifying those qualities— love, respect, devotion, admiration, self-sacrifice, etc.—that characterize the good marriage. Even those with a cursory knowledge of the subject know the importance of a good, warm, accepting, affectionate home for rearing affectionate, loving, social-minded children; how the example of a good marriage, as witnessed by the children, becomes a prototype for their own marriage.

It was not by chance that children who are reared by happily married parents offer the best prospects for good husbands and wives. Incidentally, children who are lucky enough to be born in such homes and reared by such parents become the good people of tomorrow. From disturbed homes, divorced homes, broken homes, bickering and hostile homes—from such homes come all too frequently the children who are a burden to themselves and to society. It is the two parents who create by their love and affection a home from which good things flow, including children who will become an asset to society. From bad homes come the enemies of society, delinquents, criminals, the hostile, and the angry.

Fourth come parents. It is necessary that before entering marriage each of the partners be an independent person; that each be psychologically weaned from their parents. Children—pliable, flexible, impressionable—become in values and outlook essentially what their parents are. If the parents are mature adults, the children are fortunate in having good models to imitate. To achieve mature conduct and living, both parents need to live active, independent lives. If children are to develop well, they need devoted, solicitous, loving fathers and mothers. This holy task—the rearing of their children—becomes the joint responsibility of the two parents; and it becomes their main responsibility and it takes precedence over all other obligations, including that to their own parents.

In stating this position, I do not say the married pair should be cruel to their own parents. No, not at all. But they should come to their own parents not as children, but as independent persons. This does not preclude kindness or generosity. It only means that once as children they went to their big powerful father and their warm, soft mother for comfort, strength, security. Now they themselves as parents should stand independently on their own feet and be a big powerful father and a soft warm mother *to their own children.*

"The relationship between the adult offspring and his parent is characterized to a certain degree by a reversal of roles," writes Robert F. Winch. "During the offspring's childhood, the parents have appeared to him as great, powerful and wise. When the offspring achieves maturity, however, his physical strength is at its ascendancy, whereas that of the parents is declining. Depending upon health and financial and class position of the family, the young adult may soon be in a better financial position than the parents. Depending upon class and educational status, he may also be regarded as better informed and

to have the potentiality for exceeding the accomplish-
ments of the parents. Finally, this situation will in most
cases portend a reversal of dependence.[1]

*Fifth and last comes friends, the community, the na-
tion, the government, the world, hobbies and whatever
else you want to include.*[2]

---

[1] Robert F. Winch, *The Modern Family*, New York, Henry Holt Co.,
1952, pp. 304–5.
[2] Helena Lopata, a sociologist at Roosevelt University, Chicago, made
a most revealing study of the marital relationships of 299 suburban and
323 urban housewives. She asked them: "What are the most important
roles of a woman in order of importance?" By a substantial majority
they said the most important role was "mother." The role "wife" emerged
a poor second. In fact, 61 per cent of the older and 72 per cent of the
younger women did not regard the role of "wife" as of "primary importance." Third came the role of "homemaker."
    Asked: "What are the roles (in order of importance) of man in the
family?" 63 per cent of the urban and 64 per cent of the suburban
women, a goodly majority, said "breadwinner" or "provider." Next came
"father" and last of all, a poor third, came "husband," mentioned by
46 per cent of the participants.
    Queerly, even the women who regarded their husbands as "breadwin-
ners" were not particularly interested or concerned or knowledgeable
about their husbands' work. The women appeared preoccupied with
their homes, but their concept of "home" was not centered around people; they seemed to be obsessed with things—furniture, curtains, refrig-
erators, dishwashers. In their minds, the husband was some sort of an
"appurtenance" of the home, necessary to it, but essentially an outsider,
not someone involved in a close, intimate, household relationship.
    As we look at these responses, if they are at all typical, and they very
well might be, all we can say is "How awful!" Who would like to take
on a life-long role of "breadwinner"? Or even the role of "father"? It
seems to me that when one marries one feels he is embarking on a
human relationship. When that relationship is reduced to work and duty,
then the person is reduced to a "thing," a machine by which to achieve
purposes foreign to him; he becomes a utility used for ends foreign to
him. In this relationship, the duties loom large and the person becomes
small.
    "The most common revolt of the accessory-husband," writes Marya
Mannes, "is silence. He stops communicating, letting the talk of his wife
and the clatter of the children sweep over him like a form of static,
turning to television or papers or the golf course to insulate him from
the household he pays for."

I feel greatly embarrassed in making this schematic arrangement. I do know that life does not proceed in neat, orderly compartments. I sometimes suspect that there is no real order in the universe; it seems so many times chaotic, and that may be its nature.

I remember once discussing the merits of two philosophers with another philosopher whom I admired greatly. This philosopher said that he thought Philosopher A was superior to Philosopher B. I asked why. He said Philosopher B had no system; there was no consistency in his thinking, while Philosopher A was consistent and had a rationale and coherent system. I remember saying: "Perhaps that's the nature of the universe; the universe itself may be without system. Maybe some day we will get right out of this planet—move out of it, as Europeans moved into America when Columbus discovered the continent—and settle on another body in space and from there who knows what." I remember this philosopher whom I admired so much saying: "You made your point. I concede. There may be no order in the universe."

It was William James who talked of the "universe with the lid off," meaning this was a novelly developing universe, not working out a predestined course. And John Dewey spoke of the difficulty of finding an absolute, a law, a principle that holds good under all circumstances and in all situations.

"A lot of third-place husbands take to drink or the company of men who treat them as himself. To others, 'outside' sex, vicarious or actual, is part of the incessant search for a male self uncluttered and uncastrated by domestic trivia and preoccupied wives. Bunnies, stag films, call girls, sex parties, girlie magazines—the huge proportions of this market can only mean that whatever it is a man needs he doesn't get with a mother-housewife who puts his paycheck before him." (Marya Mannes, "I, Mary, Take Thee, John, as . . . What?", *The New York Times Magazine*, November 14, 1965. Facts and quotations taken from this article.)

I suggest the foregoing priorities with a great deal of
diffidence. When parents are sick, or even a friend is sick,
then you may have to give them first and prior and primary consideration. When the order of involvement and
commitment is broken, I generally find a great deal of disturbance in the marriage. I am not setting this down as
an absolute. I have an abhorrence of absolutes. One has
always to use his judgment; and do what is wise in the
circumstance. Each situation requires its own thinking
through. But yet as a workable hypothesis I am hoping it
may have some merit. It was Lewin who said that the
most practical thing is a good theory. In this qualifying
sense I am presenting the above.

13

DISTURBED PRIORITIES OF COMMITMENT

A COUPLE IN COUNSELING WITH ME HAD A TERRIBLE BLOWUP. The incident illustrates, I believe, a mixup in priorities of commitment. It also shows, how delicate are the nuances of feelings and how difficult they are to understand even by the person in the process of experiencing them.

The couple had an only child, a daughter of fifteen whom we shall call Beatrice. The husband had put a lot of thought and invested a great deal of his savings in the purchase of an abandoned farm. The marriage was a bad one and he thought that with the family working on re-modeling the place, his daughter assuming responsibilities, they would be brought together in harmonious purposes. And now the family was indeed together on their new property after a journey of more than 100 miles from the city.

Almost from the first, as soon as she arrived, Beatrice, the daughter, showed disinterest and irritation. The father was not sympathetic.

"How long do I have to stay here?" Beatrice asked.

"Do you want to leave?" questioned the father.

Beatrice said, "Yes."

"When?"

"Right now."

Whereupon the father, in great rage and anger, slapped her.

The child began to cry inconsolably and said ugly things to her father.

Mrs. R, the mother, witnessing what was happening, became hysterical. She began to console her daughter, took her in her arms and both as a pair darted looks of anger and hate against Mr. R.

I should explain that it was a rare thing for Mr. R to use physical force on anyone, especially his daughter, whom he loved very much.

Here facing him was his family, his wife and daughter, embraced in each other's arms, both weeping hysterically, clinging to each other.

And here was the husband and father, Mr. R, at the other end, feeling guilty, deserted, alone—rejected by his wife and in a stew about his daughter.

Later, in private session, Mrs. R, said: "It was so unreasonable of him to act in this horrible, uncontrollable manner. It was unforgivable. He's a brute."

Let us see what made him act in this "horrible, uncontrollable manner." Normally, he is most controlled, and he is truly sensitive and kindly and would not hurt anyone, especially his beloved daughter.

The husband is speaking in private session: "I bought the farm to bring the family together. I thought it would be wonderful if we could all join in some common activity. The farm could be such a lot of fun, I thought. As a family we have so little fun. We argue and we bicker and I figured that this would be positive and this would do it. And when I found Beatrice not taking to the place at all, being disagreeable, not wanting to do any of the work or take any of the responsibility that goes with such a place, I felt disappointed, frustrated, angry. And in all this my wife was involved. I could not stand the way she was handling Beatrice; I never can stand the way she handles her; she irritates me. She seems to shut herself up with Beatrice almost as if against me. This manner she has of excluding me, this being palsy-walsy with Beatrice, of pushing me aside. My wife started that as soon as we reached our country place. There she was with my daughter—I can scarcely feel she is mine when my wife is with her—cuddling her, fussing over her, making up to her. What I can't stand about my daughter is her whimpering, and she was whimpering more than usual; and my wife was humoring her, taking her side against me. Inwardly, I felt irritated and angry, especially since I had put such hopes on the farm and it had cost me so much. But I knew that if I got angry, my wife would be angry at my anger, and this made me still angrier."

He knew, he said, that if he showed his anger against Beatrice or against his wife, his wife would blow up and become hysterical and life would be unbearable at home. Infuriated by a sense of hurt, despair, disappointment, helplessness, he lashed out against his daughter.

"It was all mixed up," he said, "Not only was I getting at Beatrice but also at my wife. And then, later, when the two of them began to carry on, I felt alone, dangling in space, guilty. That day and the day thereafter was ruined for me, so that I could hardly work. If I haven't a bitch for a wife . . . and that daughter. . . ."

Mrs. R, is now talking in private session. "How could he be so unreasonable. Children do get cranky. He ought to know it. Beatrice is fifteen; she has her own friends. So she doesn't like a farm. That's no crime. Why did he get so violent? And then when he got angry, I knew how he would carry on afterwards—how he would sulk, and how miserable I would be. I can't stand it when he's angry. I can't live when he's so angry; it affects me so badly. That's why I become so hysterical—for myself, for my lot, for Beatrice."

And then she spoke of her own father. "When I was a little girl I would become violent when my father would do anything I didn't like. I remember once throwing something at him. My father was a cold person and I so wanted to be petted by him. I wanted to be his little girl who was adored. So when I became hysterical I was thinking of my daughter; I was thinking of my father; I wanted to be a little girl; I wanted my husband to look after me; and I felt sorry for myself. Also, I remembered the time when I wanted my father to love me and I threw something at him. At that moment I couldn't stand the thought of Beatrice being abused. So it was all mixed up and I was all mixed up."

These feeling are not simple, not at all. They are "all mixed up."

From my own standpoint, I make these observations:

Obviously there was irritation on the part of both husband and wife; neither liked the way the other was behaving. What hurt the marital relationship, the primary relationship, was, it seems to me, the misplaced order of commitment. Instead of the wife being by her husband's side, she deserted him, joining her daughter against him. It was a father–daughter disagreement—at least for that moment. Naturally, the mother would like her daughter to get along with her father, and understandably she would feel badly if they did not. But still, her first and primary duty was to her husband. Instead of being close to him when he needed her so badly, she deserted him— leaving him dangling in the air with his anger, his irritation, feeling alone and guilty, for one does feel guilty after administering hurt, and he did. It was he who needed solace and support from his wife, not condemnation and judgmental attack. And his wife should have been right there to give it to him.

Does that mean that she need necessarily agree with him? Not at all. But she should have perceived the need for being sympathetic to the grief her husband was experiencing. It is precisely at such junctures that a good spouse can best serve. Instead she left him and comforted her daughter.

Further—and this cannot be emphasized sufficiently— it was a father–daughter problem; it was not a mother– daughter problem against the father. No one has the right to take over another's problems. This problem was by all rights the father's and the daughter's. It was only the mother's incidentally in her concern for her husband and the need of the father and his daughter to work it out between them. It was the wife's role to be beside her husband, there in support of him, no matter what. By deserting him she did, it seems to me, a terrible thing.

Further, the mother did not help her daughter; she harmed her. Her daughter had an ally in her mother against her father. She was a wedge between the two. It is the daughter's problem to get along with her father; and also the father's problem to get along with his daughter. In this instance it was the wife's role to be by her husband's side. One of the reasons for the bad marriage was that she violated this role so often that the husband never felt that from his wife he got any support.

Without in any way yielding her primary loyalty to her husband, the mother when alone with her daughter—since she saw that her husband was so wrought up and unable to discuss anything calmly at this point—could have discussed the situation with Beatrice, and made it plain that she could not be happy unless Beatrice managed with her father. As she has concern for her husband so she has concern for her daughter, but it is of a different quality and kind.

It seems to me that this would set each role in the right place: the husband and wife together, and both concerned about Beatrice. Every encouragement, every consideration should be given the daughter as she attempts to work out a better relationship with her father.

If the daughter learns that it is her responsibility to get along with her father, there is the hope that she will in the same way learn how to manage other relationships—including friendships—and eventually her own husband. Even if the mother wants to take over the daughter's problem, it is futile. Certainly it would not help the daughter, since only the principals in a relationship can work out a modus vivendi.

One has a right to one's own problems. No one has a right to take them over. You help no one in that way; you only do harm.

Beatrice and her father had a problem. They had to work it out and they did. In truth, despite the clash, the relationship of father and daughter was intrinsically better than mother and daughter; and both father and daughter had a great love and regard for each other. It was his wife, in the habit of running to her daughter's aid, who complicated and exacerbated the father–daughter relationship.

Another observation: If all those involved in the situation could have only managed to speak their feelings as they experienced them in the way they did to the therapist, they would have saved themselves a great deal of hurt and grief. Unfortunately, as in many cases, this was a couple where the communications were of a volcanic kind since there had been so much suppression in the relationship. If the husband had spoken of his hopes and his disappointments as he was feeling them, and the wife was able to express what made her become so emotional, I believe they would have reacted differently. Since there was practically no communication of a deep and vital kind, they were apart in the situation, each nursing grievances and wounds, and each coming out of the incident feeling angry and misunderstood.

14

SILENCES IN MARRIAGE

WHAT PART DOES SILENCE PLAY IN A MARITAL RELATIONSHIP.
I know all kinds of mystic feelings exist about silences.
I myself have experienced fleeting moments, some episode,
where speech would have been a disturbance and an in-
trusion. Or where between two persons the understanding
was so complete and sensitive that words would only act
as an abrasive. Said Sydney Smith of Macaulay: "He has
occasional flashes of silence that make his conversation
perfectly delightful." And William Hazlitt said: "Silence
is the one great art of conversation."

Withal, I suspect silence in a marital relationship. I
have seen too many couples with walls between them,
saying nothing to one another, having nothing or not
wanting to share or to communicate. I have been privy
to the pain and the tension of such relationships, couples
who face each other evening after evening in what should
be the most intimate of relationships, staring at each
other, not touching, a world apart.

There is a story by Dorothy Parker which had and has
for me enormous psychological significance. I believe it
portrays a profound truth. I read the story many years
ago and it has stayed with me because it revealed a wise

and perceptive insight. It tells of a newly married couple living in Manhattan. The young husband comes home from work at his office and after supper he sits in the easy chair reading his newspaper. After his wife is through with her chores, she joins him. As they sit facing each other, he thinks: "There is no sense telling her what happened at the office. It is too trivial." She on her part, also silent, thinks: "How silly to tell him what happened during the day—shopping at the store, cooking, cleaning, really nothing intelligent to talk about." Thus they sit facing each other, night after night, he engrossed in his newspaper, she mending and silent. One night, he does not return; and neither the next night, nor ever. She does not miss her husband at all; in fact, she is relieved.

I suppose they both are. There was nothing between them to begin with and at the end there was nothing to regret.

I regard the silent person, as a stammerer, unable to ventilate feelings, with all the corollary frustration, bitterness, and grief. In a good marriage, there should be the freest flow of communication, unimpeded, full, and complete. To the extent that there are impediments, blockages, to that extent the marriage, I would say, cannot achieve its optimum good.

Even in relationships that are not close, there is, I believe, the need for communication. This became clear to me in several group experiences I had. I will relate one instance to illustrate what I am trying to say. We were a group of about twenty, all professional people in psychology and psychotherapy. There was one member who session after session said not a word, not a single word. Feeling a sense of compassion for him, I said to him privately: "You never speak and I would like to hear you.

I have the feeling that if one does not speak he is a stammerer, and I cannot imagine a more suffering person."

He felt, I suppose, my concern, but, nevertheless, on the first occasion I broached the subject, he cavalierly brushed the whole business aside. He was most comfortable, he said, listening. He learned a lot, he said, from listening; and he liked to listen. People who talk he said "shoot off their mouths"; he learns by listening; and that is why he is there.

As the sessions continued, he still remained the only silent member in the group. Sometime later, I again brought up the subject. I taxed him for not speaking. Visibly, I saw his defensive outward facade break down, and moved by my interest, he said: "Do you really want me to speak?"

I said, "Yes."

He asked "Why?"

"Because," I said, "I want to hear what you have to say. I like to feel your person in the group; that you're part of it. It's my sense of obligation to another human being."

During the session following this incident he did speak up, and as he did, he turned to me and I nodded to him in acknowledgment to indicate how glad I was. As he looked at me, I detected in this person, a professional psychologist, a sense of triumph, relief, euphoria such as I have not seen before. I suppose it is somewhat similar to the child who speaks his first words and learns the goodness of words.

The philosopher, John Dewey, could never get over the wonder and the magic of words. He could never quite understand how bits and scraps of sound can make a person happy, exhilarated, depressed, triumphant, sad, stirred, contemplative, joyous; how words can make a person feel attacked, abused, elated; how it can arouse him to fury, to protect, hate, kill, and be killed. The wonder and the magic of sounds!

The world, the Bible tells us, was created by words. "In the beginning was the word." How important words are, how fundamental they are to life, is told us in a fascinating book by Mark Zborowski and Elizabeth Herzog called *Life is with People: The Culture of the Shtetl,* which describes the life of the Jews in rural areas in old Russia. "Shtetl" is the Jewish word for the little towns in which this old and ancient people lived for centuries; and these good and wise people had a highly spiritual and beautiful culture. To these good people, words were synonymous with life itself; it differentiated civilized man from animals. They could not conceive of life without words. They literally believed that when one's quota of words was expended, one would die; for how could a civilized human being live without talking.

Quoting from this book, I am setting down how Shtetl Jews regarded words:

The emphasis on reason and its corollary, law is linked with an enormous emphasis on words. It takes endless words to rationalize all of life on earth and in heaven, to bring all within a framework of order, reason and purpose conceived in justice and mercy. Words are required not only to explain how past history and present facts conform to divine Law, but also to interpret and apply that Law. Day-by-day existence can be carried on only to the accompaniment of elaborate verbalization.

. . . The incessant communication indispensable to social well-being is achieved through words, which serve incidentally to communicate far more than their verbal content. . . . The paramount role of words is suggested by the popular notion that every human being has assigned to him at birth a definite quota of them. When his quota of words is expended he will die, since obviously to live without talking is impossible.

. . . The negative power of words is suggested by the strong feeling that silence is unsocial or even anti social. It is not a passive state, but a notice of withdrawal or exclusion from family, community or individual relationship.

In this highly verbalized culture, words are more than a medium of communication. The word is a force in itself, a tool. More than that, the word itself embodies substance—the Hebrew root is the same for "word" and for "thing" or "object." Thus the word endows its reference with existence.[1]

In a good marriage, I have said, there is full expression of feelings. When there is sparse communication, most often I find walls have risen between the couple; and the walls invariably arise because of the hurt each has given the other, so that one has learned to withhold thought and not to confide, out of fear of attack or ridicule. As one husband said: "My wife stores up what I say as evidence against me. I wouldn't tell her a thing. I've learned that." Or else they have learned the futility of trying to share feelings and experience, of not being understood, in fact, misunderstood, so instead of sympathy and support, they experience rejection.[2] Or else, they maintain walls out of spite and anger, refusing to share with a spouse. Fre-

---

[1] Zborowski, Mark and Herzog, Elizabeth, *Life is with People: The Culture of the Shtetl*, New York, Schocken Books, Paperback Edition, 1962, pp. 412–414.

[2] A member of Alcoholic Anonymous said: "It's a funny thing. I can't discuss certain things with my wife because I know she wouldn't understand. Yet I can come down to a meeting and discuss intimate affairs with a stranger. I can because I know they understand."

quently, it means that one of the partners has given up, for whatever the reason, and he doesn't want to pursue the relationship further. Sometimse the kind of escape may take the form of work, or business trips or golf or a mistress. Bickering, it seems to me, is better than silence. There is still fight in the relationship and still a fighting chance for it. Silence often represents surrender.

The importance of communication is made clear by Dr. Karl Menninger. He writes:

. . . Especially differences, disagreements, and dissatisfations should be talked out by friends—or lovers. The reason that the course of true love never runs smoothly is the fact that true love can endure only if the provocations of anger and resentment which inevitably develop are freely expressed and discussed and adjusted to. I certainly do not mean wrangling; both parties must make some conscientious effort to achieve objectivity and not simply indulge in temper tantrums. "A soft answer turneth away wrath but grievous words stir up (more) anger." It always seemed to me significant that among the Jews, where there is such a noticeable tendency to express aggressions in argument and verbal combat, there are so few divorces and so little physical violence. It is my idea that, even if the Roman Catholic church did not forbid it, divorce would still be infrequent among the Irish and Italians, because of their relatively great facility in expressing their emotions. It is often assumed by the silent, dignified, sulky Anglo-Saxon that the avoidance of verbal and even physical conflict between husband and wife promote peace and happiness. The story of the European peasant who wept because her husband had not beaten her for a month seems grotesquely and pathetically amusing, but it is psychologically true. If a woman has to choose between being ignored and being beaten she will certainly choose the latter. Although this might be construed as a recommendation of wife-beating, that is certainly not what I mean; I do mean that if hostilities cannot be repressed or diverted, it is better to have them *out* than to have them *in*."[3]

Marriages have been known to improve when some untoward or tragic family event occurred, such as serious illness, the delinquency of a child, the marriage of a daughter, or an escapade of a son. Such occurrences sometimes succeed in breaking down barriers and open clogged lines of communication. The husband and wife find themselves talking freely and openly as they haven't before. In their sorrow or joy, they draw together; they view and they relate to each other differently. The hope stirs that perhaps now they have found the person they need and want. And sometimes it does happen. More frequently what happens when the incident has quieted down, communication also stops and the couple face each other as of old and another hope is dashed.

It is for this reason that I am so suspicious of silence. In a good marriage, as I have said, each brings the other choice little "talk tidbits," incidents, gossip, stories; first, to entertain the other; secondly, to be close to the other. In the talk, there is human exchange, banter, laughter, comment, a sort of touching each other, a delight in each other, a closeness. It did not surprise me at all to learn that a study made in Syracuse, New York, with middle income families by the Department of Child Development of Cornell University concluded: ". . . The more time husband and wives spend talking with each other, the more likely they are to report a high level of marriage satisfaction."

Do these bits and pieces of conversation have to be profound? No, not at all. The talk is used, I repeat, to

---

[3] Karl Menninger, "Love Against Hate," N.Y.: Harcourt, Brace & World.

touch each other. It serves the same purpose as two lovers touching each other physically. The physical act of sex is of short duration, but the touching of each other by speech—that can be prolonged and lasts indefinitely, as long as the two have a mind and a loving heart. Watch two lovers. See how sensitive they are to every sound they make. What they may say may be silly and insipid, but that does not matter. They want to give each other love and affection and regard. Of what consequence is the content of the conversation if it can be used as a vehicle?

You might say that there exist kinds of silences that are mystically soul-stirring, which to break with harsh sounds would be sacrilegious; where the understanding is so complete that nothing need be added. I do not say that such moments do not exist and blessed indeed are such moments. I wish I myself experienced many such. In therapy I know that there are silences that are the outgrowth of two persons in a highly sensitive moment of understanding, and I do believe that such moments are good and healing.

Nevertheless, I end the way I began. For the most part, generally, I suspect prolonged silences in the marital relationship. I have been privy to too many silences that have connoted separation of the partners, loneliness, grief, cultivated and nursed hostilities, hatreds; silences that have been the prelude to the termination of the relationship whether in actuality or even worse, in a spiritual sense. I use the word "worse" for the latter contingency. The couple may remain together because of lack of courage—only to torture one another.

15

BLOCKING FREE COMMUNICATION

MAN CANNOT LIVE ALONE WITHOUT HURT.

In marriage, there is the chance to develop the most intimate, the closest, the frankest communication possible to man. In a good marriage, the skin that encloses man and isolates him can become as thin and permeable as one human being can manage with another. In this resides the strength of the good marriage. In marriage, the two can become nearest to being one vasomotor system. Through generous openness to the other, the one learns about the other. The thou best confirms the I. As Martin Buber has told us, when there is no thou, man is nothing; we become human beings in the presence of another. The "thou"—the other—confirms the "I." Alone, the "I" is like vibrations on an island where there is no ear to hear, and hence, technically no sound.

The tragedy of our culture is that in so many instances, one human being will not listen to another. He is quite willing to tell, direct, instruct. Even better he likes to assail, deny, reproach, but he does not like to listen so as to understand.

This is the greatest tragedy in marriage. The couple will

116

not listen to one another in generosity, understanding, acceptance, respect.

There is no person who has explored human relationships, what it does to human beings, how it affects them for good or ill, with the creativity, the insight, the unremitting perseverance as has Dr. Carl R. Rogers. I am convinced that if his work, his philosophy and outlook were more generally known and acted upon, it would have the power of revolutionizing the ways and behavior of society; of changing man himself and man's conduct to man, and make man and his universe kindlier, more humane, more loving.

I myself have been deeply influenced by Dr. Roger's outlook and philosophy. In this portion of the work, I shall quote him frequently.

Carl Rogers maintained that if a husband and wife listened to each other and were made to repeat what each said, it would reveal, first, how little they have listened, really listened; secondly, how little they understand what was being said and what was being heard. Once a married couple succeeded in repeating and understanding with some accuracy what each said, then the number of bad marriages and bad relationships would decrease enormously.

Discussing what sharing of communication means to him, not only as a person, but as a therapist seeking to enhance the emotional health of others, Carl Rogers says:

The first simple feeling I want to share with you is my enjoyment when I really hear someone. . . . I believe I know why it is satisfying to me to hear someone. When I can really hear someone it puts me in touch with him. It enriches my life. It is also true that it is through hearing people that I have learned all that I know about individuals, about per-

sonality, about interpersonal relationships. There is another
peculiar satisfaction in it. When I really hear someone it is
like listening to the music of the spheres, because beyond the
immediate message of the person, no matter what that might
be, there is the universal, the general. Hidden in all of the
personal communications which I really hear there seem to
be orderly psychological laws, aspects of the awesome order
which we find in the universe as a whole. So there is both the
satisfaction of hearing this person and also the satisfaction
of feeling one's self in some sort of touch with what is universally true.

At another point he says:

I find, in therapeutic interviews, and in the intensive group
experiences which have meant a great deal to me, that hearing has consequences. When I do truly hear a person and the
meanings that are important to him at that moment, hearing
not simply his words, but him, and when I let him know that
I have heard his own private personal meanings, many things
happen. There is first of all a grateful look. He feels released.
He wants to tell me more about his world. He surges forth
in a new sense of freedom. He becomes more open to the
process of change.

I have noticed, both in therapy and in groups, that the more
deeply I hear the meanings of this person the more there is
that happens. One thing I have come to look upon as almost
universal is that when a person realizes he has been deeply
heard, there is a moistness in his eyes. I think in some real
sense he is weeping for joy. It is as though he were saying,
"Thank God, *somebody* heard me. Someone knows what it is
like to be me." In such moments I have had the fantasy of
a prisoner in a dungeon, tapping out day after day a Morse
code message, "Does anybody hear me? Is there anybody
there? Can anyone hear me?" And finally one day he hears
some faint tappings which spell out "Yes." By that one simple
response he is released from his loneliness, he has become a
human being again. There are many, many people living in

private dungeons today, people who give no evidence of it whatever on the outside, where you have to listen very sharply to hear the faint messages from the dungeon.

Not only in a good relationship is it important to listen but also it is important to be heard. In this connection, Dr. Rogers writes:

Let me move to a second learning which I would like to share with you. I like to be *heard*. A number of times in my life I have felt myself bursting with insoluble problems, or going round and round in tormented circles or, during one period, overcome by feelings of worthlessness and despair. I think I have been more fortunate than most in finding at these times individuals who have been able to hear me and thus to rescue me from the chaos of my feelings. I have been able to find individuals who have been able to hear my meanings a little more deeply than I have known them. These individuals have heard me without judging me, diagnosing me, appraising me, evaluating me. They have just listened and clarified and responded to me at all levels at which I was communicating. I can testify that when you are in psychological distress and someone really hears you without passing judgment on you, without trying to take responsibility for you, without trying to mold you, it feels damn good. At these times it has relaxed the tension in me. It has permitted me to bring out the frightening feelings, the guilts, the despair, the confusions that have been a part of my experience. When I have been listened to and when I have been heard, I am able to reperceive my world in a new way and go on. It is astonishing how elements which seem insoluble become soluble when someone listens. How confusions which seem irremediable turn into relatively clear flowing streams when one is heard. I have deeply appreciated the times that I have experienced this sensitive, emphatic, concentrated listening.

What happens when a person is not appreciated, is deflated, feels rejected?

Another learning I would like to voice briefly is one of which I am not proud but which seems to be a fact. When I am not prized or not appreciated I not only *feel* very much diminished. I *am* greatly diminished in my behavior. When I am prized I blossom, I expand, I am an interesting individual. In a group which is hostile or unappreciative I am just not much of anything. People wonder with very good reason, how did he ever get a reputation? I wish I had the strength to be somewhat more similar in both kinds of groups but actually the person I am in a warm and interested group is very different from the person I am in a hostile or a cold group.

So in this third area, prizing or loving and being prized or loved is experienced by me as very growth enhancing. A person who is loved appreciatively, not possessively, blooms and develops his own unique self. The person who loves nonpossessively is himself enriched. This at least has been my experience.[1]

I feel that communication—a free flowing, open relationship where each in it feels understood, appreciated, prized—is the central and crucial nub of a good marriage.

Have you every observed a couple in love? The popular term, "They are deeply interested in each other," is indeed descriptive and appropriate. You can recognize two lovers by their total absorption in each other; they have eyes only for each other; they are as if glued to one another. Even though surrounded by the hustle and bustle of many people and many activities, the two are apart, as if they were an isolated island. They are highly sensitive to each other; the slightest remark evokes from the other the strongest reaction; they smile, their faces are mobile, their whole bodies seem to want to merge; they are open to one another, fully, completely. If you should

[1] All the above quotations from Dr. Carl Rogers were taken from an address delivered by him at the California Institute of Technology, Pasadena, California, November 9, 1964.

overhear what they have to say, you will probably wonder why what they say—so simple, even inane—should beget such total absorption.

For the marital pair, talk is not only a means of communication, important as that is. For them, the actual words frequently are not meaningful, in the sense of two persons trying to come to an understanding; the talk goes beyond words; it reaches and permeates the entire person. In talking, the two feel close, they touch one another. If they didn't talk, they would be apart, each with his own self; but now, in talking, they have bridged the gulf that divides man from man, and they touch each other, and they feel warm and good from the power that resides in the capacity of one person to give to another. They are excited, exhilarated, yes, I suppose, we can say happy.

In a good marriage, this communication—free, open, accepting—is the key to all the good and the health in the relationship. In a good marriage, each of the partners tries to think of incidents, impressions, ideas—really anything—to bring to the other. Is what they bring to the conversation important? Not necessarily so. Then why bring these bits of talk to the other? It is, I believe, so that in the exchange, in talking together, they can feel close and near one another, and give each other warmth and affection and love.

The first sign of a deteriorating marriage is the blocking of free communication. When man needs to communicate for health and life, why should there be a blockage? Blockage will occur in the relationship when from it there develops a sense of futility in getting warmth and understanding from the partner.

Let us revert back to a previous illustration—to Mrs. A, who was told by her husband that he was in fear of losing his job. If the marriage were a good one, the wife would have sensed her husband's anxiety and despair. She would not have needed coaching or prompting; she immediately would have felt it. Mr. A was up in years, he had worked for the company a long time; and with the prevailing prejudice of industry toward older men, Mr. A had realistic cause for concern. She would have felt his sense of being unjustly treated. At this juncture in his life her husband was in desperate need of a good, understanding wife. She could have filled him with her admiration, regard, faith; her conviction that he would be able to lick whatever befell him. The experience would have been a uniting one, and a good marriage would have become closer and better. Mrs. A would have been a therapist to her husband, giving him strength and support. When she depreciated him, when she expressed her lack of faith in him, she only added to his already present insecurity, his sense of inferiority, his doubts about himself; she furthered his self-depreciation and depression.

If once a partner in a relationship begins to understand that from his wife he can get little appreciation, he is less apt to tell her of untoward happenings, for he learns that from her he is only the recipient of hostile, deprecatory feelings; that she only exacerbates whatever ails him; if he for the moment may be suffering from inferiority, anxiety or guilt feelings, she only adds to them. He learns that from her he can expect no comfort, only condemnation. So he holds back.

The insidious process continues. Instead of looking for tidbits of conversation to share with his wife, he tends to suppress. No, he will not tell her that; he will not tell her this other thing. Like a faucet where the pipes are clogged, the trickle becomes fainter and fainter. Likewise, in the relationship ominous silences develop, until there is nothing between the two.

Sometimes the hostility is more open, and then the couple resort to attack, hurting and injuring one another, finding ways to make each other small and stupid and ignoble, so that the sight of one creates such violent emotions of hostility that there can be no conversation, no friendly intercourse, only the expression of hate. When this relationship exists, we have underhand warfare.

By and large we meet our fears by fight or flight—we struggle or we run away. Of the two it is better to struggle, for in the struggle there is always the hope of some kind of accommodation. Unfortunately, in marriage there is a great deal of flight; it is even respectable. There is the husband who works hard all day, very hard, and he comes home late, later than any of the neighbors' husbands. After supper, he relaxes with his newspaper or television. On weekends, he plays golf, or is caught in traffic jams on the crowded roadways. He is consuming his energy and his life so that when he gets home he can flop his weary body into bed, and then start a hard week of unremitting toil.

He talks little to his wife or his children; his family contact is minimal. He is living physically at home but his true life, his real life, is somewhere else. His wife has physical possession of her husband, but spiritually her husband is far away; he is absent; he is a deserter; he has run away.

Yet all of it is within the bounds of respectability. This is no marriage and this is no family and this is no home. The husband has departed.

I was reading a collection of letters by D. H. Lawrence,

and among them, I found one written to a friend in which Lawrence with remarkable insight sensed the health-giving qualities and the joy of a deep understanding relationship in which there is "entire nakedness of body and spirit." The contents of the letter follows:

I can't help thinking that you wouldn't be quite so down if you and Mrs. D. didn't let yourself be separated . . . by this trouble. I think the trouble ought to draw you together, and you seem to let it put you apart . . . it seems a shame that her one cry, when she is in distress, should be for her mother. You ought to be the mother and father to her. Perhaps if you go away to your unhealthy post, it may be good for you. But perhaps you may be separating your inner life from hers—I don't mean actual and eternal—but you may be taking yourself inwardly apart from her, and leaving her inwardly separate from you; which is no true marriage, and is a form of failure. I am awfully sorry; because I think that no amount of outward trouble and stress of circumstances could really touch you both, if you were together. But if you are not together, of course, the strain becomes too great, and you want to be alone and she wants her mother. And it seems to me an awful pity if, after you have tried, you have to fail and go separate ways. I am not speaking of vulgar outward separation; I know you would always be a good reliable husband; but there is more than that: there is the real sharing of one's life. . . . One must learn to love, and go through a good deal of suffering to get to it, like any knight of the grail, and the journey is always *towards* the other soul, not away from it. Do you think love is an accomplished thing, the day it is recognized? It isn't. To love, you have to learn to understand the other, more than she understands herself, and to submit to her understanding of you. It is damnably difficult and painful, but it is the only thing which endures. You mustn't think that your desire of your fundamental need is to make a good career, or to fill your life with activity, or even to provide for your family materially. It isn't. Your most vital necessity in this life is that you shall love your wife completely and implicitly and in entire nakedness of body and spirit. Then you

will have peace and inner security, no matter how many things
go wrong. And this peace and security will leave you free to
act and to produce your own work, a real independent work-
man.[2]

A couple—we will call them Mr. and Mrs. Richards—
who entered therapy to save their foundering marriage
may serve as an illustration. The bridge of communication had narrowed. Mr. Richards dreaded coming home.
He would dally as long as possible at public bars or his
club. He wanted to preserve appearances and he could
not go as often or stay as long at his club as he would have
liked. The nights when he stayed home there was silence,
except for perfunctory talk, but not real talk.

"I'm afraid to say anything at home," Mr. Richards explained. "If I do, my wife attacks me. She accuses me and
makes me feel low and degraded. If I utter the slightest
adverse remark, she interprets it as an attack on her, even
when that notion is farthest from my mind. She sort of
uses what I say against me. She stores it up, mulling over
it; and sure enough, when I least expect it, what I said in
innocence becomes charged with emotion, distorted from
the way I meant it. So I have learned to keep quiet."

Mrs. Richards had only a faint notion of what was happening between them. She knew the marriage was a bad
one, but she was sure it was her husband's fault. She
thought she was good and kind. He did the attacking; she
was only defending herself. She had no notion of the
desperation of her husband, his despair, his hope some-
day of severing the marriage. The tensions of the nightly
silence, the lack of real, meaningful communication were
unbearable. What baffled and infuriated Mrs. Richards
was her husband's vehemence, his volcanic outbursts

---

[2] D. H. Lawrence, "Selected Letters," pp. 73–74. Penguin Books, Great
Britain, 1954.

about a minor incident, out of all proportion to what occurred.

When there are walls between a couple, and there is no openness, and each bears his grievances in silence, not airing them, not working them out, not coming to terms with them, such outbursts are common. The suppression acts like a poisonous stew, brewing within without any safety valves; and when it bursts forth, its noxious gases erupt with great violence.

"For no reason at all, in the middle of some quiet conversation, he begins to scream and shout," said Mrs. Richards. "I don't even know what I have done. He has a terrible temper. I'm scared of him. Sometimes I think he's just plain crazy."

You would think that such attacks would have little meaning for Mr. Richards. You would be wrong. And he in turn—yes, this powerfully-built, extraordinarily successful business man—would be in fear of his wife, fear of her unmerciful attacks, her calling him "selfish," "ingrate," "callous." "I take care of your children, your house. I entertain your business associates, but never a thank you. I work from morning till night. I try to protect you in every way. But all you do is shout and scream."

After such an episode, Mr. Richards experienced anxiety, guilt, shame, also anger and hate for his wife. Unfortunately, none of these feelings is a good base for a cordial, creative relationship. After such clashes Mr. Richards would try harder than ever to avoid his home and the inevitable tensions of an evening where both would occupy opposite corners, conscious that in each there were seething hostilities.

In such a relationship the individual is not prized, not accepted; on the contrary, he is rejected and condemned.

16

VIOLENT OUTBURSTS

I READ OF MARRIED COUPLES DOING MAYHEM TO ONE AN-
other. In a fury beyond understanding, they will attack
their spouse with the most horrible weapons. The ostensible cause seems out of all proportion to the offense.

Below is an item from the *New York Times,* and the
aggression described is comparatively mild when compared to more heinous deeds, such as a husband throwing
a wife out of the window or taking an axe to her, but it
is still sufficient to show indignation and fury. The item
follows:

WIFE GOES ON RAMPAGE
BUT IT'S ALL IN THE FAMILY

DALLAS (UPI)—There was a family argument and the
lady of the house was peeved, so she:

Got into one of the two family cars and rammed it into the
side of the house.

Rammed the other car, which was in a carport.

Ran down her husband, pinning him to a wall.

She refused to tell the police what the argument had been
about or give her age.

Her husband was hospitalized with a broken pelvis. Their
7-year-old son got hit by falling boards, but was just scratched.

The husband said he would not press charges. The police said there was nothing they could do because the incident occurred on private property. (July 23, 1965).

Here is another item:

LAST ARGUMENT

New York (AP)—During the last five of their 41 years of childless marriage, Leo Braun told police yesterday, he and his wife argued about many things.

Yesterday, the 71-year-old retired garment industry executive was charged with smothering his wife, Fannie, 69, with a pillow as she lay in their apartment bed.[1]

Their last argument—over the sharing of a blanket.

As one who has listened to marital couples in distress, I believe I understand how these maniacal outbursts can happen. If the surface facts are told, you might say what a demon lies in this person to be driven to such fury for such a silly reason. But I am certain if you dug more deeply, you would find pent up hate and anger beyond endurance and a sense of grievance sufficient to drive a person out of his mind. The person who commits the violence may not be fully conscious of what really motivated him. I have to resort at this point to a rather trite and hackneyed illustration, the favorite of those writing in a psychoanalytic vein. The iceberg that we see floating on the water has six-sevenths of its mass buried beneath and only one-seventh appears on the surface. In the same way the ostensible reasons, those reported by the person, are only surface reasons, little pieces of the iceberg that bob above the water surface, leaving its vast bulk buried deep, deep under.

---

[1] The San Juan Star, September 2, 1965.

Psychologists talk of the precipitating cause and the pre-disposing cause. A man gets a telegram saying that his mother has died. He begins to act queer, shuts himself off from others, quits his job, becomes morose, and one morning he is found attempting suicide and then he is hospitalized. You say the death of his mother was the cause of his psychosis. But why didn't his two brothers and his sister who received identical telegrams develop these symptoms? They grieved over the death of the mother; but nevertheless, they continued doing what they had to do, working normally and living normally. The psychologist is not nearly so interested in the overt, the precipitating cause, as he is in the predisposing causes, what went on before, what made him so unstable that this untoward event could cause such a total collapse of the personality. We all have to lose our parents. It is rare when parents survive their children; and if each of us responded in this manner, we would be a world of psychotics. Healthy people, functioning well, can cope with such a loss. It is his previous background, his weaknesses, his malfunctioning—it is these that determines the overt, the outward act. If each of us responded to vicissitudes, with crises in our life, with psychotic experiences, who would escape being institutionalized? In whose life do not such experiences occur—horrible, seemingly unbearable—and yet we survive them, live through them, frequently are the better for them, coming out of such experiences kindlier, more understanding.

So we have to go back to more fundamental causes. Generally before the commitment of the horrible deed, you will find in the aggressor a boiling caldron of poison, a sense of injustice and of grievances, possessing him, driving him obsessively, until it reaches a point beyond control.

We are not talking here about right or wrong. There are, it is true, paranoiac people, hostile people, emotionally disturbed people, who require little or no cause to generate great hate. Even among those you would describe as normal, obsessive hate can take control and blind reason.

We act on what we believe to be true, not what is true. A moment's reflection will make this obvious. Once it was taught that tomatoes were poisonous. You may say how ridiculous. But if you believed that tomatoes were poisonous, would you eat them? As the white man landed on American shores, the Indians saw them as Gods, and, hence, they were powerless, for how could they, what right had they to stand up against them? We act on what we *believe* is true, not on what *is* true. The man who holds up a gun against someone is likely to be met with arms upraised. Later, it may be discovered that it was a toy pistol. If the victim had known this beforehand, then his response would in all likelihood have been different.

For good or ill, man, as William James tells us, is a speck of reason bobbing around in an ocean of emotion; and we are held and bound by our emotions; and reason is so weak in comparison. The story is told of a man who was visiting a psychologist, and he said: "I am incorporeal. I am dead." The astonished psychologists looked at him and said: "You are talking. I hear you." The response was: "You are hearing a ghost, not a live person. I am one-dimensional." Whereupon, the psychologist proceeded to reason. "You know a ghost has no heart; and no blood comes through his arterial system." "Oh, yes, yes," eagerly agreed the patient. "I know a dead man has no heart and cannot bleed." Whereupon the psychologist thrust a needle in the finger of the patient, and he drew blood. The patient held up his hand for scrutiny, somewhat puzzled and mystified. As he squeezed the finger to examine the blood that had accumulated, he remained quiet for awhile, and then, seeing the blood continue to trickle, he said with strong conviction: "That only proves a dead man can bleed."

The more I have worked with people the more I have come to realize what a small role reason, pure intellect, plays in man's affairs, and how large and mighty a role the emotions play. If we view a person as good and kind and helpful, we will respond one way. If we view the person as wicked, sly, dishonest, double-dealing, sinful, and hateful, we will respond in another way. In incidents involving mayhem, the latter view takes hold. And violence may be the result, not because of any particular incident, although it may take some incident to trigger off these feelings, but it represents essentially a long history of unresolved grievances and a sense of rankling injustice, not necessarily as a fact, but as the person views the facts. "As a fermenting new wine to which no vent is given damages the cask," wrote Jerome Gaub, "so a raging mind that reason tries to control but cannot calm attacks the body more violently within to the extent that it is not allowed to discharge itself without."

In marriage, when it is bad, there is a great deal of battling and warfare and the desire to inflict hurt out of a sense of grievance and injustice. It is rare that middle class persons commit physical violence. Middle class people generally attack themselves, not others, not society. Most of my work has been with middle class people and I find they are hard on themselves; they make terrible demands on themselves and they constantly feel guilty.

I have colleagues who work with lower class people—

delinquents, convicts, and the like—and they tell me that these people seldom feel guilt; they feel put upon by a hostile society, and they are more apt to commit crime, murder, and violence from a sense of righteous indignation. Middle class people commit suicide, lower class people tend to commit murder; they kill others.

The middle class are suffused with a sense of fear, anxiety, guilt, shame, self denigration. Further the middle class weapon is words; their tongues develop great power to cut, bite, hurt, attack. These words come to be used so expertly that they wound more sharply and more accurately than any physical weapon. The lower class has a much more ineffective weapon, their physical power, acting out their aggressive feelings.

As I said at the outset, I can understand violence in marriage. When walls of separation become thick, then human beings cannot reach out to other human beings as human beings.

17

THE SOURCE OF GOOD SPOUSES

THE WAY TO GOOD MENTAL HEALTH AND TO GOOD HUMAN
relationships resides in the capacity of a person to like
people, have regard for them, be animated by good will
to them. Once you feel this way, all you need do is to
be your natural, unaffected self and people will seek you
out. William James wisely tells us: "The deepest feeling
in human nature is the desire to be appreciated."

What sort of person can envelop another with warmth
and affection? We are beginning to understand that for
the most part they comprise mature, healthy persons with
good self-esteem; those who, in a measure, are living realistic, effective lives and finding some pleasure and meaning out of living.

Who are the persons who cannot give to others regard,
esteem, affection, warmth? For the most part, we are
coming to believe that they are persons who are insecure,
frustrated, bitterly disappointed, seething with hostilities,
rankling with resentments of all sorts. Insecure and miserable themselves, they cannot give comfort and support
to anyone, including themselves.[1] As a group, they are

---

[1] Speaking of his training as a physician at St. Thomas's hospital, W.
Somerset Maugham wrote: "I learned more about people than merely

133

emotionally infantile. For the most part, their thinking does not extend beyond their own navels. Their conversation and thinking begin with "I" and end with "I." As they talk to you, they do not relate or give of themselves to you. Foremost in their mind is "I." As they talk to you, they are thinking, "How am I impressing him?" "Does he think I'm smart?" "What am I getting out of this?" "Does he see I'm better than he is?" His big, fat ego looms so large that you, the person to whom he is talking, get lost. From such persons, one cannot find comfort; one leaves such persons with feelings of emptiness, of nothingness. They are like children, who constantly ask you for and want things from you, and if you cannot or refuse to satisfy them, they go off uninterested or pouting or sulking. Such conduct is all right for the child because he needs to be given to, but a child cannot make a good husband or a good wife.

When John is bound on the north by John, on the south by John, on the east by John, on the west by John, then John cannot have a good marriage; and pity the person who attempts a marriage with John. When patients of mine are involved in some pivotal relation with a John, and they seek what we all seek from a relationship, warmth, appreciation, understanding, I have had occasion to say to such patients: "There is no sense in fishing in a pond where there is no fish." When they are married to a John, it is amazing how long and unremitting the hope lingers that they will catch this fish, this appreciation, this

what their bodies had to tell. And what I learned—and what seems to me the most important of all the lessons—is that pain and suffering do not ennoble the human spirit. Not at all. Pain and suffering breed meanness, bitterness, selfishness, cruelty. It is only happiness that ennobles." Garson Kanin, *Remembering Mr. Maugham*, *New York Times*, September 4, 1966.

affection we all seek. Sometimes they think they almost
have the fish hooked—almost caught. But no, they are mistaken. Despite disappointment after disappointment, they
cannot really and deeply believe that their quest will remain unsatisfied. Again and again they think they almost
have the fish they seek so eagerly. But it is an illusion.
There are no fish in the pond and there is no use seeking.
This is the hardest fact for the marital partner to learn,[2]
and even harder for the marital partner to accept. From
such a partner they will never get a sense of appreciation,
warmth and affection. No, there is no sense in fishing in
a pond where there is no fish. The Johns have no capacity
for a deep, warm relationship.

In Greek mythology, we are told of Narcissus who rejected all love, instead concentrating such feelings on himself. He saw the reflection of his own image in a pond,
the story goes, and he fell in love with it; and unable to
communicate with this image, he pined and pined away
and eventually he died. Freud called such love of self
"narcissism," an incapacity to relate to others with affection or to be genuinely concerned with others outside of
self.

Such a person has the characteristics of a child; he is
infantile, and like a child, he is narcissistic, self-centered,

---

[2] It is equally hard for a child to know, deeply know, and accept that
in his parents he will find a pond empty of fish; that from his father or
his mother he will never receive what every child wants from a parent—
love, admiration, regard, warmth. Frequently he thinks he almost has
a fish hooked, but it somehow escapes him. This need, this desire for
parental love and acceptance haunts the child through adulthood; and
he continues to seek, never quite giving up. I have heard patients, thirty,
forty, fifty years old, say, "Before I die I would like my mother (or father) to say to me, 'I am proud of you.' I want once to feel that my
parents think I am a worthy person and that I have lived up to what
they hoped." It is pathetic the way they seek this approval and how
hard and bitter it is for them to learn and to know that this will never be.

egoistic and egocentric. His thoughts and feelings center about himself—his health, his person, his sensitivities; he adorns himself endlessly, both in dress and physical attention. Like Narcissus, he is in love with himself and seeks satisfaction in terms of self. Whereas the mature person has merged his lot and his life with the society in which he lives and is more concerned with serving than receiving, the infantile person is obsessed with vanity and self-love. Like the infant, he finds it impossible to love in a mature way.

In some primitive tribes, the sign of maturity is the capacity to suffer. The infantile person suffers more than his share, but even his suffering is infantile; it centers around his own slights, wounds, and vanities. He has never learned that the extent to which he can help others is the extent to which he can strengthen and build himself up. As Mark Twain said, "The best way to cheer yourself is to cheer somebody else." Neither have they learned the Biblical injunction, "It is more blessed to give than to receive." Neither have they learned that one who thinks primarily of self shall have a wretched and sickly self. He who loses his self for unselfish purposes shall have a psychologically healthy self and, to boot, will have a good life. The infantile person has never learned to give of himself and to merge his self and his lot in common cause with others. He bears an intolerable cross; he is really a cripple for good, healthy living. Stunted in development, never having grown emotionally to maturity, he finds it hard to live with himself, and others find it impossible to live with him. Such a person cannot grapple with the profound complexities of a marital relationship; and pity the spouse who attempts one with him.

In another context, we shall further discuss the subject

of maturity. Sufficient now to say that the kind and the quality of a person's maturity is the key to his marital adjustment, as it is to all other vital adjustments. We are seeing more clearly that the home is the nurturing soil of nearly all that is good and evil in man. The best and the richest sources of good husbands and wives are homes that are kind, generous, and democratic; homes in which there exist a happy or at least a satisfactory marriage, so that the children can witness what a good marriage is like. We are learning that maturity is acquired best—this all-important desideratum in every adjustment—in a family where the parents are themselves emotionally mature; where there is sympathy and respect for everyone in the household, child as well as adult; where there resides fundamental affection for all human beings; where in it neighbors as well as strangers are enveloped by warmth, sympathy, and understanding; where children from earliest infancy are taught to contribute to the home and to the wider community, to assume responsibilities in the home and the wider community—to share the good and the bad of mankind's common lot. In such homes, there are no onerous chores, only opportunities to serve the common good. It is a democratic home, where discussion and consensus determine decisions as to what best will serve the common good. Such homes provide the richest nourishment for the development of mature personalities.

It need not be a home of numerous material possessions, for wealthy homes are not immune to neurotic parents who base their decisions and actions, not on the common good, but on satisfaction of their own neurotic needs. Certainly, the mature personality cannot develop in an authoritarian household, where father and mother know best and no one may question why but do only as told.

The kindly, permissive home, studies indicate, produces children who are softer, warmer, more considerate of others, more cooperative, who make friends more easily, exercise more initiative, are more creative. That, however, does not answer all problems, for such children, since they have learned the right to agree and disagree, can speak up for their position, can become non-conformist, rebelling against society. In school, they can become problems since they may refuse to conform; and as a result their grades may not equal those children who come from stricter homes. By and large, however, they are nicer, kindlier, more lovable, and better able to love; and they make better and more lasting marriages.

In authoritarian households—the kind where you hear, "Listen to your father," "Do as you are told," "Why?" (smack!) "You were told to do it."—the children are more conforming. They may get along in school better, make better grades and may even be more ambitious. Studies show that on the surface they seem to be doing all right, but inwardly, they harbor an enormous amount of hostility; they are resentful of their parents; they do not make friends as easily as children from permissive homes; they quarrel more; they have poorer relationships with classmates; they have more unsatisfactory love affairs; they break marital engagements more frequently; they are more dependent on parents but more resentful of them; they have less initiative; they feel more inadequate; they are shyer, more withdrawn. More conforming, they genuflect to authority and their superiors, but when they are in authority or when they feel strong enough to dominate, they can be harsh and vindictive.

From homes where parents keep closed doors, where the outsider is feared and shunned, come children who themselves are apt to grow up to be full of suspicion and fears. I have had patients reared in such suspicious, paranoid homes; and when such patients talk of walking on city streets, they give you the feeling that they are in danger of momentary attack, as if they were on a battlefield unarmed. Themselves full of hostility and hate, they cannot imagine anyone else being otherwise. I have had occasion to say to them: "You speak as if you wish you had eyes in the back of your head." They are excited by the very idea. "That would be wonderful," many have said. "I'd be able to watch them from the front and the back." For them life is a jungle and they live in a jungle.

Children who grow up in good, warm, accepting households, where the door is always open to the stranger, early learn that people are good and desirable; they learn to have faith in them and to trust them. Since they are encouraged to mingle with human beings—all kinds—they learn more about people; they understand them better; they learn how to get along with them better.

Compare a warm, trusting home, with its open door, its welcoming of the stranger, its involvement with the community—compare such a home with a home where parents keep closed doors, are suspicious of the neighbor, attend to their own knitting; where parents keep children to themselves; where parents fear that when their child mixes with other children and visits other homes, he may acquire bad habits; and because of this they do not give him freedom to learn about people, but to regard others warily and from a distance. If we live in isolation and suspicion, we grow up to be isolated and suspicious.

Family, wealth, and position cannot supplant this necessary, vital experience—learning about people by mixing with all kinds of people. The Duke of Windsor relates how as a boy of about thirteen he was sent off to Osborne, the British naval school, and of how he suffered from the hazing and the ridicule of other boys and how he was unable to defend himself, since he had never learned how to stand up for himself in this kind of rough give and take. He describes how the senior students gathered around him to ask him taunting questions, " . . . his name, who his father was, where he lived. Manifestly all the answers I could muster could not have been more damning, for, quite apart from my royal parentage and homes, the fact that I had never been to school before caused me to be regarded as a freak." He tells how several seniors decided that the color of the hair of "His Royal Highness," would look much better red than his own shade; and they proceeded to dye it by pouring a bottle of red ink over it, "leaving me in a terrifying dilemma for which nothing that I had ever learned under the good Hansell seemed to supply a solution."

Never having mixed with other children, never having learned to know other children, never having practiced to get along with them, he was unable to defend himself— as helpless and hapless as his most incompetent and lowly subject. Even his lofty position—as heir presumptive to the mighty British throne—could not protect him. And if the heir presumptive to a mighty throne cannot defend himself because of this lack, who can?

Also there are the legions of unfortunate children, ill-fated children who are raised in broken homes filled with hatred; or in severe homes, where they are subjected to cruel authoritarian discipline; or in poverty-stricken homes, where both parents are made waspish and irritable by their merciless struggle just to exist. How can children from such homes ever feel secure; how can they grow up wholesomely? These children wear crippling spiritual blows; for them to grow up to be generous, sympathetic, kind in mind and in deed is asking for a miracle. The child who has been treated justly, listened to with sympathy, learns how to treat others justly and to listen to others with sympathy. At least that's the best method for teaching and learning such traits. We are beginning to perceive that cruelty begets cruelty, that frustrations and privation beget bitterness, hostility, and hate. The child who has been beaten spiritually and psychologically becomes himself severe and brutal; the child who is reared by dominating, authoritarian parents becomes himself domineering, inflexible, harsh, and unkind. The child learns love by being loved. The child who has never had love poured into him is like a wild asocial animal, incapable of receiving or giving affection. As no or little parental love has been poured into him, he has none now to give. The unwanted, "un-mothered" child has many of the traits of the homeless alley cat, kicked about, maltreated, hungry, slinking in dark corners. When you try to approach these alley cats, they look at you suspiciously, snarl and show their teeth. Even when you come up to them with food, wanting their good, they eye you suspiciously and distrustfully; and instead of taking the food will dash away in fear of their safety. These alley cats have never known kindness.

If you should seek for his opposite, there is the beloved and well-treated poodle dog. He rushes up at you eagerly, friendly, welcoming, trustfully. If you should kick him, he'll come at you friskier than ever, wanting more, thinking you are playing a game with him. As he has never experienced harsh and cruel treatment, he lives in a world of affection and love; and in him there is trust. This animal cannot imagine anyone disapproving or disliking him. Just as unconditional regard and love were poured into him, he has it now to give out.

The evidence that is piling up is to me overwhelming and irrefutable. For a child to grow into a good, warm human being, he needs, vitally as food and sunshine, to be played with, talked to, cooed at, held admiringly to a mother's (or a mother substitute's) soft breast and to be allowed to reach freely for her warm milk. Without this love and affection, a child cannot thrive even physically, much less emotionally. He simply withers away—physically and emotionally.

In orphanages children do not thrive. Intellectually, they become stunted; emotionally, they become passive, listless, staring at space, unable or unwilling to relate to another human being. Some never learn to walk, or to talk, or to feed themselves; they are devoid of curiosity, unresponsive; in short, they lack the mysterious and divine spark that makes a human being human.

The death rate for maternally-deprived infants is scandalous. Dr. Rene A. Spitz made a study of two groups of infants, both raised in institutions. One group was cared for by their natural mothers, the other by overworked nursing personnel. In all physical respects, the two groups, both admitted shortly after birth, were treated identically. The food, the housing, the cleanliness were all anyone would want. The only difference was the care the infants received. The infant mortality of nurse-cared infants— the motherless infants—for the first year was 29.6 per cent; by the second year 37 per cent of the infants had died. What befell the infants cared for by their own mothers? Not a single child in the two years died.

Even more frightening than the physical devastation of the motherless infants is the havoc wrought on them emotionally. It is generally known, I believe, that both Sigmund Freud and Alfred Adler maintained that by the time a child is five years old he is fairly well-set in his patterns of behavior, in his style of life, in his direction of development. Experimental work by Dr. Mary M. Shirley and Dr. Patricia Neilson seems to confirm such a point of view. Dr. Shirley made a study of twenty-five babies over a two-year period. She carefully noted their behavior, their temperament, their characteristics. Fifteen years later, Dr. Neilson made independent personality sketches of fifteen of these children, who were now adolescents. She had never seen Dr. Shirley's studies. Then they matched these two independently done personality sketches, made at a fifteen-year interval, and it was found that the subjects could be identified with an accuracy beyond all expectation. Concluded Dr. Shirley when she made her study of infants: " . . . each baby exhibits a characteristic pattern of personality traits that change little with age."[3] Concluded Dr. Neilson fifteen years later: " . . . personality similarities in an individual persist over a period of time."[4]

And now we come to a book written by Dr. John Bowlby and edited by Margery Fry called *Child Care and the Growth of Love.*[5] This book has made a profound impression on me. In my opinion, it establishes its thesis brilliantly. If a child, says Bowlby, is to become a *humane*

[3] Shirley, Mary M., *The First Two Years: A Study of Twenty-five Babies,* Vol. III, Minneapolis: University of Minnesota Press, 1933.
[4] Neilson, Patricia, *Shirley's Babies After Fifteen Years: A Personality Study,* Journal of Genetic Psychology, 1948, 73:175–186.
[5] John Bowlby, edited by Margery Fry, *Child Care and the Growth of Love,* Great Britain, Pelican Books, 1963.

being, he needs the love of a mother or a mother substitute for a minimum of three years. All separation between mother and child till seven is harmful, depending on the length of the separation. If a child is deprived of the maternal love of a mother for more than nine months during the first three years of the child's life, then that child cannot become a good, warm, loving human being. He may look like a human being; he may be well-dressed, physically may be well-developed, but emotionally he will act and behave like a zombie. These children will never be able to relate to another with any depth or closeness.

Dr. Bowlby maintains that the stunted emotional development is irreversible; nothing can be done afterwards to erase the evil. These children become difficult to control; they become delinquents; they are egotistical, violent, sexually troublesome. They cannot maintain close relationships; to outsiders they appear weird, apart, unable to give warmth or develop deep social interests. In popular language we describe them as "cold fish," "lone wolves," "queer, clammy guys." As patients, I find many with such a background harbor deep hostility, and from this hostility come the many aggressive actions against individuals and society. Seething with hostility, they feel others want to act in kind toward them. Such persons are in frequent altercations, and in explanation they will say: "I got them before they got me." It is these adults, who have grown up without tenderness and affection, who are able and probably do commit out of all proportion the heinous crimes that fill the newspapers; they are the ones who are capable of shooting from rooftops at innocent human beings below; they are the ones capable of terrible sex crimes which make you wonder how depraved a human being can become. I am beginning to believe that a person cannot have a deeper, a warmer, or closer relationship than that which he had with his mother or his mother substitute.[6]

Dr. Bowlby summarizes the findings dealing with children deprived of maternal love because of long institutionalization or frequent shifts of foster parents:

"The symptom complaints . . . include, frequently, aggressive and sexual behavior in early life, stealing, lying, often of the fantastic type, and, essentially, complaints variously expressed that indicate some lack of emotional response in the child. It is this lack of emotional response, this shallowness of feeling that explains the difficulty in modifying behavior.[7]

Dr. Bowlby describes more specifically the characteristics of maternally deprived children:

Early in the work a third group of girls was recognized who were asocial (i.e. unaware of obligations to others), but not obviously neurotic, and with whom no treatment methods seemed of any avail. Later it became clear that the features common to them was an inability to make a real relationship with any member of the staff. There might seem to be a good contact, but it invariably proves to be superficial. . . . There might be protestations of interest and a boisterous show of affection, but there was little or no evidence of any real attachment having been made. In going over their previous history, this same feature was outstanding. . . . [These girls] have apparently had no opportunity to have a loving relationship in early children [and] seem to have little or no capacity to enter

---

[6] Although for the most part, it is usually the mother who is the significant figure in the child's early life, it need not be. It may be a father, a relative, a servant or someone outside the family. I have found that once a person has experienced a good, warm, tender relationship with another person, the kind where the two light up with pleasure at the sight of the other, a prognosis for a favorable outcome of therapy can be made.

[7] John Bowlby, *op cit,* p. 35.

in an emotional relationship in early childhood with another person or with a group."[8]

Dr. Bowlby here writes of deprived children who have been reared at home:

Prolonged breaks (in the mother–child relationship) during the first three years of life leave a characteristic impression on the child's personality. Such children appear emotionally withdrawn and isolated. They fail to develop loving ties with other children or with adults and consequently have no friendships worth the name. It is true that they are sometimes sociable in a superficial sense, but if this is scrutinized we find that there are no feelings, no roots in these relationships. This, I think, more than anything else, is the cause of their hard-boiledness. Parents and school-teachers complain that nothing you say or do has any effect on the child. If you thrash him he cried for a bit, but there is no emotional response to being out of favor, such as is normal to the ordinary child. It appears to be of no essential consequence to these lost souls whether they are in favor or not. Since they are unable to make genuine emotional relations, the condition of relationship at a given moment lacks all significance for them. . . . During the last few years I have seen some sixteen cases of this affectionless type of persistent pilferer and in only two cases was a prolonged break absent. In all the others gross breaches of the mother–child relation had occurred during the first three years, and the child had become a persistent pilferer.[9]

---

[8] *Ibid*, p. 35.

[9] John Bowlby, *op cit*, pp. 36–37. What is set down here seems also to apply to macaque monkeys. Dr. Harry F. Harlow, at the University of Wisconsin, removed macaque infant monkeys from their mothers at birth. In place of real mothers, he substituted two figures, one made out of mesh wire and another made out of cotton terry cloth. Although the wire mesh "mother" was the source of milk, the infant monkeys clearly preferred the soft, terry cloth "mothers." It is the latter that they clung to and hugged and when frightened they dashed to it for protection. When the "mother substitutes" were removed, the infant monkeys acted very agitated and alarmed. When threatened with danger, they became transfixed with fright when the "mother" figure was removed. So these "mother" figures did play a role resembling the maternal. In the matter

Here Dr. Bowlby writes, not in generalities, but of one particular child:

My first example is an eight-year-old girl who was adopted a year and a half before being examined. After an illegitimate birth, the child was shifted about from one relative to another, finally brought to a child-placing agency, and then placed in a foster-home for two months before she came to the adoptive parents. The complaints were lying and stealing. The parents described the child's reaction to the adoption as very casual. When they took her home and showed her the room she was to have all for herself, and took her on a tour of the house and the grounds, she showed apparently no emotional response. Yet she appeared very vivacious and "affectionate on the surface." After a few weeks of experience with her, the adoptive mother complained to her husband that the child did not seem

of physical care, food and cleanliness, they were treated well, except in one respect: they had no mother.

When the "motherless" monkeys grew up, it was obvious that they were badly neurotic: they did not relate to one another; they kept themselves isolated and apart; in them there was no zest of living and no joy.

Comments Dr. Harlow: "We have seen them sitting in their cages, strangely mute, staring fixedly in space, relatively indifferent to people and other monkeys." When approached, some became so disturbed that they went into violent rages. They appeared to be uninterested in sex; male did not approach female; and it appeared as if they would not reproduce, and that life would end them.

Whereupon Dr. Harlow introduced into the group a gentle, persevering male Casanova, who had a "normal" mother and who had amply proved his prowess in previous such affairs. After the most painstaking efforts, this persuasive male succeeded in impregnating only a few of the monkeys.

What kind of mothers did these "motherless" monkeys make? Horrible. As their infants sought them out, they cuffed and bit them mercilessly, drawing blood; from the top of the cage, they would beat their infants violently with both paws and throw them to the floor. "We eventually realized," said Dr. Harlow, "we had a laboratory full of neurotic monkeys."

Said Dr. Harlow: "Month after month, female monkeys that never knew a real mother, themselves became mothers—helpless, hopeless, heartless mothers devoid, or almost totally devoid, of any maternal feeling."

able to show any affection. The child, to use the mother's words, "would kiss you but it would mean nothing." The husband told his wife that she was expecting too much, that she should give the child a chance to get adapted to the situation. The mother was somewhat mollified by these remarks, but still insisted that something was wrong. The father said he saw nothing wrong with the child. In a few months, however, he made the same complaint. But this time, also, it was noted that the child was deceitful and evasive. All methods of correction were of no avail. . . . The school teacher complained of her general inattention and her lack of pride in the way her things looked. However, she did well in her school subjects, in keeping with her good intelligence. She also made friends with children, though none of these were close friendships. After a contact of a year and a half with the patient the adoptive father said, "You just can't get to her," and the mother remarked, "I have no more idea today what's going on in that child's mind than I knew the day she came. You can't get under her skin. She never tells what she's thinking or what she feels. She chatters but it's all surface."[10]

You may ask: What has all this got to do with marriage? In my opinion, it has everything to do with marriage; it is vital. As we have indicated, each of the partners in a marriage enters with a life pretty well formed and made.

Stressing the importance of early childhood in establishing the quality and kind of sexual relationships, Dr. William H. Masters and Virginia E. Johnson, authors of *Human Sexual Response*, write: " . . . what is perfectly clear is that sexuality does not suddenly emerge at puberty, that it is not born of glandular change or the ability to reproduce. . . . The infant 'learns' sexuality at his mother's breast, from the touch of her hand, the warmth of her body, the sound of her voice. He learns it from

---

[10] John Bowlby, *op cit*, pp. 33–34.

the different ways in which his father holds him, the different sound of his father's voice. He learns it by touching and being touched when he is bathed. He learns the pleasure of sensual stimulation, the pleasure of sounds, of smells, of warmth, of embrace. And it is from this learning, from these beginnings of sexuality that his capacity for tenderness, for warmth, for love and sex is nurtured."[11]

It is not surprising to learn studies agree that the kind of home from which the spouse comes is the crucial element in predicting marital success. Dr. L. M. Terman, better known for the Stanford Revision of the Binet Test for Intelligence which made the I. Q. part of the language, is also known among students of the subject for his pioneer study of marriage. Subsequent studies have only confirmed and strengthened Dr. Terman's original findings. According to Dr. Terman, the ten factors which are predictively highest for marital happiness are the following:

1. Superior happiness of the parents
2. Childhood happiness
3. Lack of conflict with mother
4. Home discipline that was firm not harsh
5. Strong attachment to mother
6. Strong attachment to father
7. Lack of conflict with father
8. Parental frankness about matters of sex
9. Infrequency and mildness of childhood punishment
10. Premarital attitude toward sex that was free from disgust or aversion.[12]

---

[11] Dr. William H. Masters and Virginia E. Johnson, "A Defense of Love and Morality," November, 1966, *McCall's*.
[12] L. M. Terman, *Psychological Factors in Marital Happiness*, p. 372.

Summarizing the studies concerning marriage, Dr. Bowlby writes:

They agree in finding three things to be of the greatest importance for married happiness: the married happiness of the couples' parents; happiness of childhood; no conflict with mother. One pair of investigators analyzed answers to questionnaires by 526 couples, mostly young middle class Americans. From this part of the inquiry they conclude that the condition of their childhoods which was most relevant to the happiness of their marriages was the happiness or the unhappiness of their parents' marriages. Next in importance came the degree of their affection for their own parents, particularly for their mothers. These research workers made a more detailed study of 100 couples. From it they came to the conclusion that the love-life of the grown person is conditioned by his love relationships during childhood.[13]

The evidence is mounting that it takes a minimum of three years of love, affection, cooing, being held closely to the body of an admiring, warm, loving mother or mother substitute before we can create a good, warm, loving, affectionate human being. We are beginning to understand what kind of home produces good, kind, generous people; and it is these homes, we are coming to perceive, that provide the best breeding environment and the richest source of good husbands and wives.

In America our marriages have not been particularly good. Our divorce rate is scandalously high. In most other cultures, marriages are more stable, solid, lasting. It is interesting to note that these cultures, without studies and investigations, instinctively and intuitively knew that the home resembled the trademark of an old and respected establishment. In arranging a marriage, the par-

13 John Bowlby, *op cit,* p. 93.

ents considered the status of the family, its integrity, its repute, its stability, its community involvement. The assumption was that if the family rated high in these criteria the product would in the same measure be trustworthy, reliable, responsible. Further, that the spouse which came from a particular family would eventually head a family that in a large measure resembled the family from which he came.

We are beginning to perceive more clearly that bad parents breed bad parents and the tragedy is that they in turn will breed children who will breed bad parents and there is no hope for a better society till we learn how to break this vicious cycle.

18

INEVITABLE DIFFERENCES IN MARRIAGE

NO MATTER HOW ALIKE THE MARITAL PAIR MAY APPEAR, there will still exist and there will continue to exist enormous differences between them. At best they will be vast. The extent of individual differences in man is suggested by Julian Huxley who writes as follows:

"The differences between a somewhat subnormal member of a savage tribe and a Beethoven or a Newton is assuredly comparable in extent with that between a sponge and a higher animal. Leaving aside such vertical differences, the lateral differences between the mind of, say, a distinguished general or engineer of extrovert type and of an introvert genius in mathematics or religious mysticism is no less than that between the insect and the vertebrate. This enormous range of individual variation in human minds often leads to misunderstanding and even mutual incomprehensibility . . . "[1]

Since these differences are so vast, it is best for the two in the marriage to be as alike as possible, in social class, in familial background, in religion, in values and outlook. You may say how monotonous; they will act as a soporific

[1] Julian Huxley, *Man in the Modern World,* The New American Library, New York, 1948, pp. 11–12 © Harper & Row.

on each other. But again the fact is that no matter how exactly the two are matched, differences will still remain, ramified and wide enough to require a lifetime for both to learn to understand, to accept and to find a satisfying modus vivendi. More than necessary initial differences only add to the burden of the marriage and make a difficult task more difficult.

Even in a good marriage will there be conflicts, disagreements, sometimes fierce and harsh? The answer is an emphatic yes. Man harbors hostilities, hates, grievances, angers; he makes demands; he suffers from frustrations which elicit from him all sorts of defense mechanisms. Marriage is a most difficult relationship; it taxes man to the utmost.

I suspect a marriage when the couple say they never differ. In significant and meaningful relationships, there will be differences. If there are really none, then it means that the relationship has no depth; it is only a surface thing. To repeat what Freud said: there can be no quarrel between the lion and the polar bear because they occupy different geographical areas; they never meet. Havelock Ellis has said the relationship in a marriage resembles violin strings, always taut, stretched and tensed, keyed up. If otherwise, then there would be placidity and slack and lack of interest.

Strong, pervasive, interlocked relationships between two people are taut, keyed up, and tense, and such relationships develop differences, sometimes fierce. What matters is how the couple handle the differences. Marriages proceed best, not when the couple ignore the differences, but when hostilities, irritations, frustrations and angers are ventilated, aired; then this ventilation acts like a safety valve. It becomes the spout of the teakettle; without the

spout there would be complete wreckage. Yet I should
not like anyone to think of marriage as some dreadful
experience, similar to sitting perpetually with a dentist's
drill in his mouth. That wouldn't be true at all. Nowhere
but in marriage can two human beings stay together so
long and so well. Benjamin Franklin said that after a
three-day visit even by one's mother, a guest begins to
smell like three-day-old fish; a married pair spend their
days and nights together. If a marriage amounts to anything at all, it develops a rhythm and a way of life peculiar to itself; and any outsider interfering with this
rhythm makes the couple's day hard and burdensome. But
the married pair alone and together—they can manage.
Frequently an outsider will ask: "What do they do?"
That would be difficult to answer. To an outsider, what
the couple do may seem dull and insipid; but for them,
this rhythm, this what they do, is deeply satisfying and
gives them a full and rounded day.

But that does not gainsay the fact that every married
pair has to overcome differences that create irritations. It
would be futile to make even a stab at attempting to catalog all or even a fraction of them. As each marital pair is
unique so are their differences unique. How numerous
indeed are the irritations that may exist between two
persons!

One likes a cold bedroom; the other fears cold like an
enemy. One likes the movies; the other is bored by them.
One likes to read; the other is threatened by reading since
reading reminds him of school where he had been a failure; he hates to see his wife wasting time, doing nothing,
reading; he favors activity. One seeks out the new and
is exhilarated by it; the other dreads the new, wanting
the old and the familiar. One needs to follow a pre-set

routine; the other wants the day to be free, open, unstruc-
tured. One is timid and frightened by experience, the
other is open to and welcoming of experience. One has
faith in the next person, being permissive and letting the
next person alone; the other feels he must direct, manage,
and oversee each step. One believes in giving freedom
and being indulgent toward mistakes; the other demands
absolute perfection and is full of guilt and self-accusation
when he makes a mistake. One likes himself and is easy
with others and accepting of others, while the partner dislikes himself, dislikes others, and makes terrible demands
on himself and on others. One is confident, buoyant, op-
timistic, sure in confronting life; the other feels inferior,
inadequate, has low self-esteem and expects failure. One
has a natural trust of human beings; the other is wary and
suspicious. One demands of himself that he live up to
high moral values; the other seeks self-gratification and
pleasure. One lives for idealistic purposes outside of himself; the other seeks egocentric pleasures of a material
nature. One is dedicated to causes and finds pleasure in
lavishly giving of himself; the other can conceive of no
pleasure outside of his own person. And thus one can go
on endlessly.

At best the differences in a marriage will be enormous,
so that it will take a lifetime of living to reconcile them,
even under the best conditions. In America, the first five
years of marriage are the hardest; after that the divorce
rates drop precipitously. Even in Russia, during the early
post-revolutionary period when a divorce could be obtained simply by mailing a post card, after three years the
Russian marriages proved to be fairly stable and durable.
What does this mean? By this time the couples have sur-
mounted some of these differences or have learned to cope

with them, at least sufficiently to make both want to maintain the marriage.

It is what the couple does with the differences that counts. If they use the differences to attack and browbeat each other, if they use the differences to show off the superiority of the one and the inferiority of the other, then these differences generally are destructive of the relationship. If, however, they use the differences for further understanding, then the quarreling and the disputes are ameliorative and desirable, for thus the marital pair can come to perceive the attitudes and the feelings of the other. If there is generosity and good-will, these differences, when worked through, lead to greater knowledge of and sensitivity to the other, and hence, to less acrimony and better accommodation of these differences. The marriage is strengthened and the relationship becomes more secure and solidly founded.

Does this mean that these differences are resolved, removed? Not necessarily. They should, however, be understood without reproach or recriminations, so that no matter what the final outcome of a difference, the accommodation is made not in vindictiveness, but in kindliness and good will. *There are degrees of acceptance; and they need not be full acceptance or full rejection.* Whatever the outcome, each should understand how the other feels and what prompted the original dispute. The degree and extent of acceptance, to repeat, may vary. It may run this gamut:

"I know how you feel, and I'd love to say yes, since I know how important this is to you. I am really sorry that I cannot agree to do what you wish, since I know how strongly you feel. If I did agree, I could not maintain my self-respect; so it is impossible to comply with what you

want, even though I know how it hurts you." Or it may
take this track: "I myself don't feel as you do, but since
it means so much to you and you are so set on it, I'll do
it to please you. On my own, I would not do it." Or the
outcome may take this felicitous turn: "I'm glad to do it.
I feel exactly as you do and it pleases me to do it."

It is in working through differences by agreement and
disagreement that one gains insight into the varying values and feelings of the partner and also in this way one
acquires more sensitive understanding and grows in the
capacity to give the happiness that becomes his happiness;
in making oneself a slave to the marital other, one acquires
a slave. There is no finality to marriage, as there is none
in life. If it is a healthy relationship, it expands, it grows,
it is creative, it is unfolding; it satisfies so many aspects of
man that it is as fathomless as man; it satisfies man's desire for a mother, for a father, for a wife, for a comrade,
for a mistress, for an erotic partner, for a lover, for a nurse,
for a parent of one's children, for a social partner, for the
head of a household, for a therapist, for a companion, and
one can go on. In an outstandingly good marriage, the
two are so close they become like one, for they are in-
extricably woven together by common needs and purposes.

19

LISTENING TO ONE ANOTHER

IN THERAPY, I CONSTANTLY URGE PATIENTS IN MARITAL counseling to "Listen to one another."

I am eager that they learn to listen because I have discovered that even in bad marriages there exists an amazing eagerness for each to please the other, a willingness to sacrifice oneself for the other; and also, and most important, a strong wish and need for maintaining the marriage.

If each listens to the other sympathetically, open to one another, trying to understand, not trying to demolish the other, not trying to prove to the other how superior and better he is, it is truly amazing how much good will, how much binding cement exists even in a badly functioning marriage.

The tragedy is that there are so many judgmental qualities in all relationships. If one differs, then the other is wrong; or worse, a scoundrel, a menace, a no-account, a horrible person.

This is aggravated in marital disputes. Love and hate, said Sigmund Freud, are the opposite side of the same coin. By the very token of hate, there is also love; for, if there were no feeling for one another, it would be simple and easy; there would be distance and calm; one would go one way, the other another way. When there is nothing between two people, there can be no quarrel, for they do not inhabit the same territory. They are distant and apart.

So I say: "Listen to one another." If a marital pair truly learn to listen—generously and in good will—there is the hope that one may come to understand the other. Beyond such understanding, it seems to me, one cannot go.

I have faith in the person, a great, abiding faith. And my work as a therapist has abundantly confirmed this faith. It has been my experience that once you see a person without his façade, his defenses, once you see him as the poor, suffering, hoping human being he is, gropingly and painfully trying to make sense out of life, you can't help being drawn to him, feeling for him, and, yes, liking him.[1]

Students of mine in a group dynamics course relate what happened to them as a result of trying to learn how to truly listen.

One student writes:

I would like to point to one particular area in which I have learned a great deal about myself in this course. I have learned how to listen. I realize now that most of my life I have listened, not to understand, but to make an evaluation and judgment so that I could respond. The emphasis has always been on the response and not the thing to be listened to. Listening, therefore, in the context described has only been a means to an end—a means by which I could express myself.

Through this course I am learning how much one can learn

---

[1] This is not an absolute. It generally holds. If, however, there is a great gap between the two in values, honest expression of thinking and feeling may only exacerbate the breach.

about and feel for another person by listening—not with half an ear, not with both ears, but with the third ear. In this way I am learning what it is to appreciate the essence of another person. In learning this, I am also learning to be myself and not be afraid of what I am. To be sure, this process and the task before me is not one to end with the course. It is a lifetime pursuit.

Although still new and unpracticed at it, what this student has learned appears to be having desirable effects.

The positive therapeutic outcomes of learning to listen are that people can learn to be themselves, fully accepting of themselves, and that they can learn to accept others. This implies that one loses, to a great extent, if not completely, his hostility and suspicion, does not regard others as a threat to himself and above all learns to communicate with others so that he can share and express his feelings. In so doing he learns the essence of communication and that is to listen to others completely, not for the purpose of making a judgment or evaluation, but for the purpose of really understanding what the other person feels, what he is.

Another student writes:

I think the most important thing I have learned in this course and which has not been an easy lesson is—to listen to what people have to say without evaluation. I think we are all guilty of judging whether we realize it or not. I never realized that I was as guilty as I am because I had never been made that conscious of it. But upon examination, I know I am very guilty. All of our lives our parents have told us (me anyway) that is good, that is not. As a little girl I remember my mother saying, "Don't say that. It's not nice." When I hear someone say something, I think I unconsciously say "How awful," or "Isn't that nice?" I must try to practice unconditional regard. Also, practice this on my children. (Let them think for themselves.)

Second on my list of needs is: I must try to take myself as I am. I must realize I have faults, know what I am. I know some people will like me and some will not and that's that. It is important to be oneself and not be one thing inside and another outside.

If I can accomplish these two things I have done a tremendous amount. But, perhaps the fact that I am in the *process* and going in the right direction is the important thing.

Another student tells what is happening to him as he tries to listen to his son. Although he loved his son deeply, and wanted much and hoped much from him, his relationship with his son had deteriorated badly. The father wanted above all else to have a good and cordial relationship with his only son. But he found that his son listened to him sullenly, resentfully, impassively. The walls between them were becoming higher and wider. This remoteness from his son gave the father sleepless and anxious nights. From his anger and frustration, he was apt to speak harsh words. His son was passive, said little; but the father saw that the boy was drawing away from him further and further. The father would note that his son spoke freely and openly to others, but to him the boy was distant, formal, and respectful. And then something happened. For the first time, the father tried to listen to his son, to hear him in a way that was understanding and compassionate; he did not come to him with demands, judgmentally, but with open ears and an accepting heart. Let the father himself relate what is happening as a result.

I have had something called to my attention although I was quite aware of the fact that my quick temper in handling certain problems is perhaps a sign of immaturity.

Reflecting on this trait in the past always brought promises within myself to overcome it but to no avail. I was forced to realize, not by what was said to me directly, but by the conversation of others in relationship to the ways they solved their problems that I was not acting in a mature way.

I feel that I have done my son an injustice in this respect but I am proud of the way he has stood up for some of his rights. I no longer look upon this action as disrespect. I feel that his rights as an individual had in many instances been violated by me.

I feel that I have matured to the point where I am able to recognize that I have done wrong and that I am now doing something about it. I won't say that I have completely changed because an individual cannot do so easily. But I certainly have come to realize my problem and am attacking it.

You are aware of the problem which existed between my son and me. We have been working toward overcoming the problem through the means of group dynamics. Whenever a problem arises which affects my wife, my son, and me, we discuss it together. Instead of quick tempers resulting in hasty remarks and actions for which we are sorry, we have learned to talk out our problems. At times we are able to reach an understanding which is compatible to all of us but at times this is not possible. Whenever possible we try to work out some temporary arrangement by which one idea might be carried out to see its effect. If that does not work out, we attempt something else. This has helped both my son and me to express ourselves more openly and yet with a feeling that the others must be respected. Through an interplay of ideas and suggestions, we sometimes are able to find a solution to a problem which none of us had thought of before.

I feel that we have made good progress in an effort to control our [the father's and the son's] explosive natures. Our tensions are released in a more decent way and we generally are more satisfied.

I suppose when you ask someone to listen to another and try to understand him, there is always the possibility that what one hears and understands may be exactly what one may dislike. There is, I say, a possibility, and this, I suppose, underlies the fact that not all marriages are good; and if so, the two should not stay together. This can occur, but it very rarely does. The very acrimony in marriage, the fact that patients come at great expense and inconvenience for counseling, would indicate that there is something in the union, something between the two, that they are loath to sever. "Those we can love," said Thoreau, "we can hate; to others we are indifferent." The lion and the polar bear, to repeat, never quarrel; they occupy different territories. In hopeless marriages the two are really apart and between them there is nothing, not even a quarrel.

Therefore, I have this faith that once they listen to one another, that which binds them, that which keeps them together, that which brings them to the therapist, will become evident; and that this—once understood and appreciated—will draw them together.

We have not yet learned how potently therapeutic is simply listening to another human being with compassion and understanding.

The most elequent testimony for this contention comes from a passage quoted by Dr. Menninger. He writes:

"Perhaps more important than talking is just plain listening. I believe listening to be one of the most powerful and influential techniques of human intercourse. The principal element in the technique of psychoanalysis is listening—uncritical but attentive listening. A good many pages have been written about this in the technical literature, but I do not recall anything else so eloquent and, at the same time, so sound as an article by Brenda Ueland, published in the *Ladies' Home Journal*. In the November 1941 issue, Miss Ueland writes:

Listening is a magnetic and strange thing, a creative force. . . . The friends that listen to us are the ones we move toward, and we want to sit in their radius as though it did us good, like ultra-violet rays. . . . When we are listened to, it creates us, makes us unfold and expand. Ideas actually begin to grow within us and come to life. . . . It makes people happy and free when they are listened to. . . . When we listen to people there is an alternating current, and this recharges us so that we never get tired of each other. We are constantly being re-created.

Now there are brilliant people who cannot listen much. They have no ingoing wires on their apparatus. They are entertaining but exhausting too. I think it is because these lecturers, these brilliant performers, by not giving us a chance to talk, do not let us express our thoughts and expand; and it is this expressing and expanding that makes the little creative fountain inside us begin to spring and cast up new thoughts and unexpected laughter and wisdom.

I discovered all this about three years ago, and truly it made a revolutionary change in my life. Before that, when I went to a party I would think anxiously: "Now, try hard. Be lively. Say bright things. Talk. Don't let down." And when tired, I would have to drink a lot of coffee to keep this up. But now before going to a party, I just let myself listen with affection to anyone who talks to me, *to be in their shoes when they talk;* to try to know them without my mind pressing against theirs, or arguing, or changing the subject. No. My attitude is: "Tell me more. This person is showing me his soul. It is a little dry and meager and full of grinding talk just now, but presently he will begin to think, not just automatically to talk. He will show his true self. Then he will be wonderfully alive."[2]

It was Rousseau who said that man is born naked and free and dies in clothes and in chains, gagged and bound. Despite the mountain of evidence that has piled up to show the healing power of regard, acceptance, and understanding to give man the strength to function healthier

[2] Karl Menninger, "Love Against Hate," © Harcourt, Brace & World, Inc.; also with permission *Ladies' Home Journal,* © The Curtis Publishing Co.

and better, it has made little dent in our culture. As in
Rousseau's times, herculean efforts are made from his
birth to push man around, reshape, remold, reform him;
we are scarcely able to keep our hands off him, to let him
be, to let him live. We may ask: Who is sick, the patient
or society?

Our "success orientated," pressurized culture has made
man anxious, neurotic, feeling inadequate and wrong. I
was reading Ernest Hemingway's *A Movable Feast.* In
one passage of the book, he speaks of a good day; he had
worked hard at his writing and he thought it went well,
and Paris this day was at its loveliest; and one has to
know Paris to understand how lovely such a day can be.
And then Hemingway makes the remark that nothing
could ruin this day excepting a person, a human being.
And I understood what he meant there, too.

There is something in our culture, especially middle
class culture, which makes us make terrible demands on
ourselves and in turn on others. Further, we seem to think
we are doing the best for the next person when we try
to alter, change, influence, direct, instruct, insist on, warn
against, modify the next person. It is so hard—so very
hard—to accept, understand, let be.

Says the Russian proverb, "Love me black as I am.
When I am white everyone will love me." Said Vauven-
argues: "No man is weak from choice." Jean Tabaud, a
portrait painter, understood well what so many in our
culture cannot: "To paint is an act of love whether the
subject is a tree or a woman." The best way to preserve
the love object and the love relationship is through acceptance, compassion, generous giving of oneself. One
who loves best, I would say, understands best. One who
is permeated with hostility and hate cannot love and

therefore has the least understanding of man or beast or anything. "Even God himself, sir," said Dr. Johnson, "does not propose to judge man until the end of his days."

Our whole culture is built on *not* listening. We must *first learn to listen.* We do not listen; we are eager to tell, to argue, to outwit, outsmart, to show up the other. Man does not talk to one another, articulate what he truly feels and thinks. From earliest childhood we are taught to alienate ourselves from our selves. It is as if each child almost at birth—this holds particularly and especially true for the middle classes—has been entered into a lifetime competition, a lifetime struggle to outdo, outperform, to get ahead of all others; and there is no limit, no end, for the goal itself is insatiable.

As Tennyson has so well said:

Ambition

Is like the sea wave, which the more you drink
The more you thirst—yea—drink too much, as men
Have done on rafts of wreck—it drives you mad.

Our society is obsessed by a desire to achieve and to outrank family and friends and to make family and friends feel inferior compared to our own achievements. We have no compunction in consigning to ridicule and public scorn those who do not succeed. We have built up a whole vocabulary to describe such unfortunates. We call them lazy, stupid, incompetent, "good for nothing." They are even regarded with contempt by their own children and family. How many good, hard-working, conscientious, kindly souls have been broken and made human debris by our society's insistence on success and more success!

In the very nature of our competitive society—each trying to out-achieve the other—there is inevitable failure.

Demands on the child in our culture start from infancy. An advertisement of an insurance company shows a soft, cuddly baby, no more than three or four months old, being held by his father, who looks earnestly and with concern at the bitsy mite of life in his hands, and says: "Thomas, I want to talk to you about college." I am sure that our culture would approve of such a parent and regard his attitude as highly commendable. How many parents have looked at their offspring and at first thought silently and then vocally, "There goes the future president of the United States." Like a Greek chorus, cultivating the insidious seeds of ambition, our books, our cinema, our radio and television have chanted endlessly the story of eminence, success, achievement. "Hitch your wagon to a star," Emerson told us.

And the misfortune is that so many fine and good people build their lives around such fanciful dreams. Some work ceaselessly to achieve this miracle, never giving up no matter how unrealistic the goal; and at the end all they have to show for their spent lives are failure, inadequacy and despair. They never stop trying to break the Empire State Building by banging their heads against its walls, although it is obvious that they can never make a dent. They succeed in bashing their heads and wrecking their lives. Even those who go through the motions of quitting this hopeless struggle do so with severe damage to their personalities, for there simmers within them a black stew of discontent, resentment, jealousy, and hate. Into psychological clinics, into psychiatric offices, into hospitals flock these victims of this debilitating struggle, suffering from harrowing emotional disturbances, from neuroses and psychoses. There is no limit to ambition, only sleepless nights and a "lean and hungry look." Even those who are eminently successful in the struggle, those who have achieved mightily and have won the acclaim of their colleagues, continue to drive themselves to ever-greater effort and set their goals for ever-higher achievements.

Says Bertrand Russell: "Napoleon suffered at school from inferiority to his school fellows, who were rich aristocrats, while he was a penurious scholarship boy. When he allowed the return of the *emigres*, he had the satisfaction of seeing his former school fellows bowing down before him. What bliss! Yet it led to the wish to obtain a similar satisfaction at the expense of the Czar, and this led to Saint Helena. Since no man can be omnipotent, a life dominated wholly by love of power can hardly fail, sooner or later, to meet with obstacles that cannot be overcome. This knowledge that this is so can be prevented from intruding on consciousness only by some form of lunacy, though if a man is sufficiently great he can imprison or execute those who point this out to him."[3] Russell recounts the story of Alexander the Great, who despite all his achievements and conquests, still felt that he had not achieved all that he wanted. And then he concluded that he was a god. "Was he a happy man? His drunkenness, his furious rages, his indifference to women, and his claim to divinity, suggest that he was not."[4]

In our culture, the emphasis is on individualism, on self-reliance and independence, on going it alone and doing things alone. In our civilization, no one can ever feel

[3] Bertrand Russell, *The Conquest of Happiness,* p. 18, N. Y. The New American Library of Literature, 1951. © George Allen & Unwin, Ltd.
[4] *Ibid.*

that he is altogether part and parcel of a group; that his fortunes, for good or ill, are ever merged in a cooperative, tribal sense. True enough, because of this, he experiences triumphs and exaltations peculiarly of his own making, but at the same time he suffers alone and he dies alone. In his grief, he has no sense of sharing; his misfortunes are peculiarly his own and are to him unique. Many individuals cannot cope with this sense of being alone, and many psychological problems result from it: many break under the strain, unable to carry the load, especially when they cannot successfully compete; and when their misfortunes seem to them so much greater than their successes. The sense of being alone, of being unwanted, of being adrift on uncharted seas, of being weighed down with Job-like despair, is indigenous and inevitable in an individualistic and competitive culture. In the great cities, where masses of men gather, many sad souls bob around like driftwood in an uncharted ocean; for here in our civilization the emphasis is not on sharing and cooperation, but on being alone. Only psychiatrists and psychologists know the high price man has paid, in broken and misspent lives, for this pattern of conduct.

How hard it is in our competitive, rivalrous culture to genuinely share and be happy over another's achievements! How easy it is to show concern and have genuine feeling of kinship and woe in the presence of ruin and death! Freud said that a funeral is a happy event for most, since their competitor is gone from the scene and they are left behind as victors.

Man does not talk to one another. As he seemingly listens, he is thinking of an answer, of a rebuttal, how to impress the other person; his ego is always there, his vanity; so he does not listen. Driven by a "success-oriented" society, he seeks opportunities to impress others with his success. He does not relate to others; he tries to impress others. He does not try to understand others; he tries to show others up. As a result there is no communication, only a sense of sadness and strain as one feels either successful or defeated in the contest. It is the most difficult thing for man to let another alone.

Our educational institutions further the sick traits of a sick society. They probably are responsible for more trauma, more hurt, more fears than any other existing institution. Our schools are permeated with grades, examinations, judgments, critical evaluations, promotion, failure—invidious distinctions of all kinds.

Man's tragedy is further compounded in that the mighty things he creates and builds—for man is a wondrous creature—further alienates him from himself and society. His mighty machines and industries in the end dominate and enslave him. Our giant industries have become too big for man. His government, created to serve him, has in its vastness become so remote that he, the little man, is lost and engulfed. Even his social life has become complex, regimented, organized like a business, and even worse—competitive. He cannot invite those he likes but those who will impress those important people he wants to impress. This sometimes results in a sense of sadness and shame, for a successful child may want to hide, not be seen, with an unsuccessful sibling or even with a parent. Especially is this true when one has risen from lowly beginnings and has become successful and important. When entertaining persons whom he regards as significant for social or business advancement, he may deny brothers, sisters, and parents.

In this atomistic society, man has frequently not only

alienated himself from himself but has emerged feeling inadequate, inferior, shamed by his own being. Isolated, suffering, alone, he cannot even resort to his nearest kin for succor, for his competitiveness, his living for success and achievement, results all too often in brother vying with brother, peer with peer. In his travail, he cannot obtain what little comfort there comes from acknowledging fear, guilt, weakness; for by our conventions he is expected to be strong and brave, so that he must hide behind a façade of fake bravado the small suffering little human being we all are. The end result is that man is now more alone than ever.

For this kind of society, it becomes imperative that we learn to listen to another human being, to understand his anguish, his grief, his hopes, his disappointments, and, also, to share those moments of triumph and high spirits that come in each of our lives.

In *Action for Mental Health,* there is this statement; and it is something which one ought to ponder slowly and thoughtfully: ". . . human understanding is achieved, not when John understands Bill, according to John's way of looking at life but according to Bill's way. In short, the usual thing in listening to another person is to hear ourselves."[5]

Good things happen when John understands Bill, not "according to John's way of looking at life, but according to Bill's way." And this requires a special kind of listening. Erich Fromm tries to explain the nature of this kind of listening.

"I mean getting wet by what the patient says, by understanding it fully, by listening with such concentration that you don't just think, you feel in yourself, you ex-

[5] "Action for Mental Health," p. 278, N. Y.: Basic Books, 1963.

perience in yourself, every situation the patient describes, and then you respond with your skill. By responding, I don't mean you tell him that to do. You tell him what you hear. You tell him, 'So this is you'."[6]

It was Herbert Spencer, I believe, who maintained that arguing only confirms one in his original convictions.

Omar Khyyam wrote:

Myself when young did eagerly frequent
Doctor and saint, and heard great argument
About it and about; but ever more
Came out by the same door wherein I went.

Said Galileo: "You cannot teach a man anything. You can only help him find it for himself."

Each of us is a world, separate and apart. It is only through honest, open communication that one can perceive this world of the other, and have the wondrous experience of entering into it and the joy of being understood.

This story is told about André Gide. When he was a little boy, he was with his nurse in the fields. He recounts that he was sad that morning and everything looked black. And all of a suddent he saw his nurse, with her beaming face hovering over him, holding before him a bunch of flowers which she had freshly picked. Gide recounts that he looked at this sweet, smiling face and the *whole valley lit up*. Certainly the valley remained the same, but the valley lit up only for the little boy who loved the nurse so much. This was Gide's world and one has to understand Gide's world before he can understand why a whole valley can light up.

Dr. J. H. Van Den Berg, a Dutch psychiatrist, relates

[6] "An Interview with Erich Fromm," *McCall's*, October 1965.

that he had had a hard day and he was looking forward to a pleasant evening with a close friend. For this occasion, he had laid out a chess set and had bought a bottle of wine. Late that afternoon, his friend called up and said he could not come. All that evening, while alone, feeling sad and disappointed, everytime he looked at that bottle of wine, Dr. Van Den Berg said, he saw his friend. Could anyone else see his friend in that bottle of wine? This was Dr. Van Den Berg's own and private world. To understand you have to enter his world.

It is when you touch another in his own world, understandingly, warmly, lovingly, affectionately—and even better, when there is a sharing of worlds, each entering the other—that we have a sense of completion and fulfillment, of excitement and exhilaration; and this is healthy and good, for we have then shed our skins and for the moment we have been penetrated and we have penetrated another person. And we are not alone.

My feeling is that these rare moments—when two people have shed skins and shared their unique special worlds and have been thoroughly understood each in his own world—that will be treasured and remembered. They will remain with us, filling us with goodness and warmth, to the very end of our alloted time.

In marriage, if it works, if one listens to one another, generously, open to one another, we can truly be ourselves. We can say the words that are truly ours. We need not masquerade and be a façade, so that our words are hollow and meaningless. Marriage can be a perfect vehicle to alleviate the sickness of our rivalrous, competitive society. In marriage, the two can become one, an island, a life and a world apart; and in marriage there can be genuine sharing both in grief and in joy.

In her poem, "I Remembered," Sarah Teasdale writes of being alone and lonesome while she "drank the wine and played the happy guest," but all the while she remembered the one who could reflect her every mood, thought and feeling, and "could ease me of its fever"; and she concludes that "the heart belongs to him who knew it best."

In marriage, this can be achieved for longer periods and more frequently than in any other relationship, sometimes even till death.

Wrote Edgar Lee Masters:

> "William and Emily"
> There is something about Death
> Like love itself!
> If with someone with whom you have known passion,
> And the glow of youthful love,
> You also, after years of life
> Together, feel the sinking of the fire,
> And thus fade away together,
> Gradually, faintly, delicately,
> As it were in each other's arms,
> Passing from the familiar room—
> That is a power of unison between souls
> Like love itself![8]

---

[8] Edgar Lee Masters, *Spoon River Anthology,* p. 95, N. Y., Collier Books, 1962.

20

MARRIAGE AS THERAPY

I HAVE TRIED TO MAKE VERY CLEAR WHAT IMPORTANCE I attach to listening. But it can't be just listening. I mean listening in a special sense. There are those who listen to attack and destroy. They are law-enforcement officers seeking evidence to incriminate and convict. This is just the opposite of what I mean. If once you listen and understand, deeply understand, not judging, not trying to alter, the results are therapeutic beyond what most people at present understand. As a therapist I have seen distraught, frightened, unhappy people change under such circumstances in a remarkable manner; and it is these experiences that have convinced me so strongly of its salubrious effects.

You yourself have been with people—the right people—and when you left them, you felt exhilarated, excited, powerful, and big. Sometimes you felt so excited, so exhilarated that, as it is commonly phrased, you "floated on air." The right kind of people can do it; they make you feel right, adequate, good, and strong. And you know that with other people, you feel small, wrong, indeed whipped; whatever you say or do you feel is not right; and it can become so bad that whatever you say and think not only appears foolish but is foolish. With these people you can't be your likeable self, your true self, your best self. And you leave such people feeling diminished, small, wrong, helpless, and dejected.

What did it? No one physically attacked you. It was words, sounds that had such a powerful effect on you. The sounds that come out of the human being have always been a source of unending fascination for me. The wonder and the mystery of such sounds! How these sounds can excite man, exalt him, sadden him, depress him, destroy him and save him. Words have moved man to love, to hate, to kill, to defend. They have driven him to suicide and saved him from suicide. Hitler induced paranoia in an entire nation; Churchill with the same human sounds gave courage to a nation to rally in its self-defense.

You have seen pictures of a distraught, desperate person ready to leap from the ledge of a skyscraper or an enormously high bridge. The New York City police have discovered that once you can get such a suicidal person talking, you can save that person.

Words are unique and peculiar to man. Through words man expresses his deepest feelings, his deepest self; and through words man communicates with others of his species; and through words he reaches and touches another so that they both can share their persons. Words are the very thing that make humans human.

Man through words can profit from the experience of other human beings, past and present. Through the printed word, he has stored up the wisdom of the ages, the words set down by its wisest and choicest souls. Words as uttered by man represent the emoting, thinking, suffering, loving, hating, hoping human being. It is through words that man thinks and reasons. The late Franklin

Delano Roosevelt said it bluntly: "How do I know what I think until I hear myself say it?" A child will ask, "What is that?" When told its name, he will feel satisfied. In truth, trees, birds, and flowers do not exist for us when we do not know their names; we pass them by, unseeing.

In some societies, rituals are built around public and private confessing, for words uttered give relief; they are a purgative, a catharsis. Erik H. Erikson tells us that in other cultures ". . . adults, when traumatized, tend to solve their tensions by 'talking it out.' They are compelled, repeatedly, to describe the painful event; it seems to make them feel better. Systems designed to cure the soul or the mind make ritual use of this tendency by providing, at regular intervals, an ordained or otherwise sanctioned listener who gives this undivided attention, is sworn not to censure arbitrarily or to betray, and bestows absolution by explaining how the individual's problems make sense in some larger context, be it sin, conflict or disease."[1]

Carl Rogers has probably shown us best—providing ample evidence for his belief—that salutary changes, therapeutic beyond anything hitherto suspected, occur when human beings give each other respect, dignity, understanding. We are learning that this is the best method to elicit from man his highest spiritual qualities; further, that under such circumstances, each individual tends to give up his defensiveness and to reach out to others in goodwill and helpfulness, frequently eager—at least more frequently than by any other method—to join with others in the common task of man to effect the good of all.

Anyone with a slight acquaintance with what happens

---

[1] Erik H. Erikson, *Childhood and Society*, pp. 222–223, N. Y.: W. W. Norton & Co.

in individual and group psychotherapy knows that remarkable changes occur when human beings, instead of
arguing, choosing sides, battering and tearing at one another, learn how to talk in terms of respect, understanding, warmth, and affection. We also know that the reverse brings out all that is sick and dangerous in man,
his defensiveness, his hostility, his paranoia.

We have not nearly begun to understand the power
and the might of a warm, accepting, non-judgmental relationship. As a therapist, I have seen persons bearing
grief beyond human endurance, who after giving vent to
their despair get up after a session, exhausted and spent,
and say: "I feel better, much better. I believe I'll be able
to manage." It is as if the venom and the poison have in
a measure been drawn from them. How many have had
the good fortune to have a relationship with another person where you feel deeply understood, where nothing is
demanded and wanted of you, where you are liked and
appreciated for being what you are? If yes, you are a
fortunate person! How rare such relationships are! It is,
I repeat therapeutic beyond what we at present even
faintly fathom.

Speaking as a therapist, Carl Rogers says:

. . . I have found it of enormous value when I can permit
myself to understand another person. . . . To understand is
enriching in a double way. I find when I am working with
clients in distress, that to understand the bizarre world of a
partially psychotic individual, or to understand and sense the
attitudes of a person who feels that life is too tragic to bear,
or to understand a man who feels that he is a worthless and
inferior individual—each of these understandings somehow
enriches me. I learn from these experiences in ways that
change me, that make me a different and I think a more
responsive person. Even more important perhaps, is the fact

that my understanding of these individuals permits them to change. It permits them to accept their own fears and bizarre thoughts and tragic feelings and discouragements as well as their moments of courage and kindness and love and sensitivity; and it is their experience as well as mine that once someone has fully understood those feelings, this has enabled them to accept those feelings in themselves. Then they find both the feelings and themselves changing. Whether it is understanding a woman who feels that very literally she has a hook in her head by which others lead her about, or understanding a man who feels that no one is as lonely, no one is as separated from others as he. I find these understandings to be of value to me. But also, and perhaps even more importantly, to be understood has a very positive value to these individuals.[2]

In another context, Carl Rogers quotes Emerson: "We mark with light in the memory the few interviews we have had, in the dreary years of routine and of sin, with souls that made our souls wiser; that spoke what we thought; that told us what we knew; that gave us leave to be what we inly were."

What holds true for the distressed and the distraught holds true for the normal. In literary circles, Mrs. Mabel Dodge Luhan is a name that is lengendary. She entertained many important literary figures who became close and loving of her. Her home guests included Max Eastman, Carl van Vechten, Gertrude Stein, Lincoln Steffens, Jo Davidson, Walter Lippman. But her most important literary friendship was with D. H. Lawrence. According to descriptions of her, she was unattractive, bluntly built and in dress and manner plain and straightforward. In

---

[2] Carl R. Rogers, "What I have Learned About Human Relationships in Therapy and Teaching." Address at the Annual Conference of the New England Teacher Preparation Assocation, Swamscott, Mass., October 2, 1959.

speaking of her, Max Eastman wrote: "She had neither wit nor beauty, nor is she vivacious or lively-minded or entertaining. She is comely and good-natured, and when she says something it is sincere and sagacious."

What made her so appealing a personality? I believe the clue lies in what Mrs. Dodge said about herself. "I have always been myself and at the same time someone else; always able to be the other person, feel with him, think his thoughts, see from the angle in which he has found himself. This has caused me many inward conflicts. . . . I flowed out to people and identified myself with them, and it has always made people want to kiss me, to manifest an actual nearness and union. . . . It is the only genius I ever had, but it has been enough. . ."

Arthur Foote, writing on "The Meaning of Love" says:

"How truly Dr. Abraham Stone speaks when he calls love 'the greatest medicine,' but that most people, even those who think themselves happily married, barely glimpse what love means. Love is the will to understand. It involves a healthy acceptance of both oneself and others. It is a relationship characterized by spontaneity and open honesty. As we learn to love we grow more able to be ourselves, able to drop our defenses, to cease our masquerading. We can let others see us as we are; our anxiety lest we be 'seen through' vanishes. Love is the opposite of self-centeredness. It is the ability to break out of the shell of isolation. It is the ability to achieve oneness with life outside the self, through union with another person, through true communion with another's mind, a genuine linkage with life."[3]

Anytime we touch another person in warmth and understanding, it is therapeutic. Anthony Storr says: "It has

[3] *Action* Magazine, Nov.-Dec., 1965.

frequently been observed that even the most deteriorated schizophrenic improves to some extent if a nurse, an occupational therapist, or a doctor takes sustained personal interest in him."[4] Something like this happened while Dr. Carl Rogers was working with institutionalized mental patients. He writes as follows:

In one of my group-therapy groups at the hospital, a woman who had been hospitalized for many years, but who had shown much improvement during the past two years, and who is now leaving the hospital, gave a moving account of what had helped her. I had been much impressed by her improvement, which clearly began before she entered group therapy, and one day when she said, "This is the first year I have felt like leaving the hospital," I said, "Gladys, why is this? What has made the difference?" She said, "Well, what changed it was when the Morses began taking me home—the ones I call Mom and Dad, although they are not. I want to get out mostly to show my appreciation to them for what they have done."

And then she told how, by chance, through their daughter, a nurse at the hospital, this middle-aged couple had become interested in her. They brought a picnic lunch for their daughter and included Gladys. They took her home. "I just sat. Wouldn't move. I was real scared." But they continued to take her to their home. Gladys says, "They've stood an awful lot. Even when I was unruly and snotty to them, they stood by me, they didn't let me down." Little by little this special-class girl who could not even read, who had always been unstable, who had been psychotic, hallucinated, and for years a difficult patient, began to respond. She says, "They helped me more than any doctor," and then adds, "Course, doctors help too. But they stood by me even when I was disgusting . . . and saying things I shouldn't."[5, 6]

---

4 Anthony Storr, *The Integrity of the Personality*, p. 36, England: Penguin Books, 1960.
5 Carl R. Rogers, "The Therapeutic Relationship: Recent Theory and Research," Unpublished paper.
6 Dr. Charles Slack, conducting a course at Harvard University for

Not all psychiatrists are equally good at helping patients in mental hospitals; some are very good at it and some very bad; and the difference in the amount of discharge of patients treated by the very good and the very bad psychiatrists is alarmingly great. At the Henry Phipps Psychiatric Clinic of Johns Hopkins Hospital, John C. Whitehorn and Barbara J. Betz made a study of the very best doctors and the very worst doctors. In what way did the best doctors differ from the worst? Simply put, the best doctors regarded their patients as persons; they seemed to know and understand them as persons; they developed a personal relationship; and they did not feel the need to instruct, advise, interpret, and set straight. The worst doctors were structured, authoritarian, tight people; they thought in terms of treatment. They regarded the patient as a patient, and as a patient they viewed him

---

undergraduates, gave them this semester assignment: Go into this mental institution and see if you can't get a patient discharged. His students became involved with the patients, so loving and caring of them, that eventually the patients became visitors of the students in their campus rooms. "If we visit them, we want them to visit us," explained the students. The result: a remarkably high proportion of hospital discharges, even of patients who had been vegetating in the hospital for years. You should remember they were not professional psychiatrists or psychologists; they were ordinary students; and they succeeded where trained professionals had failed.

This movement of students to work with mentally disturbed patients in hospitals has gained momentum, and the results in nearly all instances have been amazingly good. They come to patients with good will, with affection, with friendship, with love. In one instance, within one year (*Action for Mental Health,* p. 91) "11 of 15 patients visited by student case aides were released from the hospital—some came back later, others to remain in the community. . . . The attendants saw the patients' needs as new furniture and clothing; the students, as friendship and love." A patient who had been institutionalized for five years and who had been aided by a student volunteer said after her release: (Action for Mental Health, pp. 92–93) "What you did for me was to treat me like a human being, like someone you wanted for a friend and could like. What you did for me is too much to explain."

as sick, and hence as a sick patient, he required instruction; he had to be told what was proper and right; he had
to be set straight. This proved to be the worst approach.[7]

It cannot be repeated often enough: Wherever there is
a warm, accepting, understanding relationship between
two persons, it is therapeutic beyond what we now realize.
There is the painful, torturesome insulin treatment. The
terror and the agony suffered by patients about to undergo such treatment is akin to a nightmare. Concerning this
treatment, Storr suggests that it may not be the insulin
that helps the patient but the attention incident to the
treatment. Storr writes: "It has been recently suggested
that the comparative success of insulin coma treatment
of schizophrenia depends upon the fact that the treatment
is difficult to administer and necessitates a great many
people giving a great deal of attention over a long period
to each patient. This may well be true."[8]

In the same vein, William Schofield in *Psychotherapy:
The Purchase of Friendship* points out that new techniques for the treatment of the emotionally disturbed when
first tried out achieve remarkable results; and then afterwards, when others begin using the technique, the seven-
day-wonder disappears from professional and public
view, and eventually it is forgotten; and then a new
"wonder" treatment appears. Schofield accounts for it in
this way: When a new technique appears, the initiators,
the innovators, are deeply involved, with their whole
egos, their whole selves, heart and soul; and this deep
concern and involvement communicate themselves to the
patient; and it is this the concern and involvement, not

---

[7] *Action for Mental Health,* Final Report of the Joint Commission on
Mental Illness and Health, pp. 36–37, N. Y.: Basic Books, 1961.
[8] *Op cit,* p. 69.

the new technique that is therapeutic and creates the remarkable results. As soon as the new technique is taken over by disinterested persons and is applied routinely and uniformly, without the original deep involvement with the patient, it loses its original magic, and then we wait for another panacea and another new wonder to behold.[9]

In an unusual way, subtle beyond the understanding of even the professional therapist, was the understanding shown by Rainer Maria Rilke, a sensitive poet, writing to a fledgling poet, with whom he was corresponding. To this young poet he wrote:

"You see—I have copied your sonnet, because I found that it is lovely and simple and born in the form in which it moves in quiet decorum. It is the best of those of your poems that you have let me read. And now I give this copy because I know that is important and full of new experience to come upon a work of one's own written in a strange hand. Read the lines as though they were someone else's, and you will feel deep within you how much they are your own."[10]

I do not like to belabor the point, but neither would I like to minimize the therapeutic nature of a good relationship. Even in industry, supposedly impersonal and profit-minded, studies indicate that when workers are treated with consideration and respect, and given dignity,

---

[9] Drs. Leon Brill and Jerome H. Jaffe, of the Albert Einstein College of Medicine, have experimented with the use of cyclazocine in the treatment of heroin addicts. They have had remarkably good results, and anyone knowing the futility of traditional treatment for such addiction can only describe their success thus far as miraculous. Wisely both doctors comment: "We are fully aware that our enthusiasm may be playing an even greater role than cyclazocine." *Time,* "The 'High' Inhibtor," March 18, 1966.

[10] Rainer Marie Rilke, "Letters to a Young Poet," pp. 52–53, translated by M. D. Herter, N. Y.: H. W. Norton & Co., 1963.

their output soars. The famous experiment conducted at the Western Electric Company has had a strong effect on the thinking of industrial psychologists. You probably know that psychologists are fond of fussing with all kinds of changes in working conditions—good lights, bad lights, rest periods, incentives, variation in motivation. In this study, a group of working girls were set up in a special room, and they were told they were participating in an important experiment. They weren't told to work fast: in fact, they were enjoined to do the opposite: "work at a comfortable pace, and under no circumstances . . . try to make a race out of the test." The testers then proceeded with their nasty business. They dimmed the lights so that the girls were working with illumination that resembled moonlight. They cut down on rest periods; they cut down on lunch periods; they altered working conditions, invariably making them worse. No matter what they did, the quality and the quantity of the work went up and up. This study continued for a two-year period; and time only made the results all the more puzzling to the testers. Disgustedly, the testers complained that the girls were setting the figures askew. Finally, it became clear to the experimenters what was really happening. The girls were involved in an experiment; they were given respect and dignity. And this stimulated them, so that no matter what the working conditions, they produced better and more. After all, they were not ordinary workers. They were involved, as you can see, in an important experiment. The stimulus engendered by giving workers special treatment has come to be known as the "Hawthorne affect."

You may ask: "What has all this to do with marriage?" Where but in marriage, so close, so intertwined, can two people manage to know each other so well, be able to give to each other the understanding, the compassion, the warmth that we know is so good for the human being, so healing for him. I have tried to indicate how healing a good relationship is for the sick and disturbed. The health-giving qualities are not limited to the emotionally sick, they are also the best preventative of sickness. They make normal people strong, and strong people stronger.

In our competitive, individualistic, atomistic, success-orientated society, marriage appears to be about the sole place where this haven, this island where each wants the best for the other, can best thrive. Outside of marriage, this sort of relationship does not usually thrive; and if it does, it is against environmental obstacles. There is in our society, I believe, an enormous amount of sickness and neurosis; it's built-in, pervasive, and it takes a great deal of strength and health to withstand it. But a marriage where the two become one, both non-competitively, wishing, working, hoping for the best for the other can become the source of strength to withstand infection; and even when infection sets in, the best remedy for its cure. Winston Churchill said it rather too simply for my taste: "I married and lived ever-happily afterwards." In another context, he stated the idea in a way that I like better. Describing Clementine, his wife, as "my devoted aide," he went on to say: ". . . I could never have succeeded without her. My marriage was the most fortunate and joyous event which happened to me in the whole of my life. . ."

In marriage, one is able to achieve a therapeutic relationship—caring, affectionate, understanding—so necessary if man is to thrive and to grow to become the man he was meant to become. In marriage, each can be a therapist to the other. As simply as that. A good marriage can provide all that therapy can. And the qualities in therapy are healing for all human beings. But that does not make it an easy task. As Rainer Maria Rilke said: "I learned over and over again that there is scarcely anything more difficult than to love one another."

This sort of relationship is difficult, but it is possible and achievable—possible and achievable most easily in marriage.

21

NOT LISTENING

IF A SPOUSE DOES NOT LISTEN, TRULY LISTEN, IT IS FATAL TO the marriage, for soon the other learns not to talk, and then you have two separate people, each living a life alone —the very thing that marriage seeks to prevent. The base of a good marriage is a sensitive, intimate sympathetic communication, each of the marital pair eagerly coming to the other fully to unburden his insides, knowing that he will be understood by his spouse as by no other. This is the uniqueness and greatness of the marital relationship, for only in a good marriage can such closeness be achieved. When there is failure in this respect, how unfortunate, how tragic!

I shall cite below an illustration of what I have come to call egocentric listening, a kind of listening that revolves around one's own belly button. Before that I should like to quote several passages from an address by Dr. Carl R. Rogers delivered at the California Institute of Technology[1] regarding the kind of communication that makes him feel

[1] "Some Elements of Effective Interpersonal Communication," an address delivered by Carl R. Rogers at California Institute of Technology, Pasadena, California, November 9, 1964.

expanded and exhilarated and the kind that makes him feel depressed and whipped.

". . . . there have been . . . experiences in communication with others which have made me feel expanded, larger, enriched, in which I feel that my own growth has been accelerated. Very often in these experiences I feel that the other person has had similar reactions and that he too has been enriched, that his development and his functioning have moved forward. Then there have been other occasions in which the growth or development of each of us has been diminished or stopped or even reversed. I am sure it will be clear in what I have to say that I would prefer it if my experience in communication could have a growth promoting effect, both on me and the other . . . "

At another point, he says: "When I say that I enjoy hearing someone I mean, of course, hearing deeply. I mean that I hear the words, the thoughts, the feeling tones, the personal meaning, even the meaning that is below the conscious intent of the speaker. Sometimes too, in a message which superficially is not very important, I hear a deep human cry that lies buried and unknown far below the surface of the person.

"So I have learned to ask myself; can I hear the sounds and sense the shape of this other person's inner world? Can I resonate to what he is saying so deeply that I sense the meanings he is afraid of yet would like to communicate, as well as those he knows?"

Below is an illustration of a wife who failed to listen, to catch nuances, the tone of voice, missed the despair of her husband and ended up with the wife feeling attacked, abused and angry, leaving her husband more dejected, more alone, feeling misunderstood and somehow guilty because his wife was so miserably unhappy.

Many things had gone wrong for the husband, Mr. Greenway, a faculty member of a university. His Ph. D. thesis, which he thought he had completed, was returned to him for revision. He had hoped for a higher academic rank, but it did not come because of this failure. That same morning several students to whom he had given low final grades had come to visit him at his office, and his experience with them had been most unpleasant. He had been writing an article for a scientific publication in which he had set much store, since he felt it would increase his prestige at the institution. But the manuscript had been rejected, and he was at a loss as to where next to send it.

There was one bright spot. He and his wife had rented a summer place near a lake, and during the winter, he thought of getting away from the heat of the city; and in the calm of rural peace and the beauty of the view of the lake in front of his cottage, he visualized himself working on a book he had in mind. As soon as classes were over, he had gone back to the cottage, and to his great disappointment he found that the reality did not live up to his fantasy; the place itself, which he had visualized as so beautiful and charming, was dark and dank, and even worse, dirty. Since he was very fastidious, he could not abide the thought of spending a summer in such a place, and he decided against taking it. And that, too, was a great disappointment.

His vacation had started and instead of spending it in a cottage on a lake, he was spending it at home in the city heat. The weeks were going and soon he would have to return to his classes, and somehow he could not get down to work. He spoke a little of this to his wife and

she said, "Well, there isn't just one place. We'll go to
Europe or the Caribbean."

He said he didn't care to travel this summer—to go to
Europe or the Caribbean. He thought of working this
summer, finishing his thesis, maybe starting the book he
had planned.

She said he always liked to travel. Why not now?

Because, he said, he wanted to work; all winter he had
visualized being immersed in work in a quiet country
place. He still wanted to work.

"How about going to Mexico?" suggested his wife.

He didn't feel like going to Mexico.

The wife was losing her patience. "You're impossible,"
she said. "You're just a contrary mule."

One word led to another.

"So where do you want to go?" she asked.

"I don't know. I wanted to work and I was dreaming
of a quiet rural place."

"But you had such a place and you turned it down.
You have only yourself to blame."

He raised his voice. "You know why I couldn't go to
that country place. I couldn't stand the filth of the place.
I'd be miserable."

"So where do you want to go?"

He raised his voice somewhat higher. "I don't know.
If I did, I'd tell you."

"Why are you angry with me? What have I done? If
you act that way, the devil with you. Why can't you be
decent? Why are you so mean? What makes you angry
with me? Stop it."

This time there was real anger in his voice, and from
the exchange resulted a marital quarrel that lasted for
weeks.

His wife had not listened, not really listened. True enough he was angry. He was angry, disgusted, and miserable about his lot, his fate, himself; he had raised his voice in anger against himself, and also, I suppose, in a measure, because his condition was so misunderstood. His wife had missed completely what bothered him. It wasn't the summer cottage. It was his general misery; the terrible disappointment about the dream he harbored, about the book he planned to write; about the waste of time—precious time for which he had planned so much; his disappointment about his Ph. D., his university situation, and just the misery of his mood. But his wife felt nothing of all this. This anger she interpreted as anger against her, rather than anger with the misery of his being.

As soon as she said, "Why are you angry with me?" he was infuriated, for every time he did show displeasure or anger, his wife would carry on as if he were at fault, as if he had done something horrible; and it would end up with the issue that brought up the disagreement forgotten and in her a sense of hurt and anger. So he was left high and dry. And here it was the same thing over again—his wife's inability really to listen and understand, fully, deeply, generously, with compassion and affection. This time, as so many times before, she introduced her big ego into what was being communicated, and it ended up with her feeling insulted, injured, abused. And the husband, bearing all this within, seeing his sulking, angry wife, knowing that she would carry on in this way for how long he did not know, only increased his misery and isolation; and also, the resolve, henceforth, to keep his grief within himself, to bottle it up, for from his wife he could get no comfort or aid.

Thus are walls built and thus are relationships destroyed.

Here are two people trying to please each other but cannot, because of the wife's "stuffed up ear," her inability to listen sympathetically and understandingly.

It was a bad marriage, and both husband and wife were in therapy; they were in the process of trying to communicate and be sensitive to each other. "Let's get away to some lonely spot, near a beach," said the husband, in a revival of endearing feelings. They were both fond of aquatic sports. "We haven't had a vacation together for years. I have a good assistant and I can leave the business without worry. And certainly we can afford it; we have the money. We'll get a chance to know one another again, away from the children."

He was in an expansive mood and he had in mind a renewal of the romantic days of the early years of their marriage. One of the terrible irritants of the marriage was that the wife always met her husband's suggestions, generally proposed with great enthusiasm, with so many but's and if's and maybe's and "we cannot," that his enthusiasm dried up, leaving him feeling flat and hanging and angry. Now in therapy, which was having its effect, she said, "Fine, but let's not go now."

"Why not?" asked her husband.

"The children—with whom shall we leave them?"

"With Liza," said her husband. "You know we have kept their children; and hers and ours get along so well. You know that she's always eager to have them. And we'll be away for a week or so; maybe less if Liza and Herbert will find it hard to manage."

"I wouldn't want to impose on them."

"Let me talk to her. You know she's frank enough to tell us how she feels," persisted the husband. "I'll talk to her. Let me do it."

But the wife said no; she wouldn't hear of it.

Soon there was irritation, followed by anger, in their exchange.

As he explained later, he wanted to surprise his wife, "but all the spontaneity was going out of it, and she was the same dead weight I felt her to be, taking the joy out of life."

At another time, she reverted to the subject. "You work hard. I know you need a trip. Why don't you go alone?"

He turned that suggestion down flatly. "I'd feel so guilty," he explained to me later. "And I know she'd throw it up to me afterwards, and I'd regret it. Really she was killing the whole pleasure of the trip."

To his wife, he said: "I thought of this trip as a sort of second honeymoon; we two together, alone, by ourselves without the children, on some sandy beach, maybe walking barefoot, jumping into the water when the mood strikes us."

That's the vacation as he conceived it and wanted it.

After his wife had worked on him, the entire family was on an airplane flying to Virginia Beach. Her mother had a house there. "It'll cost us nothing," she reasoned with him, "and she'll be glad to have us."

When the family returned back home, the wife said: "He was cranky and uncivil all the time he was there. I hate the man. He appreciates nothing. My mother couldn't do enough for us. And yet you ought to have seen him— grouchy, insulting, not a civil word out of him."

She wept hysterically. "He's a hard, unfeeling man; and I can't stand him."

The husband was speaking to me: "I had in mind a nice, quiet vacation—both of us together, alone. How did it end up? Exactly the way she wanted . . . with her mother and her other horrible relatives. We were shut up every night with them. We couldn't go to an outside restaurant or a show or take a side trip. Nancy [the wife] said it wouldn't be right leaving them, especially since they were so nice to us. So the few times we went out, we dragged them along. And that was the dream vacation I fantasied; and for that I spent my good money."

He was bitter; and he spoke vile words, especially about his wife.

The trip was the cause of many violent disputes and almost broke up the marriage. And the wife could never understand why her husband could be so unreasonable.

Let us end with several observations by Carl Rogers.

"But what I really dislike in myself," he says, "is when I cannot hear the other person because I am so sure in advance of what he is about to say and I don't listen. It is only afterward that I realize that I have only heard what I have already decided he is saying. I have failed really to listen. Or even worse are those times when I catch myself trying to twist his message to make it say what I want to say, and then only hearing that. This can be a very subtle thing and it is surprising how skillful I can be in doing it. Just by twisting his words a small amount, by distorting his meaning just a little, I can make it appear that he is not only saying the thing I want to hear, but that he is the person I want him to be. It is only when I realize through his protest or through my own gradual recognition that I am subtly manipulating him that I can become disgusted with myself. I know too from being on the receiving end of this how frustrating it is to be received for what you are not, to be heard saying something which you have not said. This creates anger and bafflement and disillusion."[2]

" . . . I am terribly frustrated and shut into myself when I try to express something which is deeply me, which is a part of my own private, inner world, and the other person does not understand. When I take the gamble, the risk, of trying to share something that is very personal with another individual and it is not received and not understood, this is a very deflating and a very lonely experience. I have come to believe that it is that experience which makes some individuals psychotic. They have given up hoping that anyone can understand them and once they have lost that hope then their own inner world, which becomes more and more bizarre, is the only place where they can live. They can no longer live in any shared human experience. I can sympathize with them because I know that when I try to share some feeling aspect of myself which is private, precious, and tentative, and when this communication is met by evaluation, by distortion of my meaning, I have very strongly the reaction, Oh, what's the use! At such a time one knows what it is to be alone.

"So, as you can readily see from what I have said thus far, a creative, active, sensitive, accurate, empathic, nonjudgmental listening, is for me terribly important in a relationship. It is important for me to provide it. I feel that I have grown within myself when I have provided it. I am very sure that I have grown and been released and enhanced when I have received this kind of listening."[3]

---

2 *Op Cit.*
3 *Op Cit.*

22

LEARNING TO ACCOMMODATE TO DIFFERENCES

A FUNCTIONING MARRIAGE, AS I HAVE SAID, IS LIKE A FORTRESS, closed for the most part to outsiders, and even to the participants there are hidden and subterranean passages unknown to themselves. In relating any marital incident we should remember it is hardly ever the complete story.

Both in this marriage are estimable people, and I believe in their own way they love each other. But they are killing the love they have by making life hard for each other. They irritate each other, and this leads to attack; and in time the good feeling, the love they bear for each other, will die out, crushed by the lack of understanding and respect for each other's feelings.

As I have said, there are differences in any marriage. I would suspect a marriage where there are none; to me it means that one in the marriage is extirpating his honest feelings and cannot be his true self. To chronicle differences does not make the marriage per se bad; it only indicates the extent of the need for accommodation—the task of every marriage.

The wife was timid, fearful, frightened. When she was a child, her mother had continually warned her to make

197

sure to come home before dark, and was always concerned that the doors at home were securely locked. As one of her early childhood memories, she related how she was gripped with terror when she thought she was alone at night at home. She rushed wildly about the house, but fortunately found a servant in the basement and clung to her hysterically. As an adult she lived in Manhattan and when she went outdoors, she was as scared as if she were on a battlefield, expecting mayhem to befall her. Born in a household that was frightened, she lived in a world that was frightening. This timidity and caution extended to her children. She was always bundling them up, warning them against catching cold, constantly impressing them with possible danger. Her husband wanted his children to be hardy, venturesome, free of fear. He felt his wife was smothering his children, making them as timid and frightened of the world as she was—an eventuality that he dreaded. The wife felt her husband's disapproval and resented his attitude, particularly his disapproval of the way she was rearing the children. Within her there smoldered a flame of anger against her husband, and within her husband there smoldered a flame of equal anger. The marital hostility came to the surface at unexpected moments—sometimes with great fury, sometimes mildly—but it was always present.

The husband was of another temperament and kind. He came from a warm, democratic home, and early in life he was encouraged to venture. He went on trips, he worked during summer vacations from school on ships, he hitchhiked; and nothing made him happier than to be meeting people, strange people, all kinds of people, and to be traveling, in any way, by car, by airplane, by ship. He approached experiences expectantly; he lived in a kindly and friendly world. He wanted his children to have a similar sense of excitement and adventure when confronting the world.

When he saw his wife bundling up his children in heavy clothing, gathering them inside the house to shield them from the dreaded night, he cringed.

He wanted his home open, full of people coming and going. During the course of the day, he might invite guests for supper or friends to visit after supper. Whenever Mr. Reynolds would come home and tell his wife what he had done, she would upbraid him, make him feel as if he were a selfish, insensitive brute. "It's all right for you to have every Tom, Dick, and Harry over to litter up the house. Why would you care? You don't clean up after them." Once he came home to announce: "Charles and Mary are coming over Friday." They were a couple they both knew.

"So you invited those two for supper. What do you care about my having to be in the kitchen all day Friday!"

"They're coming after supper," explained Mr. Reynolds. "All we'll need is some sandwiches, and perhaps cake and ice cream."

But she wouldn't hear of that, either. "If they're coming, they may as well come for supper. I'll call them up."

Mr. Reynolds knew his wife would invite them for supper, but he also knew he would be taxed for the whole week about his thoughtlessness and selfishness. Mrs. Reynolds was a spotless housekeeper, somewhat on the order of Craig's wife. This tightness, this closed-in quality, this meticulousness typified all her behavior.

The husband's continual sense of grievance, irritation, and lack of sympathetic communication had caused him to withdraw, and with time, the walls between the two had become almost impenetrable. The trickle of communication had diminished to skimpy drops. And thus the marital bond was disintegrating.

The couple were about to separate formally but before doing so they entered therapy. At the initial stages of therapy, there was a great deal of wailing and hysterics on her part and a great deal of guilt, misery, and a sense of inadequacy on his part. When he tried to open up to her, explaining his irritations, she would become violent, insulting, hysterically angry. In therapy, it became clear that the wife could not stand even the slightest hostility on the part of her husband. She did everything for his approval—in her own way—and any evidence of disapproval would make her collapse. Instead of working through disagreement, she would become defensive, fighting him viciously, as if her world was being threatened. So these disagreements—inevitable in any marriage—instead of providing further insight into each other made her appear to her husband unreasonable, disagreeable, and obnoxious.

There is an explanation for the wife's behavior. As I have said, the mystery of a marriage is like a citadel, the inner fortress hidden from outsiders, with many inner passages as frequently hidden from participants. Both had married for wrong reasons. Mr. Reynolds had had some bad heterosexual experiences with strong, dominant women; and had been rejected by one just previous to his present marriage; and he was seeking a weak, compliant, hero-worshipping partner. When he married Irene, he thought of her as a child whom he could instruct and look after. She, on the other hand, frightened of life, with a practical absence of heterosexual experiences, with low self-concept and low self-esteem, wanted a strong man whom she could admire.

As they both discovered, it is impossible for a child to play the role of a wife; and also, in marriage, there is nothing so deadly as someone playing the father figure. Marriage proceeds best when there are two mature peers, both equal, each functioning from strength; and each a unique self contributing to and enriching the life of the other.

In therapy, the Reynolds became aware of the differences that made them act so abrasively on each other. As they learned to talk more openly, it became apparent why Irene, the wife, dreaded guests. The main cause did not stem from her obsessive need for cleanliness or being irked by the work involved. No, not at all! They were defenses, rationalizations. What made her avoid guests was fear, yes, plain unadulterated fear. She suffered from terrible inferiorities, and people to her meant anxieties of all kinds, fear that she would not carry out her part as a hostess successfully. She wanted each of her meals to be a masterpiece; each visit of guests to her home to be a memorable event. It was this demand on herself, this expectation, that made her behave in a way that seemed so unreasonable to her husband. If she had honestly admitted her fears to her husband and said: "I appreciate how you like and need people. I wish I could be as strong and healthy as you in this regard. I shall try, however, for I want you to feel good about and free in your own home." Or even if she had said she could not, explaining, "it takes too much out of me," such candor would have cleared the air. Instead of his wife making her husband feel like a brute, it would have made him feel as if he were understood by his wife. Of if she said she just couldn't, explaining frankly: "It takes too much out of me."

If she felt badly, really felt badly, that she could not satisfy her husband's legitimate need for people in his own home, that too, would have been better.

Instead she in effect implied: "You, my husband, are a selfish, insensitive brute." She talked of the house being littered, and his having a good time, while she drudged away. If she had expressed her true feelings, her husband might have sympathized; he might have been drawn more closely to her because of her need.

In the course of therapy, it worked out that way. As they understood each other better, he from his strength gave to her. While entertaining friends, he took special pains to join her in the kitchen, to reassure her, to tell her how well things were going and how proud he was of her. And that made a world of difference. Hitherto, not knowing how she truly felt, in fact, feeling aggrieved at her unreasonable accusations, during the evening he would glower and could even be offensive, so that she would break down before her guests. That only added to her anxieties when contemplating future entertaining. Once honest feelings were aired, her husband proved to be most sympathetic. Not only did they both work on this problem, but they widened their area of sharing and they deepened the need for communication.

I wish I could report that the problem was solved. It is true that man likes Q.E.D., the problem is solved and "they lived ever happily afterwards." I suppose Mr. and Mrs. Reynolds still have their differences, in this and other areas, but I have the hope that they are continuing to learn to understand each other more deeply, and as they do, they are learning to cope with and to accommodate themselves to their differences ever more intelligently and ever more adequately.

I shall relate one other strong difference in this marriage; and how helpful sympathetic communication proved.

Mr. Reynolds itched to travel, but he was held back by his wife. Now that the marriage was functioning better and they were communicating more honestly, he toyed with the idea of a European trip with his wife. He wanted to go badly. He had been working hard; he needed a rest. But I believe the trip meant more than that to him. He was excited both by the trip and the idea that he now had a brand new marriage and a brand new wife; and the trip represented for him a sort of test for the marriage. He thought of speaking to her about the trip but he was timid. If her first reaction would be no, he knew he would be disgusted with his wife and again feel that he was trapped in a bad marriage. He knew she would raise problems about the children. "When she talks this way," he said, "I feel she's lying, not talking honestly, and I feel disgusted. The children will be away at camp anyhow, so why should she bring it up?" If she did raise the issue, he felt he would get so annoyed that whatever good had come from the reconciliation would be destroyed. He was in a quandary, but he did put the question.

While they were both in a good mood, he said: "You know I've been working hard and I am tired."

Yes, she agreed, and she was very sympathetic. "I've tried awfully hard to save you, and wherever I can, you know I do."

He readily conceded that and he told her how much he appreciated her thoughtfulness of him. And then he said: "I'd like to make a trip."

He observed how she stiffened, her face flushing.

And then he said: "I know how hard it will be for you, how frightening such things are. I won't insist on it, but if you can possibly make yourself go, with all your fears, it would mean a great deal to me. I'm not insisting since I know how you suffer when it comes to such things."

Irene had never heard such talk from her husband. She listened quietly, though obviously disturbed.

She did not have to defend herself. She wasn't attacked and she didn't have to counter-attack. "I know," she said, "I haven't been much pleasure to you, but you know how hard these things are for me."

For the first time Irene admitted real, honest feelings. Hitherto, it was never herself; it was the children, or money, or it couldn't be done for this or that reason. This time it was clearly she. There was no doubt about that.

It would be nice to say she immediately agreed; she hesitated, not saying yes or no and so it was left.

Later, when alone with me, I asked Mr. Reynolds: "Are you really giving Irene a choice or are you using this new approach as a strategy? Will you truly understand if she says she cannot go?"

He smiled sheepishly. "I never thought of that. I suppose I want her to go, and if she doesn't I think she's a drag and a pill."

"So you haven't given her a choice?"

"I suppose you're right." And then he said: "If Irene is my wife, I suppose I'll have to learn to live with her the way she is."

This time he really meant it when he gave her the choice. She could go or not as she chose.

You would think that now that Irene knew and felt that she had the choice her answer would be easy. In truth she did not want to go.

It turned out to be the hardest choice she ever made. What was her final answer? She said: "If it means so much to you I'll go, although I know I'll be miserable in strange countries, in strange beds, with strange people." Even as she spoke her fear and terror asserted itself. "But I want to go because I know how much it means to you," she said.

Mr. Reynolds was appreciative of his wife's sacrifice; and I am sure that the next time Irene wanted something, he would be ready to make an equal sacrifice.

Was there a final, end solution in terms of full agreement even in this situation? I cannot say there was. But if there continues to be this understanding, this desire to please, this acceptance, especially if it is mutual; and if both continued on this track—communicating, understanding, working through, accepting, appreciating differences, sensitive to the other's feelings, even when not approving —this marriage, despite its strong, basic, fundamental differences, may develop into a good, healthy marriage and the two may learn to give to each other a great deal.

Even when full and open communication prevails, is it possible to experience irreconcilable disagreements? I wish I could say no. Unfortunately, the answer is yes, a resounding yes. There are times when a spouse will have to say: "I understand you fully. I am sorry I cannot comply. I wish I could, but I cannot. It violates too many things which I hold precious."

The outcome may be the final result of working through a difference. From it, there may come the understanding that one cannot conform or agree. If both persons are mature, they will realize the limits of the other; and if the relationship is a sound one, both may come to respect these limits and differences. If crucial, fundamental differences are involved and compromise or accommodation might jeopardize the integrity of the person, then, it seems to me, the only alternative is separation.

23

COPING WITH DIFFERENCES

HERE IS AN ACCOUNT OF A MARITAL DIFFERENCE. IT IS SET down to illustrate what I have come to feel is a desirable way to cope with differences that inevitably occur in all marriages.

Dr. Andrew K. is a dentist who has become fed up with his work. Daily it is harder for him to get up in the morning and harder for him to see his patients. He is in his late thirties and he would like to change his occupation. He doesn't know quite what he would like to do, but he knows that he doesn't like what he is doing. In his thoughts he visualizes becoming a journalist (he was editor of his school paper); and when he is more practical, he thinks of teaching biology, since that was his favorite school subject. These thoughts may be fantasies, escapes from what at present seems drudgery. They may be dreams, unrealistic and not right for him. He readily admits that. But as he bends over his patients in his dental chair, he knows he hates what he is doing; and he feels trapped. He also knows that it is "later than you think," especially for him.

While in therapy, Dr. Andrew K. talks nostalgically of

his youth, saying that his profession was not his choice, but his father's who himself was a dentist and who wanted his son to be a dentist. Since Andrew couldn't make medical school, he accepted this compromise. He would like to talk about his present dilemma to his wife; and as he discusses this he shrugs his shoulders in a helpless fashion. There is a sense of despair about him; he is angry that he cannot share these thoughts with his wife. "She would first think of herself, her security, the children, the home," he says, "and then she'll tell me I don't know when I'm well off; that all work is unpleasant; and that I don't appreciate how lucky I am to have such a good practice; and that I'll get over it; it's only a passing phase, like a male menopause." So he spoke, and as he spoke, reflecting her feelings, he became angrier and angrier. Even the thought of what she might say upset him. "All she can think about is herself; she begins and ends with herself."

Andrew got up the courage to communicate his desire for a change of occupation to his wife. *His wife responded exactly as he feared.* When next he saw me, he was more despondent than ever, and in a weary, depressed tone, he said: "I can't go on; that practice of mine is more hateful to me than ever."

His wife had become more abusive. "I struggle with the children," she said. "I give you a good home. But there is something in you that wants to destroy all this—your home, your family, yourself. You want to run away as you always do. I loved the country and I begged you to establish yourself there. But you wanted a practice in the city, and if that was what you wanted, I went along; and you know how I worked and struggled; how I found a night job so that I could be your nurse in the office by

day since we couldn't afford to hire one. Now at last
when everything seems to be going well, you want to quit.
It's typical of you. You shirk responsibility. What would
happen if I weren't here to take care of the children and
the home and keep you from these crack-brained ideas?
I'm the only stable influence here. You're an anarchist."

What was Andrew's response? It was to counterattack.
"You use me for a meal ticket," he would shout, "and I'm
fed up with being a sucker. You want me to provide you
with security. Why don't you work like other women,
and then maybe you'd understand what it means to work
at something you don't like."

And thus it went, on and on and on and on, each finding openings and holes through which to shoot darts,
edged with salt so they could hurt more. Each was highly
practiced in this art from long knowledge of each other's
weaknesses.

They were both in therapy with me. Despite their
abuse of each other, I knew they both had a fundamental
respect for each other; and that beyond all things, they
wanted their marriage preserved and they wanted from
each other what such a relationship can give, namely,
warmth, understanding, affection, appreciation, and, yes,
admiration. In fact Dr. Andrew K. could not go ahead
with any project, he was immobilized until his wife would
give him the consent and the support to proceed. He
would not have the strength to make it on his own. On
her part, in her own way she had a high regard for him.
Fundamentally, each had a great need for the other, but
the tragedy lay in the fact that each wanted to remake
the other, refused to accept the other as each was. Hence,
each found the other irritating, exasperating, frustrating.
What communication they had was only an outlet for the

expression of hostility and anger; each pressed upon the other in an attacking way, hurting the other deeply.

Once you knew their background you could understand how wide were their differences. Andrew came from an affluent, solid, middle class home, where money had never been a matter of too great concern. He therefore felt financially secure. Many things bothered him, but never money. Jane, his wife, came from a poverty-stricken home; her father was on relief during the depression, and the life of her home was made anxious by financial need. Money was vital and was the frequent cause of quarrels. In her early childhood, she remembered vividly the constant family concern about money in order to obtain the necessities of life. Existence for Jane's family was made hard and bleak for the lack of money. Jane went to evening school and worked by day; she had attained her present position in life by hard struggle. She had overcome many vicissitudes but she was branded traumatically by them. She was frugal, even hoarding, not only about money, but about nearly everything else. Dr. Andrew K. was generous and carefree about money; and if Jane did not hold a tight rein on him, they would be penniless and probably in debt.

In the very nature of their personalities, there were bound to be differences. This was only one clash in one aspect of living, a token of many other differences in many other areas. It was the wife who felt constantly threatened and aggrieved while the husband felt trapped, constrained, frustrated, and angry. These differences were ingrained in the very fabric of their personalities.

In terms of maintaining the marital relationship, despite these permeating intrinsic differences, what modus vivendi might be suggested?

It cannot be repeated sufficiently that in any good relationship first and foremost is the need for generous understanding and compassion, and crucial to this is sympathetic listening.

If the wife truly listened to her husband, with understanding and sympathy, which does not necessarily mean agreement; if she did not act defensively, if she did not try to show her husband up as evil and sinful, she could have expressed these feelings without implying agreement or disrespect for her own person. It would have meant articulation of honest feelings. If she spoke in the following vein she would have generously reflected the feelings of both:

"How awful that you have to feel so trapped and that I, being what I am, cannot help you. I wish I were more courageous about such things; I wish I were a stronger and a more self-reliant person; then I could be by your side and give you the encouragement and strength you need at this juncture. I know you must be going through a personal hell, and I know how hard it is for you to go to your office and face the day. With a wife such as you have, it must be harder. Not only am I of little help to you but I am a burden."

If Jane really felt this way, if she were sincere and honest, if she uttered not mere words, this sympathy, this feeling for, this understanding would have come through. The husband's knowledge that he had a wife who felt for him, understood him, might in itself have mollified him. Even if not, they would have preserved a communicating relationship and the wife would have given of herself—her compassion and understanding—to her husband. The very distress of her husband would have served as a bond and strengthened the ties between them. Knowing

Dr. K. I have the belief that once he perceived his wife's true despair and mortification, her confessed helplessness, he would have ended by consoling and reassuring her out of gratitude for her sympathy.

You observe that Mrs. K. did not give up her fears and timidities; she merely expressed them. Best of all, she was not defensive and did not attack. In effect, she said she could not go along, but her refusal was couched in such a way as to show her sensitivity and concern; and that is the binding tie.

If she could muster the requisite strength and courage, she might take a mid-way position, not full acceptance and yet not a complete rejection. In that event, the response might take this form:

"What you tell me is naturally very disturbing to me. We do have a home and children and I have fears about money. I know that's a weakness of mine and probably a fault. But your irresponsibility about money is also a terrible fault and a terrible burden for me. I don't want to hold you back. I shouldn't want you to suffer because of my own problems. Your work seems so dreadful to you and the change so important. Realistically, however, you know that you are old for such a change and we have responsibilities—a home and children—but yet if it is at all possible I'll be by your side. Get it down to more practical terms; work it out; and we'll see how far I can go along with you in terms of what courage I can muster. You know how frightened I get about such things. Yet I feel so badly that you're doing a work that has so little meaning to you that I can't stand the thought of your going on in this way. If you can figure out any sort of reasonable out, I'll do my best to be by your side. But again I want you to know that I understand what a horror this work is to you."

And there is still another position if she could summon up the requisite courage, if she had confidence in her husband and herself, could bring herself actually to dare to venture, and the response might run along these lines: "I have faith in you and whatever you decide to do, I'll be by your side. We've struggled before and we can again. I shouldn't want you to do work that has no meaning for you. It's ridiculous. You're a good man, and whatever you do and wherever you are, those qualities will show up. You're bound to stand out. I know it's hard to change at your stage of life, it's frightening, but it's even worse frittering away your life at what you hate. And I myself won't have it. I myself can't imagine anyone who can excel you in integrity and responsibility and intelligence; and I wouldn't worry a minute. I know you won't make a hasty decision. But I want you to know that whatever you decide, I'm with you and I know you're going to make good. There's no one who can compare with you. But meanwhile, I'm so sorry that you're going through this horrible period. It makes me feel very badly."

Who could resist such a response?[1]

---

[1] A couple with essentially a similar problem tried this way of coping with differences based on honest exchange of feeling, yet at the same time being aware and appreciating differences in feeling. After the couple changed their method of relating to each other, the husband was so moved by the strong faith of his wife, her understanding of him, her desire to share, that at the end he consoled her, saying that his work was not nearly as debilitating as he had depicted it; and that if he had managed this long, he could last longer. It was the wife who insisted that her husband give up his profession when both were convinced that he could never be happy at it. She obtained a position to ease his anxiety in reaching a decision since the financial concern was the main desideratum. It turned out well for both. Even after he had established

I have tried to illustrate communication of feeling, two human beings, each different, coming to each other and giving to each other the support and understanding, the warmth and sympathy that are the ingredients of a good marriage. Even in their disagreement, there was concern; there was no attack.

In their initial response, each had attacked the other; there was no understanding, only a strong feeling of resentment. The wife felt angry, put upon, injured since her husband, for no apparent reason, outside of whim and selfish unreasonableness, wanted to jeopardize her security. How could anyone feel kindly to a husband who was so selfish, thoughtless, egocentric, who thought of no one but his own convenience, who forgot his obligations and his family?

The husband on his part felt his wife, like his work, kept him trapped; he saw for himself a bleak, black future, bending over that dentist chair, breaking his back; that's all there was and there never would be more. He saw his wife as one who thought of him in an exploitative way, who had no feelings and understanding of him, other than as a provider who bolstered her material security. She was his doom.

Worst of all, neither had learned how to talk to one another without hostility, resentment, attack; they talked to hurt one another. They conducted a sort of underhand war, trying to show each other up; to prove that the other was at fault in the marriage; that one was good and the other bad.

---

himself in his new work, she continued on her job and would not hear of leaving it. She had become valuable to the firm for which she worked. She herself grew as a person, in her self esteem and in her sense of self-worth. In sharing the vicissitudes they at first encountered, the couple became closer and the marriage was strengthened.

The truth and the facts were that Dr. K. had these feelings about his work, good or bad, right or wrong, there they were; and they should have been discussed. In a queer way, he needed his wife's cautiousness, her timidity, for she stabilized him and kept him back from doing reckless things. She could have functioned this way, and yet not alienated him. How? As we saw. By showing concern, understanding, empathy, compassion. These are healing qualities; and no one can help but be moved by them. The dog is the best loved creature on earth. Why? Simply because he can give affection and love; and those qualities are irresistible. He frisks his tail when you enter and wants to paw you in joy at your presence and lick you from affection. And in payment for this, there is no sacrifice that man will not make for his dog. How much more true it is when two human beings can give to each other this unconditional affection!

In the marriage, each wanted to make the other different; each did not like the other as each was. In this was the tragedy. They would like each other "if"—if she or he were this, that or the other thing—but they did not like the person they saw before them, with the result that each had a baneful influence on the other; they communicated a sense of inadequacy: you are not quite right, you'd be right "if." The "if" never eventuates. The needs of both in this marriage, as I came to know it, were great, more on her part than his. Jane was very dependent on her husband for the satisfaction of those needs; and she was highly judgmental when they were not met or when they were jeopardized.

She was unusually articulate, very verbal, of high intelligence and she managed to convert most differences into moral issues. It is true she did work hard and faithfully and conscientiously, day and night, and when it came to her home and children, nothing was too hard for her; and she wanted a husband who would respond with the same dedication to what she regarded as important. When he didn't, she became hostile and angry and felt her husband was callous and cruel, especially when he appeared to be unappreciative of how hard she was working to be a good mother, wife, and home-maker.

Although undoubtedly a factor in a good marriage, all this is extraneous. What is crucial and important in a marriage is a good, generous, accepting, loving relationship.

24

THEY STRUGGLE

BELOW IS AN ILLUSTRATION OF A RELATIONSHIP THAT PRE-
sents hard-core problems. If the marriage is to function
in any satisfactory way, many of them will have to be
worked through: Why the advance of one is a threat to
the other; why the need for a social life is such a problem
to the other; why sexually the wife finds the husband repulsive, etc., etc.

Joseph, newly-married, has a teaching fellowship at a
university. He is a brilliant student and his work shows
great promise. On graduation from his university he was
at the top of his class in chemistry, and he was asked to
stay on by the head of the chemistry department. He
began to work for his Ph. D.; and as he progressed, his
whole person became more and more involved with the
work, so that it became the center of his life. He began
to fantasy about his future; he visualized himself as a
great chemist, adding to the knowledge of the world.
Achieving the Ph. D. became an obsession with him. He
wanted that degree beyond all things.

Rebecca, his wife, appeared to share her husband's en-
thusiams. She led him to believe that she, too, supported

him strongly in these academic ambitions. In reality she regarded his work in a rivalrous way; she resented that Ph. D., and thought that with it her husband would out-pace her.

"When I speak to Rebecca about my work and my hopes for the Ph. D.," Joseph said, "I find her mind wandering. Instead of being happy, she'll talk about our having to move out-of-town should I get another job and then about her mother, who'll be far away. She doesn't care at all about me."

He continues, however, to speak to Rebecca about his hopes and dreams. While he is in the midst of being carried away by them, his wife will suggest a weekend in the country, or going to a movie, or a restaurant, or visiting a friend. It's all perfectly innocent on her part, and she cannot understand why her husband bursts out in anger, sometimes so violent that he can scarcely control himself.

Listen to the way he explains his conduct in a therapeutic session. "My wife is not interested at all in me. While I am working so hard to get ahead, all she can think about is a movie, or having a good time. I feel as if she resents me and my work. Just as I'm settling down to study, she jabbers away on the telephone and before I know it there are people in the house."

Listen now to Rebecca as she explains her conduct. "You can't imagine how obsessed he is about his Ph. D. He can't talk of anything else. He studies week-ends; and what does he want me to do—just watch him? Sometimes late at night, after nine, I beg him to go out and then we go to a restaurant or a movie."

This is Joseph speaking: "Even when I ought to be studying, we went to a restaurant, and then to a movie, and it cost us money which we can ill afford. I didn't enjoy a bit of it. I felt guilty because I didn't study. You would think she would appreciate that I took off, going to that damned restaurant and spending all that money. But no, if I let her, we'd be going out every night."

Once he went "berserk," as Rebecca described it. "He was wild, wild! Crazy," she said.

Why? Listen to Joseph: "Rebecca knew I was having an exam the next day, and that it was my toughest course. I was tired and frightened by the coming examination. The instructor of the course is my thesis sponsor and I wanted to impress him. I was so anxious and frightened that I couldn't get near my books and I was lying in bed. So Rebecca says: 'Let's go to the movies.' In the middle of my most important exam. I tell her I can't. She acts as if she doesn't know about my exam and cares even less. When I try to tell her, she says: 'You're not studying anyhow.' She doesn't understand a thing. And I'm getting to hate her."

As I have indicated repeatedly, one can't hide one's true feelings. In a moment of frankness while with me, she says: 'I'm not at all interested in that damned degree of his. He can keep on talking about himself forever. He never listens to my trouble. I find my work so hard. [She's a teacher.] I come home after a terrible day at school with the children, whom I find so hard to control. A parent complained and the principal came to visit me; and I, too, want someone to talk to. In fact, I'd like to quit my job; but when Joseph hears that he gets furious."

A marriage is like a citadel with many intricate, unexplored subterranean passages. I myself was somewhat surprised to discover the extent she resented Joseph's work toward the Ph. D.; that came much later in our relationship. But once when she was truly herself, fully revealing herself, she said: "I resent his Ph. D. He'll be getting ahead, and where will I be? Still an elementary school teacher. And he'll be a big shot. But if he never got his Ph. D., he'd have to teach in a public school, just as I do."

Yet in the marriage, withal, there were moments of softness and concern.

Joseph is talking: "Maybe I do demand too much. Maybe I don't listen to Rebecca, as I know I should. But these exams—I've just got to get 100 per cent, and I get worried. Doesn't she know what that money means to me? How will I be able to continue going to school? How will I get my Ph. D.? She ought to know how much that Ph. D. means to both of us!"

So the irritations mount.

In desperation, he once beat her, although he is not a sadistic man or a hard man. Rebecca surprisingly understood; and even more strangely forgave him. "I was out with friends," she said, "and we had a good time, and I came home very late without letting him know in advance. When I came home, I knew he would be angry, but I led him on. I think I wanted to be punished. I didn't do right. He works so hard. I give him so little. He needs someone very strong and healthy. You can't imagine how he can suck at you, hour after hour, until I'm ready to scream."

In turn, Joseph in moments of regret and guilt will say: "I know she's good and kind and I demand a great deal." He is now speaking frankly and gives me an insight into himself which he would like to hide. "You know this business about going out with people. Partly it's the Ph. D., but that's not all, nor nearly all. Often I'm just scared about visiting, so I have a handy excuse. But it's easy for Rebecca; she gets along; she enjoys herself."

It is quite true he is frightened of people and Rebecca does not help him when in company. This fear goes back to his childhood and his harsh judgmental parents who always found fault with him. Even as a child when Joseph had to visit a relative, the prospect loomed as a dreadful event for him. In large measure, this fear was induced by cold, unloving parents, who wanted their son to shine brightly, and a father who was constantly disappointed. Upon reaching home after such a visit with relatives or friends, the parents would enter upon a long analysis as to how young Joseph compared with the others. "Seymour did very well," his father would say, "You notice how people looked up to him. And Roy—he's real smart; you notice how well he talked. Vincent has a fellowship to the university." And then he would shake his head and say: "Some people have luck with children," implying that his own son, Joseph, could not match up; and Joseph was made to feel like a failure.

This fear of not measuring up was constantly before Joseph in any social relationship; as also this need to excel and this prevented him from being natural and spontaneous. In any group, he was always evaluating himself, asking himself, "How am I doing? What do they think of me?" Instead of relating to people with warmth and understanding, there was always this wall—his big, egotistical self—so that he was self-conscious, not listening to people, not trying to understand them. Carrying out as an adult the precepts taught to him by his parents as a child, Joseph tried to win the regard of others by gaining their admiration, by impressing them with his superiority. He wanted others to admire and love him. To achieve that aim, he was doing exactly the wrong thing. We like and admire those who make *us* feel big and important and worthwhile. We like those who love us. So it is this capacity to give that is paramount. And since he did things in the reverse, he was socially isolated, friendless, and whatever social contacts he had filled him with dread.

In this respect, he also was not helped by his wife. When visiting, Rebecca was ashamed of Joseph; she found him dull and boring, and she hated the way he tried to make himself the center of a conversation, monopolizing it. She did not understand his insecurity and fears; and even worse, she argued with him in public, invariably taking the opposite position, really venting her hostility in the safety of a social situation. At the end of the evening, when returning home, there was little good feeling between them. They bickered and attacked.

These differences also affected their sex life. Said Joseph: "I wonder whether she loves me." He felt that Rebecca was trying to please him sexually, but he would describe how in the midst of the sex act, she would become indifferent to him and he could not go through with it. Rightly, he suspected her lack of passion for him. "She tries to avoid me. At night she makes out she is sleeping. Or else she stays up so late and waits till I am asleep and then goes to bed."

Instinctively, he hit on the right explanation. She wanted to please him but the irritations were so great that she was in a state of constant anger; and this is the worst preparation for the sex act. But there was another aspect which he never suspected; she was too kind to hurt him. She found his body and penis repulsive. Why? Again we have to go deeper. She was still emotionally involved with her father whom she loved sexually. Nothing had ever happened between them, but they both carried on a sexual involvement that was so bad, even if not consummated, that they could not be in the same room together unless chaperoned. This was something shameful and devastating for Rebecca. This secret relationship—with no words passed and no overt action—caused her a great deal of guilt and shame. Before marriage, in her home, to protect herself she slept with a knife under her pillow to fend off any attack by her father. "Let him dare," she said. Of course, the attack never came.

You may ask, "Why did she marry Joseph?" Out of loneliness, out of fear that she would never find another man so strong, so intellectual, with such integrity, a man who would look after her.

Why did Joseph marry Rebecca, although, as he would bitterly complain, "She never once said she loves me." First, he was genuinely fond of her, admired her; and he, too, was lonesome; and he, too, thought that if he let her go, he would never get anyone else, that no one would want him.

Why did he have such low self-esteem, such insecurity about self? You would have to probe ever deeper. Man is fathomless; he has no bottom. No complete story can be told.

In this marriage, there were irritations of all kinds; and they were mounting. If the marriage was to go on, they would have to understand one another, communicate with one another, learn to accept one another, accommodate themselves to one another; and above all, respect, admire, and love one another, despite the many compromises they would have to accept, deeply accept.

Quite a task you may say. And you would be right.

25

AS THEY STRUGGLE

THERE ARE COUPLES WHO NO MATTER HOW MUCH THEY may discuss their differences, how much they may understand one another, are so fundamentally different in values and outlook, in character and personality, that discussion only reveals the wide gap between them. It is of these, I suppose, that the late Dr. Abraham Stone, a pioneer in the marital counseling movement, wrote: ". . . the majority of bad marriages are those in which the individuals are quite normal and average, but are wrong for one another, but each might have been right for somebody else."

Here is an illustration of such a marriage:

It is a young marriage; there is much hope and expectation on the part of both. He is a lawyer and she is a school teacher. In the therapy session he says: "I have a weight on my back. I feel unhappy and unsatisfied. I don't know why."

He continues: "I was held up at the office. I called up Elaine and told her I thought I'd eat out; it would be too much bother coming home. She readily agreed. I don't know why, but that bothered me. It is true I suggested the idea and it seemed sensible; and I don't know why it bothered me when she agreed." There was a silence and then he said half to himself. "I wanted her to want to make a meal for me, to urge me to come home."

Reflecting, freely associating, he speaks of Elaine entertaining his family. "She wanted to know what to make, how to make it, what to buy; and in the end, I did the buying and I almost made the meal. It was nice doing it with her and yet why am I angry? You take the matter of the apartment. It was my apartment before marriage and she moved in. It was nice having her. I remember being lonely, very lonely in that apartment. In sex, she is generous and good, and yet, damn it, I find she irritates me by what she does. She keeps the apartment sloppy. I always kept a tidy apartment and it doesn't mean so much to me to look after things, especially since we have help. But I resent the fact that she doesn't take over; that she doesn't assume responsibility." A long silence. "Of course, we have good moments—when we go to the theatre, or to a restaurant; she is lovely-looking, very beautiful; and it's nice to go places with her. But now we're going on a vacation, our first together. And you know I dread it. She's like a weight. You ought to see her packing last night, fussing with her dresses, setting them out. Would you believe it, she showed no interest at all in anything beyond her own; none at all in my things; she didn't think of anything but her own things."

After his return from their vacation, he spoke of a terrible blow up they had. It was something simple that set it off. He wasn't feeling well; he had eaten something that disagreed with him, and he hadn't slept all night. Early the next morning Elaine awoke with much commotion, full of energy. She showered and was eager for breakfast. While the two were driving in the environs of the resort area, they got into a terrible quarrel, and he said: "Take the car and go back to the hotel and I'm going off." And he went off.

This is the way he spoke about the incident: "It was a new area of the country for me, and I was eager to explore it early in the morning—alone. Out of deference to Elaine, I would lie awake in bed till she was ready to get up; I didn't want to disturb her. But here I was, feeling sick and alone, and Elaine proceeded gaily about her business, not thinking of me."

In a therapy session Elaine is talking: "He'll drive me crazy; stark, mad, out of my mind! Dick called up one night and said it was too late to come home for supper; and I said all right, if that was better for him. When he did come home, he ignored me completely. I know him, especially when he's bothered. And when isn't he bothered? And I wanted him to talk about it, for both of us to talk. I wanted to get him out of his bad mood; but he sulked. And I tried to make love to him, for he generally comes around in bed; but he wouldn't have sex with me." There was a silence and she meditated: "When we go visiting, it's terrible. They're all his friends and I feel left out of things. He's close to them and they talk a great deal, and half the time I don't know what they're talking about. In desperation, I flirt a little with a man—only to make Dick jealous, so he'll notice me, so that I'll feel I count and am attractive—to someone at least. But you ought to see him afterwards. He sulks and will not talk and I can't reach him. When he gets that way, I get hysterical; I get frightened. I think he's going to leave me; and I know I carry on like a child. And Dick can't sleep all night, and then he screams; 'I have a hard day in the morning. Please, let me alone. Please get off my back!' He just won't talk and I don't understand him. What have I done wrong? Just tell me and I'll try to do what's right. Please tell me what I'm doing wrong? Since I learned how Dick feels, I tidy up the house, I go shopping, I try to take care of things. I beg him: "Let me know what bothers you and I'll do it.' He's going to drive me crazy."

Her loss of weight, her drawn face, her terrible fear of being deserted by Dick—so frightening to her—all this is exacting an outward toll, but that does not indicate the inward toll which, as she says, has made her a "nervous wreck," and is "driving her crazy."

If there were communication before marriage, real communication, there would have been no marriage. They both married for the wrong reasons. She married because her parents wanted her to marry; because her friends were marrying; because she went to movies and saw young women marrying; because she wanted to be married and "to have all that marriage represents." And when she said this, she thought in terms of a proper marriage, being respectable and doing what a nice girl ought to do.

She had had several previous affairs, and none of them turned into marriage; and these were traumatic experiences for her. When she met Dick, she was desperate, ready to do anything to get married. For her, Dick embodied an ideal husband, a professional man, a lawyer, intelligent and respected; certainly he was an excellent marital catch in the sense that he was superior in status to the husbands of any of her friends. She came from a poverty-stricken Polish home; and by hard work and ambition, she had become a college graduate and a teacher. She was the only one in her family who had left the home for a broader world. She saw marriage as a necessary accomplishment, like being graduated from college; and she wanted to be successful at both.

But Elaine had no sense of a relationship. She was infantile. She could not think of anyone but herself. A husband represented someone needed for her purposes. She was quite willing to play a part, but she couldn't successfully play the role that her husband wanted. This was beyond her. What her husband found so burdensome was her infantilism. She had to be told to cook a meal; she had to be told that when he came home he was tired and wanted solace, attention, fussing. Whatever she did irritated him, for it came out of duty, not out of devotion and concern for him, not out of love of him. She wanted to be a good wife, and was willing to work hard at it; but she had no capacity for being a *good* wife, in the sense that Dick wanted.

As Dick said, there was something wrong; he did not know what. Sexually, he was delighted with her, but often his sense of anger and grievance over her infantilism would be such an irritant that in the midst of intercourse he would lose interest and even become angry, leaving her in distress, making her cry and plead, which made him feel guilty. That did not change his ways but only made him unhappy.

She could not understand what was happening. She was bewildered. She said: "I don't know what makes him so angry. Sometimes he doesn't talk, but sulks; if he only told me what's the matter, I'd do it." But that was the very crux of the disagreement. He wanted her to do it without being told; he wanted her to do it out of her sensitivity, concern and understanding of him, out of her ability to sense what he needed, out of deep involvement with him.

This he did not get from her and his disappointment was constant and infuriating. Before marriage, Dick was as disappointed and infuriated with Elaine as he was now. He thought he didn't understand her; that deep down she had the makings of a good wife; that she would tend to him when he was depressed; love him when he felt alone; give him support when he felt weak; that she would do what a good wife should do.

There was no factual basis for his hope but he hoped.

Dick entered the marriage with demands, terrible demands on Elaine. It is true that socially he was many notches above her. He came from a good, solid achieving family. He was regarded as somewhat of a failure, not by ordinary measures, but by his family's standards. He was highly intelligent, sensitive, well-read, artistic; he had hoped for a time to be a concert pianist. As a lawyer he was not too successful, certainly not in accordance with what his talent or merit warranted. This was due to personality defects rather than his knowledge or ability. He was aloof, withdrawn, snobbish, in manner cold. He was exceedingly lonely, and at times would stay in bed for the entire day, unable to face the burdens of the day and its demands. He lived in fear that his clients would find him wanting and inadequate. He had low self esteem. He said, "Once anyone knows me, he will dislike me." His natural taciturnity was reinforced by his dread of any close revealing relationship.

So there he was—lonesome, frightened of life, fearful of contacts with human beings, with low self esteem, feeling inadequate, insecure. In reality, as a therapist I saw him as an unusually good looking man, highly sensitive, highly intelligent, highly artistic, graceful in every way. But, unfortunately, reality has nothing to do with the way a person feels about or perceives himself. He had had many previous affairs with women but they had all turned out badly. He was now in his forties. In the loneliness of the night the fear would come to him that he was destined to grow old and die in his silent, empty apartment, unwanted, shunned, and these feelings grew as each of his affairs ended badly. His heterosexual relationships were with impossible partners, young girls, often fifteen or twenty years his junior, or sad lonely girls. Why did he choose such? As he said, "A worthwhile woman would not bother with me."

When he met Elaine, he also desperately wanted a marriage. Somehow he became obsessed with the notion that this was his last chance. There were many difficulties to the marriage. For one, the difference in class. Elaine came from the lower class; she was the only one in her family who had managed to acquire a college education and middle class work status. The lower class background of Elaine bothered Dick, for he was essentially a snob. But Elaine was very bright, eager to please, and highly attractive. He had never previously experienced a relationship where a woman tried to please him. As he said, "I do women's bidding. I try in all ways to please them." Elaine knew what she wanted and she wanted Dick; and before marriage worked hard at pleasing him.

Dick had a sex problem. He worried about impotence, for with many women he was an inadequate sexual mate. But Elaine was so respectful of him and sexually so kind she made him feel that with her he was a powerful, potent male.

What, basically, did Dick want from a wife—way down in the vicera? He wanted a woman who was bright, sophisticated, scintillating, who could make a social life for him. "I need a woman who can make friends. I myself cannot." Because of snobbery, he also needed a woman who could not only win the approval but the admiration of his family and professional colleagues. Many of his previous affairs were confined to back streets, for he feared what his social acquaintances would think and say. He described how once, while walking with his wife and her parents, he met a professional colleague and how embarrassed he was; and how he tried to avoid him. Also, he sought a woman who was not only socially engaging but also sensitive, well read, cultivated, artistic. And Elaine had none of these traits.

These differences represent quite a task for a marriage to absorb. Meanwhile, as they struggle, pity the two. There is no villain in the piece.

The lack of communication made the marriage possible, and after marriage communication would have destroyed it. I believe that if they spoke, spoke truly and from the heart, if there was honest communication—and not hope that blinded reality—there would have been no marriage in the first place. It is better not to have any marriage than have a bad one. What I don't understand is how many enter such profound and pervasive relationships with pipe dreams, and hopes and fantasy, not based on the reality of what they see and hear, but on what they like to believe. They feel that deep within the other it will be there—their fantasies and dreams, the source of their imagined happiness. Since reality is often painful, it is brushed aside. Both have the hope and the faith that deep down, within the two, there are these wondrous things that will transform the terrible, burdensome premarital relationship into one of deep happiness. It is amazing how this hope, this self delusion, remains with both despite the harshness of reality. They will not give up this hope. They feel that once they patch things up and come to an understanding, once the other reveals himself, eternal happiness will be theirs. And it is this faith, this hope, that keep many marriages going, despite the reality of grief, hate, debilitating angers and rages.

Once real communication reveals feelings about the other person that denote dislike, egocentricism, selfishness, exploitation of the other for purposes other than what should exist in a good marriage, then such communication can very well lead to its termination.

26

ANOTHER STRUGGLING COUPLE

AS WE HAVE SAID, THERE ARE COUPLES WHO CANNOT ACCOM-
modate themselves to each other in a deep, fundamental
sort of way. Whatever honest communication they may
have will be denigrating and derogatory. Their very person, what they are and who they are, begets condemnation, so that neither can give to the other the respect, the
regard, the admiration so essential in a good marriage. In
such instances, honest, open communication would be
destructive of the relationship.

Here is recounted a marriage in which there is a great
deal of affection and need for each other, and yet the
differences are pervasive and deep-seated.

Linda comes from an upper middle class family, proper
and right, and she has always lived that way. She was
reared in a substantial home, and she wanted for nothing
that was material. She was attracted to a fine young man,
whose socio-economic background was altogether different. His parents were immigrants, and he had worked
since he was a boy. He was and is of an artistic bent and
he was encouraged by a settlement house worker to paint.
He left school even before completing high school to

233

devote himself to his art. Life was hard for him and to make a living he did all sorts of odd jobs. Physically, he was attractive and outgoing and friendly, and happy in his work.

When Marc met Linda, there was a mutual attraction of a kind. She was attracted by his artistic flair, his good looks, his verve for life, his sense of dedication and purpose. Life for her was proper enough but dull and lonely. Linda herself was shy and not too attractive. On his part, he was strongly drawn to her because she represented for him a novelty; her middle class manners, her material well-being, the fact that she was a college graduate. He had never been close to such people—well-dressed, well-mannered, well-heeled. So the two hit it off at first. But as the relationship continued, difficulties began to arise.

In Linda's mind an artist represented something special and exciting. At the beginning she saw all this in Marc. His carefree life with friends like himself, meeting in studios, or in apartments, or restaurants, staying up all hours of night, many with irregular employment and some with no employment, many dressing slovenly and carelessly—all this had for her excitement and adventure. Linda's parents had opposed the relationship, and that in itself was a bind, for there is no better way to draw two people close than to create for them a common struggle against some obstacle. It should also be said that although Marc was not materialistic, he knew quite well that Linda was well-provided-for and that, too, added to the attraction he felt for her. He lived in a drafty, unheated tenement and he suffered from lack of necessities.

They married, and life became a lot better materially for Marc. Linda set him up in a decent apartment; but this wasn't a major factor in Marc's choice of Linda. In fact, he was at first reluctant to use her money, and even wanted to continue living in his tenement apartment. It was Linda who insisted otherwise. I want to emphasize that there was no villain in the piece; they were both estimable people in their own way.

The differences developed after their marriage. What had seemed so attractive before became irritating later. For one, there were Marc's Bohemian friends who did not observe proper hours and dressed so shabbily. As Linda said, "They're filthy. After they're gone, I feel like fumigating the house." Reacting to this, Marc became defensive and counter-attacked: "These friends of mine have talent and more guts and are more real than those shadowy, proper, prim, dull people that you have as friends. Save me from them." She didn't like the way Marc dressed and the way he behaved and the irregularity of his working; but I feel pretty sure the two would have accommodated themselves to this area of their living.

Marc was an avant-garde painter, and he could scarcely wait till Linda saw his new work. She would mutter, "Very beautiful. Very interesting." And then she would talk about some successful artist, and mildly wonder whether artists who paint like Marc ever become successful. "But I'm sure you'll make it. There is a great future for you; and I know you'll be a great artist." And they would both embrace and he would feel good.

No one can hide one's true feelings. Linda had visualized an artist as someone very successful who displayed his work in East Side galleries, with people eager to buy his paintings, and as one who gets a lot of publicity and becomes famous. Simply stated, she wanted a successful, respectable artist. Once after Marc had painted some abstract thing, she said, "Yes, very nice. But why can't you paint portraits. I'm told that there is a lot of money in that."

"I don't want to paint portraits; and I'm not out to make money."

"What's so bad about making money? Why do you have to paint these monstrous things. . ."

And then she stopped and said she was sorry.

But unfortunately, it was no slip. She had revealed her true feelings. Linda disapproved of Marc—his very being, the very thing that made him Marc, what attracted her to him, and what made him so attractive as a person.

In this marriage there can be no honest communication. If there were real communication, this disapproval, this rejection could not help but come through. Marc's wife could not give him what he needed from a marriage— understanding, admiration, encouragement. From this marriage there could be no growth of Marc, for Linda disliked his very being, the very thing that made him unique and special. She would like Marc if he were a proper middle class artist, but if he became that he would not be Marc. From such a marriage, there can come nothing but acrimony, dissension and hostility, for the very best in Marc, his art, in which he poured his very being, would not be appreciated by the one who in a good marriage should be his greatest admirer and his greatest strength.

27

IRRITATIONS IN MARRIAGE

WHAT ASTONISHES ME IS HOW OFTEN, UNWITTINGLY, WITH-out intending to do so, married couples will irritate one another beyond belief. Sometimes they even think it is a joke and josh about it. What is funny about humiliating another person or being so insensitive to him as to keep him in a constant stew is beyond my understanding. When the harm they do is pointed out, they frequently act surprised, which indicates that they were not even conscious of what they were doing.

I was reading a novel by C. P. Snow, *The Light and the Dark*. The scene is set in the Master's house at Cambridge University. The Master, lying in bed in the quiet house, is dying of cancer. His wife, Lady Muriel, has remained by his side for days and weeks. She is visited by two members of the college faculty, who have come to lighten her vigil. One of them, a young fellow of Cambridge University, Roy by name, is urging Lady Muriel to join both of them in a game of bridge, since he knows how much she likes to play. As the game proceeds, Lady Muriel gets Roy to confess that he detests the game and is playing it only to please her. Portions of the conversation follow:

"Do you really like the game, Roy?"

"No, not very much Lady Muriel," he said.

"It's good of you to give up the evening," she said. She added, in a low, almost inaudible murmer: "I wonder if the Master ever liked the game. I don't remember asking him. I'm afraid he may have felt the same as you."

She still did not deal. Suddenly we saw the reason. A tear rolled down her face.

She had been subjugated by the Master's disinterested kindness. She felt ashamed, she tried to imagine now things which had not troubled her for thirty years. It was almost incredible, as Roy said to me late that night in the garden, that she could have played with him night after night and never have known if he enjoyed the game. She was broken down by his heightened understanding, as he came near to death. Her imagination was quickened; she wanted to make up for all her obtuseness had cost her; she could not rest with her old content, formidable and foresquare inside her.[1]

Sinclair Lewis had a talent for caricaturing personalities. He was very witty and he could amuse audiences with these burlesques. One could guess the characters in his next book by whom he was currently impersonating. Calvin Coolidge was caricatured by him long before he became the main character of one of his novels. At the time the following incident occurred, Sinclair Lewis was married to Dorothy Thompson. Let Dr. Charles Angoff chronicle the event.

As we went in Dorothy Thompson was holding forth about the world situation, especially about the then Prime Minister Neville Chamberlain. Lewis waited till she was through. Then he got on a chair and in his truly inimitable style delivered a speech on "British Rights in a World of Sin" that was so deadly a take-off on Mr. Chamberlain's oratory that we could hardly

---

[1] C. P. Snow, *The Light and the Dark* pp. 162–3, Harondsworth, Middlesex, Penguin Books.

control ourselves with our laughter. Dorothy Thompson merely looked at her husband, stone serious, not saying a word. When Lewis was finished she said. "As a college boy prank, dear, you were funny, real funny, but that is all. You simply know nothing about world politics."

On the way home Goodman turned to Mencken and said, "Harry, did you see poor Red, how he was on the verge of crying? What a bitchy woman!"[2]

It should surprise no one that this marriage ended disastrously—in a separation and a divorce that became the subject of a book.

While writing this, I found another illustration in another book, *That Summer in Paris*, by Morley Callaghan.[3] Callaghan describes his first encounter with Paris, that lovely city, when he was young and on the verge of a career as a writer. There he met other writers whom he admired and held in the highest awe—Ernest Hemingway, Scott Fitzgerald, James Joyce, Ludwig Lewisohn. In this group was a man by the name of Titus, the husband of the late Helena Rubenstein, the enormously rich cosmetic tycoon. Young Callaghan and his newly-married wife would meet nightly with Titus and their writing friends at the Café Select, this famed Parisian cafe on the equally famed Montparnasse. Sitting with these writers, Titus was a world away from another life, that of business —the life of wealth, the chauffeur, the limousine. He was now the excited editor and owner of the Black Maniken Press, which published the works of young and promising writers. At the cafe where they gathered, the group and he would talk about writing and writers, and while deep

---

[2] Charles Angoff, *The Tone of the Twenties*, p. 70, N. Y.: A. S. Barnes & Co., 1966.
[3] Morley Callaghan, *That Summer in Paris*, Dell Publishing Company, 1964, pp. 127–8.

in talk, they would order drinks, and the garçon would pile one saucer on top of another, and as is the custom, the price of the drink was baked into the saucer. At the end of the evening, the waiter would tally the bill for each by counting the amounts as indicated on the saucers piled up before each. Titus made it a point to pay only for his own drinks. He wanted to be one of them, like them, not like some moneyed people who would occasionally join the literary group and because of the privilege were expected to pick up the tab. Titus could well afford to pay, but that would have set him apart; so he would wait patiently while the waiter calculated the sum owed by each of them, and then paid his own bill.

At times Titus would be joined by his extremely wealthy, opulent wife, Madame Helena Rubenstein; and when she would witness this picayune tallying, she would become annoyed and say imperiously to her husband. "Pay for them, Edward," and commanded by her, he did.

I am wondering whether she understood what she was doing to her husband? Although the bill did not come to much, and, according to Callaghan, he was a man of means, did she realize that she was violating her husband's concept of self, his feelings about himself?

It is this ability, this sensitivity, this empathy to get into another person's world that is so important for the good marriage. I am wondering to what extent the wife, Madame Helena Rubenstein, realized what it meant to her husband when she demanded, "Pay for them, Edward." Did she realize that she was setting him apart from them, his friends, and was making him the sightseeing rich one, and they the literary ones?

We are not discussing deliberate hurt but unconscious

hurt, where the marital partner is not even aware of what he is doing, and how it is affecting the other. There are real serious differences that cause hurt; and this unfortunately is part and parcel of the lot of two persons in an intimate relationship. We are thinking of slights, irritations, indignities which a marital pair heap on one another unthinkingly and which keep them seething with angry, hostile feelings. Sometimes one, sometimes two play at this game. Examples follow, but anyone with any sensitivity, I am sure, can multiply such examples ad infinitum.

One remarks to another when displeased, "Oh, shut up."

The wife is trying to explain something to guests. The husband: "She gets everything balled up. Just watch."

He is heavily involved in the stock market. In the morning, he can't wait till he gets at the stock page. Indifferent to his interest and his concern, his wife seems to take just those moments to seek him out to bother him with petty nonsense; and when he tries to tell her about this stock or that stock, she proceeds to tell him about some gossip. On the occasions when she buys a paper, she comes home with an early edition, which is of no interest to him. Although the marriage is an old one, she still doesn't know what edition would please him. So when it comes to this whole area of his life, the hope of rising prices or the disappointment of falling prices—all this is outside of the marriage. You may say that this is also outside the home and the relationship. But the luxurious home and the maid and the expensive furniture and the trips to Europe hinge on what to her appears silly and no-account. But even more, outside of the vital financial consideration, what goes on in the stock market has become part of a deep interest; and this interest—the risks and the possible rewards of the financial commitments he makes—he cannot share with his wife; neither the moments when his judgments were vindicated nor the moments when the reverse happens. You may say the wife is not a financier. His wife need not be an expert; not at all. If she seeks, however, a deep and satisfying relationship with her husband, it seems to me she should make every effort to learn enough about what is involved to show understanding of her husband's feelings, his sense of exhilaration when things are going well, his worries and concern when not. In this instance, I cannot imagine a single more satisfying —at least for him—bond between the two. But all of this is now left out of the relationship, a blank, an emptiness between the two.

Whenever the wife asked her husband to pick up something or do a simple errand on his return from work, he never does. He says he forgets. Over the years his wife has learned to resent it. She explains: "It is not forgetting the errand that bothers me. It is his thoughtlessness, his lack of desire to please me."

When the wife proceeds to tell her husband—what she saw, read, or has been told—her husband looks at her as if she is some simpleton and gently and firmly says: "Oh, come, you don't believe that. You mustn't be taken in."

She thinks, not daring to speak up: "That big fat lug. I tell him something and he thinks I'm gullible and stupid. Without knowing or seeing what I saw, he thinks he knows better and understands better than I do. I am an idiot for trying to tell him anything; I ought to learn to shut up and just listen while his big mouth sounds off."

"My Sally. She thinks the atomic bomb is some sort of firecraker." He laughs and thinks he is so bright.

"He's not a man. I need a real man."

The marriage had become very bad. In a therapeutic session, he explains: "She doesn't bathe often enough and there's a terrible odor that emanates from her body and I can't stand it. It takes all I can manage just to lie beside her in bed."

She says: "How he avoids me! As if I have leprosy!"

He was a very clean, fastidious man, and certainly a lot more sensitive than his wife could ever be. "It's true," he said. "I do avoid her. But I can't tell her why. I don't like to hurt her. But I pray for the time when we will have separate beds."

"You have never indicated how you feel to your wife?"

"I wouldn't dare." After meditating awhile, he said: "Why shouldn't I?"

When he did, it was something to witness the barrage, the screaming and shouting. "The nerve of him telling me that! Who does he think he is? What does he know about cleanliness. The insult! And he told that to you! My, my, my. How dare he! He'll hear from me about this. Look at that family from which he comes. And *he* thinks I'm not clean enough."

Now at least the issue was clear. It was not a matter of impotence. It was a matter of disgust. And the wife knew what she had to do if she wanted to have a better relationship.

The husband comes home from work and finds his wife watching television. His observation: "What sort of trash are you watching?" and then proceeds without by your leave or apology to turn to another program, implying that the one he chooses is much more intelligent.

The wife who goes out of her way to make a special dish for her husband or wear a new dress or do something to please him, and he is oblivious, concerned with something else. She thinks: "There is no use doing anything for this man. He appreciates nothing."

The husband has pyorrhetic teeth and has been warned by his dentist that if he does not clean and massage his teeth and his gums immediately after eating he will lose them. He is most conscientious in this duty. If at all possible, immediately after eating, he makes off for the bathroom. His wife appears completely impervious to her husband's needs. As soon as supper is over, she'll rush him to the movies, saying there is no time for dental chores; or when company is present, instead of helping him to escape, she'll hold him captive with his guests.

Before going to bed, she goes through an elaborate toilet; she wears her sexiest negligee, her most expensive perfume; she tries, as she says, to "be as attractive and sweet-smelling as possible." But her husband not only fails to bathe but doesn't even bother to wash his teeth. Although she does not like his habits in this regard, she is willing to forgive him. Incidentally, he has quite a rationale about not complying with conforming behavior, and personal cleanliness is part of it. But for the wife it has wider significance, deeper and more meaningful than even she suspects. She feels that his personal neglect is an affront to her femininity and her attractiveness as a woman; she feels humiliated. "I cannot be a very attractive woman if my husband acts that way toward me." At other times, when she feels angry with him, she will say: "He's filthy and I don't want him near me." The unfortunate part of this interplay is that the husband has no awareness of the full meaning of his behavior. He is an intellectual, and this business of being so sanitary "like one of these stupid women's magazines" is a sort of conformity against which he is rebelling. But in terms of his wife and what it means to her—well, he has no awareness.

The husband does hard physical work and he comes home sweated up and what he likes beyond all things is to take a shower before supper. Not a great sacrifice, it seems to me, for a spouse to make. I can conceive of sacrifices—gladly and generously given—demanding much more from a spouse. "For eleven years I have been married to her and every time I come home, there she is with the supper on the table, making me feel like a heel because I want to take a shower before eating. And if I should work overtime and I come home late, I feel like a wifebeater. And why she can't wait and why she can't give me that simple pleasure is beyond me."

We can go on and on. I am sure you can multiply marital irritants of this kind sufficient to fill many volumes. How can a couple living together, year after year, sleeping in one bed, be so immune, so unknowing of the feelings of a spouse; or if they know how could they not want to please? It astonishes me. Again and again I am amazed;

and in therapy, the culprit stares at you blankly, not realizing what he is doing or has done. Such insensitivity and ignorance of a marital partner with whom you are living so closely is inexplicable. What I can't understand is how marital communication—and I am now talking of fairly good functioning marriage, at least outwardly—can be so obtuse and so clogged that there can exist such unawareness, such crude insensitivity.

28

NOT MEANT FOR EACH OTHER

WHEN I FIRST BECAME A THERAPIST, I WOULD CONSIDER NO possibility of divorce. If I could not help a couple live with a marriage, I would terminate my professional relationship. I would refuse to preside over the liquidation of a marriage. I conceived as my task keeping every marriage going, and if I couldn't I would tally that up as one of my failures and resign. Theoretically, I no longer hold to this position. Many marriages, I have come to feel, are so bad that they are not worth saving; in fact, the continuance is destructive to both, and the partners can salvage for themselves a better life if they had the courage to start afresh. Although I concede the wisdom of such a step, I still find it hard if not impossible professionally to participate in a marital separation.

I once believed two mature persons could manage, no matter what the difficulty. I thought of wives married to alchoholics, and nothing in my opinion can be so destructive of the person, and yet they managed. You and I know couples where one takes awful abuse, and they remain together. I now ask: Why should one suffer a lifetime of abuse? What good is served? I know there are masochistic persons who revel in being abused, who never feel right unless they are meanly used. I have come to think of such persons as sick. I have also seen couples torturing one another because they were too weak to muster the courage to separate. I have also found that there are persons of such low self esteem that they believe no matter how bad their partner, they are not worthy of better.

Reluctantly, I have come to the conclusion that there are some couples who would be better off, not together, but separated. And the evidence is mounting that many who divorce and remarry do much better on the second try.

The more the two partners in marriage are alike—in education, in family background, in intelligence, in philosophy of life, in religion, in culture—the better the prognosis for the marriage. Differences, it is said, attract, but in marriage they are fatal.[1] A case in point is the fact that when couples of differing religions marry, the odds that the marriage will fail and end in divorce are two or three times as great as if they had similar religions. On hearing this idea elaborated, one perceptive person remarked: "You want me to marry me." The fallacy, of course, is that there is not another "me" in the entire universe. At best, the differences between any two human beings are deeper than a well and wider than the door of a cathedral, and sufficient to provide a lifetime to accommodate.

---

1 There is no "always" when it comes to human beings. I once lived in Paris and there I knew a woman in the cast of the Folies-Bergère who was married to an impecunious, unworldly Sorbonne student. She was a beautiful woman and had many admirers, some wealthy and some of high social position. But these held no attraction for her. When she heard her husband in a cafe hold forth with friends in a highly intellectual and brilliant manner, she would become sexually so aroused that she would hail a cab and rush her husband home to do his male duties. It can be said that generally differences add burdens to a marriage.

But there are chasms so wide that it is impossible for two persons ever to bridge. This is the nub of tragic marriages. What can be said about a musician whose spouse regards his playing as cacophonous noises; or the deeply religious person living with a non-believer; or the scholar who seeks the seclusion of a library married to a worldly, sophisticated person; or a night person ["I start to live at night," as one patient explained it,] married to a quiet day person who goes to bed early so as to be fresh for the next day's work? One can go on endlessly.

To repeat: It is similarity of values, aims, and purposes that bind people together in the closest spiritual unity. And such relationships are lasting and they provide a glamor and beauty beyond description to life. It is such relationships that are uplifting and strengthening. Further, relationships thrive best when there is some sort of equality between the giving and the taking. There can be no real friendship between a servant and a master, for one orders and the other obeys. Any relationship in which there is no rough equality of give and take is demoralizing. That is why the relationship between the southern whites and the slave Negroes could never turn into friendships; and that also is why the southern whites were demoralized by that relationship. There can be no real friendship between a master and a servant. The exchange need not be exactly equal nor similar; it need not be equally weighed in the balance. An artist can be a friend with an engineer, for the artist can respect the engineer and feel for him and give to him; and the engineer can reciprocate.

There is a new aspect of marriage that has contributed greatly to our marital dilemma. People are marrying at younger ages than ever and in greater proportion than ever. The figures are there to prove it. Dr. Harold W. Berman points out that in 1890 54 per cent of American men were married; in 1950 it was 68 per cent. For women, the figures are 47 per cent for 1890 and 57 per cent for 1950. "Moreover," Dr. Berman says, "the average age at the time of first marriage is also showing a decline. In 1890 the average age at marriage was 26.1 years for men and 22.0 for women while in 1950 these ages had dropped about four years to 22.8 for men and had dropped about two years to 20.3 for women."[2] Based on 1959 U.S. Census Bureau figures, Dr. Berman observes: "The peak age for marriage of women is 18 years. One-third of 18 and 19 year old girls are married. One-third of first children are born to mothers who are not more than 20 years old. The median age of marriage for women is 20.1 years. When one considers that some may not marry until 30 or older this indicates the large number who marry early."[3]

It is true our young people are marrying in greater numbers and percentages than ever but they cannot stay married. We know that the earlier the age of marriage the greater the probability of divorce. Further, many of our young people are marrying for the wrong reasons—to follow the style set by their peers, to run away from a disagreeable home, to escape from school, to seek some shreds of affection when starved for it, to legitimize an out-of-wedlock child. It is estimated that at least 35 per cent of teen-age brides are pregnant at marriage. None of the foregoing is a good reason for marriage.

The Kinsey study tells us that the strongest sexual urges

---

[2] Harold W. Berman, *Human Development in Western Civilization,* p. 306, Boston: Allyn & Bacon, Inc., 1962.
[3] *Ibid,* p. 288.

appear in the male in the late teens. Middle class parents are giving their sons and daughters increasing freedom to mix heterosexually, and some parents regard the sexual popularity of their offspring as reflecting somehow on their parental success. They throw young people together; they want them to be close and intimate short of actual intercourse. The moral code of middle class parents still demands virginity for at least the daughter, and in the vast majority of cases for their sons also.

This puts young people in a terrible bind. Many of the teen-agers haven't the emotional maturity or character to deal with their sexual urges. They are capable of sex, driven unmercifully by these urges in a sex-saturated society, but the same society demands that this be curbed outside of the marital relationship. Simply put: Our young people are ready for sex, mature in this regard as they ever will be, but they are not at all ready for marriage, not the kind of marriage as we conceive it, namely, a binding, permanent, life-long union.

At this stage of their development, for the most part they do not know their own minds, who they are, what they are, what they want from life. They aren't financially or emotionally able to assume the responsibilities of marriage. When so much of their life is still nebulous and unformed, how can they make a permanent choice?

Dr. Allan Fromme relates that while examining a baby at a hospital, he saw a number of persons around the bedside and was puzzled as to who were the parents of the child. He inquired. Whereupon an elderly man said he was one of the parents and then said he wasn't. This only increased Dr. Fromme's puzzlement. The elderly man then explained that he was really the grandfather and that he had adopted the child. He said his son, the real father, and the girl, the real mother, were too young to rear a child and too young to marry. He pointed to the real parents who were children in their early teens. "They will live with us and we are taking care of the baby," the grandfather matter-of-factly explained.[4]

As far as sex goes, young people are altogether ready to function. This is the dilemma that confronts our society. Their elders don't know quite what to do, how to handle the situation, even what to say to young people. Once they could terrorize them with the fear of venereal disease, unwanted pregnancy, and the religious ideal of pre-marital chastity. But these deterrents no longer are as effective as they once were. The "birth control pill" has wrought profound changes; so has the lessening of faith. But a solid, permanent family is as essential as ever, if we are to maintain western civilization as we have known it. The child needs a secure, permanent and forever father and a mother if he is to flourish and take his part as a good, contributing member to our society. In other portions of this work we have indicated the crucial nature of the family in developing warm, loving children, fit for marriage and fit for good healthy living. This still holds.

This whole area is a sorry mess. Since we do not know what to say to our young people, we engage in a sort of double-talk—mealy-mouthed gobbledegook. The solution, admittedly, is not simple. As long as we maintain the ideal of chastity before marriage, and as long as we wish permanent, binding marriages, the dilemma remains; and there is no ready answer. Because we have not come to intelligent grips with the problem, and have not even re-

---

[4] Allan Fromme, *The Ability to Love,*" p. 45, N.Y.: Pocket Books, 1966.

motely hit on a viable solution, horrible marriages are taking place, marriages not worthy of permanence.

Reports *Time*: . . . forty per cent of today's brides are between the ages of 15 and 18; within five years, half of teen age marriages end in divorce.

Why do teen-agers get married? And what goes wrong? Pennsylvania State University Professor Carlfred Broderick sees it beginning when they decide to go steady (more than half do), terms this "the beginning of the end."

Says Broderick: "It takes little or no effort to get more and more involved; before they know it, they are slipping into marriage." For boys, sex is the driving force; . . . the stronger the moral code, the more likely that the teen-ager will marry early.

For girls, as important as sex is the desire to "love." But an early expectation of romance can soon be replaced by harsh reality. Disillusion is especially rapid when the husband has to curtail his education or children arrive too early.

. . . One part-time secretary who was born illegitimate herself confessed she had yearned for security. A pretty cocktail waitress who was wed at 17 said: "I was marrying to get out of home." Bitterest of all was a girl who married at 17, was now in the process of getting a divorce. "My parents trusted me too much," she said. "In a way, it's too bad giving kids too much time for things they're not ready for." For her the future is bleak. Said she: "I have a little boy of two and a little boy of four, and they're too much for me. I'm not grown up yet."[5]

Dr. Mary Calderone says: "When a 16-year-old marries a 17-year-old, 80 per cent of the time, it winds up in divorce." The baby? "A child brought up by a child."[6]

Writes Leonard Gross: "Each week, 20 pregnant girls,

[5] "Teen-Age Marriage," *Time*, April 19, 1966.
[6] "Education Comes of Age," Leonard Gross, Look, March 8, 1966. © Cowles Communications, Inc.

mostly 15 or under, drop out of Chicago's public schools. Girls 17 and under account for 22% of illegitimate births. In 1964 alone, girls of high-school age aborted 180,000 pregnancies. Reported cases of syphilis among teen-agers have more than tripled since 1956; young people under 20 account for more than one in five cases of venereal disease."[7]

The number of pregnant teen-agers has become so numerous that increasingly large cities are establishing educational centers for teen-age pregnant girls. Hitherto, school authorities have expelled them with middle class righteous fury and indignation. Now they are large enough in numbers to comprise a special class of students with special needs and a special curriculum aimed to serve their needs.[8] According to a news report in the New York Times, the trend continues upward. "In 1950 one out of 25 children born in the United States was illegitimate. By 1960 the figure was one out of 19 and by 1965, one out of fifteen. The nation's illegitimate births rose from 3.98 per cent of all births in 1950 to 7.74 per cent in 1965."[9] All told there were 291,200 illegitimate births reported for 1965, probably much below the true figure, since so many out-of-wedlock mothers try to avoid public acknowledgment of such births and in many instances succeed. If this trend continues, it is estimated that by 1970, one out of ten births in the U.S. will be out-of-wedlock births. In some large cities the rate of illegitimate births is now running better than 10 per cent. Who are the mothers of out-of-wedlock children? Approximately 44 per cent of

7 Leonard Gross, "Education Comes of Age," Look, March 8, 1966. © Cowles Communications, Inc.
8 "Maturity for Unwed Mothers," Time, February 10, 1967.
9 New York Times, "Rise Is Reported in Illegitimacy," October 29, 1967.

them in 1965 were under age twenty. In 1964, there were 64,500 children born to unwed mothers under eighteen.[10]

Further, parents do not help; they shirk their duty. Instead of educating their children in sexual matters, they shy away from the task. As a result, children learn about sex for the most part on the streets, and it comes to them in clandestine fashion as vulgar, sinful, shameful. I have had college students who smirked lasciviously when an attempt was made to discuss sex with them in a frank manner. What astonished me was to see the same, furtive, smirking attitude among university graduate students, many of whom were teachers.

Each one of us—every single living human being—is a product of a sex act. You are a product of a sex act. Your mother is a product of a sex act. Your father is. So are your brothers and sisters. So also are your aunts, uncles, cousins. So also is your wife or husband. The home, family, babies, the community are all the outcome of sexual acts. When I point this out to my students, I sense their astonishment and bewilderment, as if it were a brand new discovery on my part.

Writes Leonard Gross: "Behind each ignorant teen-ager is usually a shy or ignorant parent. From 1958 until 1963, William Blaisdell, a public health specialist of Washington, D.C., interviewed 25,000 teen-agers. His findings: One in 14 receives sex information from his parents before learning it from other teen-agers; one in 22 learns from his parents about venereal disease. Two years ago, Blaisdell asked a gathering of 624 educators to indicate whether they had learned first about sex from their parents. Not one raised his hand. In this respect, alas, times

[10] U.S. News and World Report, "Startling Story of Illegitimate Children in U.S., October 2, 1967.

have not changed. Observes a husky, University City, Mo., high school senior sadly: 'My father kept telling me, "As soon as you get older, I'll tell you about it." Now, I'm too old!"[11]

Is it any wonder that America has the highest divorce rate of the Western world and that one out of four marriages goes smash?

[11] "Education Comes of Age," Leonard Gross, *Look*, March 8, 1966.

29

THE MATURE PERSONALITY

WHAT IS MEANT BY AN EMOTIONALLY MATURE PERSON?

If the explanation is groping and circuitous, it is because it is impossible, as I view the concept, to arrive at an understanding of what comprises the attributes of a mature personality in a cut and dried fashion. But that does not gainsay in any way its crucial importance in every vital personal adjustment—social, vocational, and especially marital. It should be said that the mature person exists as a theory, an abstraction; and even about the theory there is disagreement. Also from the outset it should be understood that the perfectly mature person is a rare phenomenon. As Jelliffee said, "Very few people are really grown up."

Let us start with an example of what can be described as highly mature behavior. John Dewey, the philosopher, had been working on the summation of his philosophy, his *magnum opus*. After five years of consecrated work, he completed the manuscript. A friend of his borrowed the manuscript and lost it. For about two days Dewey was disconsolate, but then he snapped right back and began the task of rewriting with his original vigor.[1]

---

[1] Benjamin Fine, *John Dewey at 90*, New York Times, October 19, 1949.

"You know," Dr. Benjamin Fine quoted him as saying, "in a way this has given me new ideas, starting over fresh again. I think I have better ideas now."[2]

Dr. Carl Binger, associate professor of clinical psychiatry at Cornell University, provides us with an excellent illustration of immaturity. He asks us to visualize an eighteen-month-old infant who suddenly becomes full grown. "Instead of being 31 inches tall and weighing 25 pounds, he now stands six feet in his stocking feet and weighs 190 pounds. But in all other respects he has not altered. He still slobbers and drools. When he is hungry, he bellows, and he goes into towering rage when he can't immediately have what he wants when he wants it. If it amuses him he might dandle his mother on his knee, but he might also bite off her nose, pull her hair out, clutch at her skirt and probably rip it off; or he might simply drop her down the stair well—just to see what would happen. In his more exuberant moments he would choke the family kitten or poke its eyes out, yank down the curtains, and generally wreck the house." And he adds: "Such a creature would be a monstrous menace to the house."[3]

An infant starts out in life as an egoist, self-centered, interested only in his own wants and needs, interested in adults only as they cater to these needs. Several months later he recognizes the importance of others, especially his parents, and he responds to them with smiles and with gurgling. This is a form of social communication, but one should not place too much meaning into this by-play. The infant is still not capable of any deep affection or sacrifice as adults understand it. He indicates this kind of emotional contentment because he knows that these moving

2 *Ibid.*
3 Carl Binger, "What is Maturity?" Harper's Magazine, May, 1951.

persons satisfy his wants. Even when he is able to walk, he makes demands; he takes; he does not give. His conversation begins with "I" and ends with "I." He cannot stand frustration. He squeals, howls, goes into rages. He wants what he wants when he wants it, and he doesn't care how or whom he inconveniences thereby. If someone comes along with a lollypop or can entertain him more ably than his parents, he is quite willing in a moment to transfer to the stranger his attention and affection. His thoughts begin with himself and end with himself and nothing counts except as it satisfies his immediate wants, wishes, and needs. One should not be unduly concerned about such behavior. If the child develops well, he will become less selfish and more social, less self-centered and more outward-centered.

There comes the day when he is old enough to march off to school. If development has proceeded properly, from that point on the outside world will become to him of increasing significance; he will be making adjustments to this outside world more and more as an independent, responsible individual. These adjustments to the outside world will dominate and possess his feelings and thinking. He will begin to have independent social relationships and become increasingly sensitive to the wants, wishes, and desires of others. This phase of his adjustment will provide him with many challenges and many problems. He will have to learn to think less and less about his own ego and more and more about the wants of others. This will be hard for him, for he has had little preparation for this role, since in his own home he has hitherto been the orbit around which the world has centered. In the process of learning how to work, play, and share with others, he will bicker, quarrel, fight, have temper tantrums. If he is normal, inherent in him will be this great capacity for learning; and he will learn—as he practices working, playing, and sharing with others—better and better social adjustments.

In his next stage of development, he will align himself with his crowd, his clique, his peers, his gang—whatever you call the world outside the home with which the young person becomes closely identified. Until maturity and marriage, this group will comprise the most important part of his world, and it will play a crucial role in his socialization. Until maturity and marriage, the outside crowd will remain his world. What they regard as the proper clothes, he will regard as the proper clothes; their ways will be his ways. In this group he will learn how to participate in joint ventures, how to lead and how to follow, how and when to assert his rights and how and when to forego them; he will learn such qualities as loyalty, perseverance, good sportsmanship. Since the crowd is a powerful educational medium, the kind of group our young man chooses will have enormous influence on his future development.[4]

During adolescence, with the help of his closely-knit crowd, our young man will try to effect some kind of

---

[4] Social-minded groups are animated by good will to man, by a desire to advance the well-being of mankind—to leave the world a little better because they were there. In this kind of group there is the resolve, implicitly or explicitly, to so live and so do as to gain the admiration of their fellow human beings. As a group, they are eager and feel obligated to assume the work and the responsibility to maintain a good society. And it is on the effort of such that a good society is built.

Anti-social groups are motivated by a desire to prey on society. They wish to live off it, not make any contribution to it. They seek self-gain and self-profit. In this kind of group, many aspire to become racketeers, gamblers, gangsters, hoodlums. I have had adults, some university students, tell me that if they had remained with their original crowd, they would now be in jail or a junkie (heroin addict), for every member who remained in it is now or was in jail or is on heroin.

adjustment to work, to marriage, to society; also, he will try to achieve a philosophy of life, to forge for himself some self-concept and the role he wants to play. He will have to make these important decisions and adjustments on his own, independently; and this will be a trying period for his home as well as for him. In fact, he will have to weaken the strong emotional ties that bind him to his family. His parents will be frequently disturbed by his assertions and demands for increasing freedom, both in terms of emotional ties and of independent action. Do not the parents know what is good, what is dangerous? Why will not their son or daughter profit by their experience? Why will he or she not listen and heed their advice? If our young person does not psychologically and emotionally "wean" himself from his parents, his development will be warped and stunted; he will never be a full grown man, a "mature" man, and fit for marriage, or fit to raise a family, or to participate and become an asset to his community or in the larger community, the city, the nation, the world.

For the adolescent this is a hard and difficult period, and this is a period of many breakdowns, some of a serious nature. And yet, turbulent as this period is, fraught as it is with crucial significance, in many ways it is a glorious period, full of wonder, full of grandiose feelings, full of high resolution, some eventually to end in fruition and some to end in bitterness and a sense of lasting failure.

Despite his apparent bravado, the adolescent is full of self-doubt, full of self-examination, full of self-torture. It does not surprise me at all that this awesome period is the theme of endless literary works. If the young person's adolescence has been good and rich, he will resolve to be a great writer, a great musician, a great scientist, a great healer, a great avenger of public wrongs, great no-matter-

262   A *Psychologist Looks at Marriage*

what. This is the time when he sees himself—as do his friends themselves—as famous, renowned, glorious. They will resolve never to live the humdrum life of their parents This is the time when the adolescent will begin to form a concept of himself and shape a role for himself to fulfill his self-concept. Each of us first has to become a person; this is a crucial task and no mean task. The healthy adolescent is continually pondering his role, is continually shaping it, and continually setting a course to fulfill it.

This is the time of close and warm friendships, deep as they never will be again, for the young have enormous need for one another. They need the group to bolster their courage to leave the safety of their home and venture into the strange, mysterious, frightening wider world. They need the closeness to make the crucial, adolescent adjustments they know they must make to become adults. They need the closeness to cut the umbilical cord that has hitherto tied and shackled them to their parents. They need support and understanding, and they get it best from the society they have formed outside their homes. They talk endlessly until the wee hours of the morning—about marriage, work, God, morality, politics, government, religion. They talk endlessly about their ambitions, their hopes, their inadequacies, their needs, their wants. If the young person has had a star-dust adolescence, he will identify himself with great persons, great deeds, great minds. To repudiate the way of life of his own family, he will have to dethrone his parents, make them small, for thus he can muster the courage to rebel and resist the pressure to hold him.

At this stage the parents wring their hands in despair and wonder what they have wrought. Haven't they made these mistakes and why can't this "wild" young one profit from them? They cannot understand that each has to learn from his own mistakes, and if their child is ever to grow up, he must learn to make his own decisions, to dare and to venture for himself.

You learn how to make right and wise decisions by profiting from your wrong ones. Your character and personality are forged from the decisions you make when confronting choices. You become the "decisions" that you make. If you make selfish and ignoble decisions and live by them, you become selfish and ignoble. If you make unselfish and noble decisions and live by them, you become unselfish and noble. Simply put, you become what you live. Said Chaucer: "He is gentil that does gentil dedis."

Parents do not understand that if they do not give the young person freedom, if they do not permit him to become emotionally and psychologically "weaned," then their child can never hope to become a mature person. He will remain a child, and all the parents will have is a child, never will they have a man for a son, nor a woman for a daughter. Nor can this child ever become a good husband or a good wife. No matter how old their offspring, the parents will be burdened with a child; and they never will have the comfort and the support that only a mature man or woman can give to another person.

There comes a time when his crowd—and so does he—begin to go out with girls; they go on picnics, to the theatre, to club meetings, to dances, to each other's homes. He learns through such group activities how to get along with his own sex and the opposite sex; he learns by a process of trial and error insights into the ways and the

A Psychologist Looks at Marriage

behavior of his boy friends and his girl friends; he learns how to evaluate and appraise them. The young people continually jabber among themselves. They talk about each other and the other sex. "Frank is good looking but he hasn't a brain in his head." "Mary wears clothes well but she's a flirt." "Alfred is smart but he's selfish." They talk about the proper way of behaving at a restaurant, at a party, when visiting. At each other's homes, they learn how different families order their lives. They embark on venturesome experiences which they would never dare alone.

During this time—if development is normal—they experience many "puppy loves." Puppy loves are learning loves. In these relationships, the boy and the girl practice their sex roles, the boy how to play the masculine role and the girl the feminine role. Each puppy love, as it ends in failure, reveals to the individual how complex the problem of marriage is; and from it he gains valuable insights as to the kind of lifelong partner he needs and wants. If these preparatory heterosexual friendships preceding marriage are bypassed, I believe a great deal of harm is done. There will remain an irretrievable gap in the young person's development. He will not be nearly as well or as intelligently equipped for the many adjustments he has to make to grow to full maturity.

It for this reason that so many sheltered young people, those who did not go through the process of having puppy loves, experimental loves, so frequently make bad choices. They have not learned what it is all about. They often make choices from ignorance, from not understanding themselves or the other sex. As a clinical psychologist, I have found that from among this group—never having had a good heterosexual adolescence—have come some of the worst marriages. It is they who most frequently marry for the wrong reasons. Even when they maintain a marriage, in it there is a great deal of discontent. The wife will say: "I have never known any other man," implying how will I ever know whether this is the right man for me. The same attitude goes for men, even in a more self-castigating form. In middle age, this hankering, gnawing for other experiences may become so acute that even a good marital relationship may develop stress. Social mingling, participating in heterosexual relationships both in groups and as couples, is the best preparation, the best way of learning how to make a wise final choice of a partner with whom to build a life. Even under ideal circumstances, marriage is a risk and a gamble. "The living together," said Arthur Helps, "for three long, rainy days in the country has done more to dispel love than all the perfidies in love that have even been committed." The actual living together is the final test, and that can only come from the actual living in a marriage. The better the couple know each other and themselves, the less the risk.

In the process of becoming a mature, independent person, many an adolescent will experience frightening moments. When things get rough, like a fledgling bird, he will hasten back to the solace and protection of his family, the home nest, which like a soft pillow will provide him with temporary safety and reassurance. If the adolescent has healthy, mature parents, they will give their young offspring their faith, their belief in him, so that he will gather the strength and the courage to venture forth again. Back and forth the young one will go, but

like the fledgling bird, he will venture ever farther away
and make fewer and fewer retreats back to the home nest.[5]
Like the fledgling bird, he keeps on trying to fly unaided
until he succeeds. If he doesn't, woe will betide that
child!

Once he is on his own, he is ready for marriage and
once married, a strange thing happens. He returns to his
old household with affection and love, but he returns not
as a child, but as an independent, responsible, uniquely
different adult. The parents' home is enriched and
strengthened, both in interests and in variety of personalities by this new marriage. The parents now have not
a child who reflects their wishes and wants but a self-
directing adult son or daughter on whom they themselves
can lean and whose experiences, new and different, en-
large their outlook and give new richness to the old home.
Instead of one home there are now two homes; instead of
one family, two families.

The new family, once they have children, will begin
the same cycle again, ever old, ever new, and ever wonderful. Again the parents will suffer as they watch their

---

[5] Wrote a graduate university student of her adolescence: "It was many
years before I accepted the fact, both intellectually and emotionally,
that *I* was not the center of the universe. Three things led me to this
inescapable conclusion: a husband, a son and a daughter, each of whom
thought he (or she) was really the center of the universe. In a way,
each of us recapitulates the experience of humanity in respect to our
conception of our position in the universe. At first, the world was considered the center of everything. The sun, the moon and the stars were
merely ornaments put into the heavens for our benefit. Finally, we realized that our earth was merely a planet, one of many, revolving about
our sun. The sun, however, certainly was the center. So we believed,
until it was shown that our sun is merely a rather small star, one of a
hundred billion stars in the spiral arm of an ordinary galaxy. And as it
happens in our personal experience, cherished beliefs are difficult to dis-
card and each one of these advances was fought bitterly until their truth
could no longer be denied."

adolescent child go through the vicissitudes of adolescence. If he is a healthy young person, like the fledgling bird, he, too, will never be content until he is able to fend for himself and establish his own nest. Unlike the bird, he will come back to the old home, to make it richer, stronger, more interesting.

And so life goes on.

As we noted, the child is egotistical, self-centered, demanding. As he grows, his love and affection expand to include his parents and members of his family; then later, it envelops his crowd and his neighborhood; then still later, the state and the nation; and if he is a fine person, fully mature, his love and his interest and his wish to serve will widen and extend to every human being the world over. When he hears of injustice or starvation or suffering in India, Africa, China, he will be as moved and as touched and as eager to help as if it were happening to members of his own family. This is admittedly a high form of social maturity, within the province of few to attain.

Signifying the highest form of social maturation, the individual will so act and so live that what he wants of good for himself and his family, he will strive to make possible for every other human being, regardless of race, color, religion, or nationality.

But always it should be understood maturity is acquired in the process of living; in growing ever more mature in behavior. It is learned on the battlefront of life, from its failures and triumphs. Each must stand his own ground; no one can avoid or sidestep the issues of life without peril to himself; and no one, no matter how well his intentions, can live another person's life nor can he shield him from life's blows without hurt to that person.

In growth from infancy to maturity, some stop literally at the childhood level; others at the adolescent; and some reach maturity in some areas and not in others. The childish approach to any baffling situation is pouting, sulking, temper tantrums, wheedling. Some adults do not go beyond that; they are assertive, inflexible, domineering, insensitive to the feelings of others. Some achieve the adolescent stage, where the emphasis is on talk and dreams and future plans, but no actualization. Our Greenwich Villagers are symbols of the adolescent mind. It is a symbol of men and women who refuse to come to grips with reality, who spend their time talking and talking about the great books, the masterly paintings, the new system of philosophy that they will create; but meanwhile they do nothing but talk. They go through all the preparatory motions of the adolescent, but instead of being better able to adjust and to find happiness in reality, they are content with going through preparatory motions.

They demand acclaim, respect, and the sensation of triumph before they write their masterpiece. Short-circuiting the actual work itself, they expect without solid achievement to gain the respect and plaudits of others. And as time goes by, they are less able to find happiness in real work and achievement, for they have bypassed the painstaking preliminary hard work necessary to perfect skills and techniques fundamental to any work.

Maturity is not synonymous with chronological age. Not even with intelligence. The studies of L. M. Terman and Milita H. Oden indicate that among the brightest, the intellectual elite, there is the same proportionate amount of emotional instability, of alcoholism and psychosis, as among those of lesser intelligence. I have seen young twelve-year-old boys and girls who are more mature than men and women of twenty, thirty, forty, fifty, sixty. I have seen twelve-year-olds who knew their own mind better, knew who they were better, knew what they wanted from life better, had a greater capacity for personal involvement, responsibility, and self-sacrifice than men and women of twenty, thirty, forty, fifty, sixty. It is not age but these other qualities that define maturity.

We should not like to imply that there is ever an end to development, to growth. It is a never-ending process. As life does not stop till death, so growth and increasing maturity should not. Travel is better than arrival, said John Dewey, for traveling is a constant arrival. We cannot speak of maturation as something fixed and static; there is no finality. In the life good to live, this growth and maturation continue on and on, forever, until death.

Discussing the mature personality, Professor Allport observes: "In the first place, the developed person is one who has a variety of autonomous interests; that is, he can lose himself in work, in contemplation, in recreation, and in loyalty to others. Egocentricity is not the mark of a mature personality. Contrast the garrulous Bohemian, egotistical, self-pitying, and prating of self-expression, with the man of confident dignity who has identified himself with a cause that has won his devotion. Paradoxically, self-expression requires the capacity to lose oneself in the pursuit of objectives, *not* primarily referred in the self. Unless directed outward toward socialized and cultural compatible ends, unless absorbed in causes and goals that outshine self-pity and vanity, any life seems dwarfed and immature. . . . These goals represent an *extension* of self which may be said to be a first requirement for maturity and personality."[6]

---

[6] G. W. Allport, *Personality*, p. 213, New York: Henry Holt & Co., 1937.

Who is the mature person? We cannot exactly say. We
can only indicate marks and characteristics of such a personality, but we should warn the reader against definitive
and categorical demarcations. But we can say that the
mature person is social in outlook, that he obtains his
strength and confidence from positive achievement in a
world of reality; that he is capable of affection, sacrifice,
perseverance; that he can assume responsibilities; that he
is interested and concerned with the world about him;
that he can cooperate and he is willing to share; that he
can join with others for the common good; that he has
some concept of his own strengths and limitations; that
he faces his failures and frustrations—inherent in a competitive world—frontally and realistically, not feeling that
he, like Job, is being picked on and that his travail and
sorrows are special and unique; that he confronts obstacles
and difficulties as interesting challenges which he faces
bravely and manfully.

Such a description, of course, is admittedly theoretical.
There are very few altogether mature persons. "It is questionable whether we should ever expect to find in the flesh
a paragon of maturity. We shall be talking more about
an ideal than about an actual person. It is significant that
when we ask people to name some person who seems to
them to have a 'mature personality' they nearly always
select someone outside their own family and of the opposite sex. Why? Perhaps because familiarity makes them
all too aware of the weaknesses of their closest associates
and of their own sex. Some people approach true maturity. But does anyone ever fully achieve it?"[7]

7 Gordon W. Allport, "Pattern and Growth in Personality," pp. 276–277,
N.Y. Holt, Rinehart and Winston, 1961.

The strongest and the hardiest among us—those who can withstand cataclysmic defeat—may show infantile behavior when suffering from a toothache. I have known of a physician of high repute, with a wife and married daughters, who when he became sick so regressed into infantilism that he wanted to have near him his very old mother who nursed him with her home remedies. Likewise, an adult who is infantile in the major areas of living may show in certain instances unbelievable fortitude and hardihood. That does not lessen the importance of emotional maturity in all the major aspects of living. We can say that the neurotic is crippled for living because he has acquired so few mature attitudes in his living. Conversely, we can say that since the mature person is grown up and adult in many of the important areas of living, he can meet life more intelligently, more ably and adequately.[8]

What has this to do with marriage? Everything. In working out accommodations, in the trials and tribulations inevitable in any deep, pervasive relationship; in the capacity to love and to be loved; to give affection and to receive affection; to sacrifice for and to be sacrificed for;

---

[8] As interesting a description of maturity as I have read comes in a report that Blaise de Montluc (1502–77) made to his king, Henry II, after defending Sienna (1554–55) against the forces of Charles the Fifth. It follows:

I told the King that I had gone off one Saturday to the market, and in sight of everybody bought a bag, and a little cord to tie its mouth, together with a faggot, taking and shouldering them all in the public view; and when I reached my room, I asked for fire to kindle the faggot, then took the bag and stuffed into it all my ambition, all my avarice, my sensuality, my gluttony, my indolence, my partiality, my envy and my eccentricities, and all my Gascon humours—in short, everything that I thought might hinder me, in view of all I had to do in his service; then I tightly tied the mouth of the bag with the cord, so that nothing could get out, and thrust it all in the fire. And thus I found myself clear of everything that could impede me in all I had to do in the service of His Majesty.

to be loyal and devoted to causes and persons outside of oneself—the maturity of the person is crucial. It is the mature person who has the capacity for good, lasting, durable, and satisfying relationships.

Marriage, as I view it, is not a romantic dream. It is a test of character requiring all the fortitude and strength that one possesses. There is scarcely a marriage, no matter how mature the participants, when one of the partners in a moment of despair does not contemplate divorce. It requires a high form of maturity for a couple to sustain the vicissitudes of a marriage and to emerge from its trials with unimpaired understanding, affection, and closeness. The immature person is more apt to feel put upon, picked on, badly used and is more apt to respond with hostility and hate. The infantile person, like Narcissus, is in love with himself; and he has no competitor, for no one can love him as well as he loves himself. The greater the maturity of the two the brighter the prospects for a good relationship and a good marriage.

30

CHOOSING A SPOUSE

IF I HAVE INDICATED THAT THERE IS AN EASY AND SURE WAY to choose a right spouse, I have given you a wrong impression. I remember the philosopher John Dewey on the occasion of his seventieth anniversary speaking on what gave him happiness. First of all, he mentioned work. "I'd rather work than eat," he said. Second, he mentioned his marriage. And this, he said, was a matter of chance.

It would appear easy to choose a good marital partner if all we need do is to find a person reared in a good home. The difficulty resides in this: What may appear to be a good home need not be. If we probe more deeply into the matter, the problem becomes more complicated, not less. We have a harsh demanding culture, so that even those children who come from what appear to be intact homes may be irretrievably damaged as *humane* beings. In the rearing of the solid, middle class child, every aspect of him becomes a matter of scrutiny, like the examination of a horse who is to be entered in a grueling contest. As an infant, he is watched closely to see what potential he has; and as he grows, he is carefully examined and trained so as to make sure that he will emerge a victor. Even the age at which he is toilet trained, starts walking and talking become matters of invidious distinction. For the middle class child there is no respite. When he starts school, the race really becomes serious. If their Herbert gets 90 per cent, the parents always know a Milton who gets 100 per cent; so what is 90 per cent? If their Herbert gets 100 per cent, the parents always know a Milton who gets two, or three, or four 100 per cents; so what is one 100 per cent?[1] If their Herbert gets a scholarship, the parents always know a Milton who has a better scholarship at a more prestigious university.

It is no longer sufficient to be graduated from college, but it must be graduation from a *prestige* college. It is no longer sufficient to work at a job, but it must be the kind of job that is important enough to make the parents proud and relatives and friends envious.[2] Just to marry

---

[1] Our schools dangle before each learner a 100 per cent objective; how wrong, how simple and simple-minded, how infantile! By insisting on this stupid and foolish standard of perfection, how many fears and timidities have we inculcated in learners, fears and timidities that have inhibited living, adventuring and venturing! Even if we could avoid failure, I question its advisability. A human being cannot become a humane being unless he has experienced the hurt and the grief of failure. We ought to make failure acceptable and respectable, part of the inevitable process of living. In the life good to live there is no perfection, no end, only growth and striving and more growth and more striving—unendingly.

What are some of the outcomes of the horrible competitiveness of our school system? For college students suicide in 1966 ranked second as the cause of death.

"Pressures grow at the better schools. As a student service, Yale's mental hygiene clinic is staffed by 20 hard-pressed headshrinkers. The University of Wisconsin has 28. Harvard does mental overhauling in a building so large that it goes by the name of 'The Farnsworth Hilton,' after the doctor who runs it." (Jane Griffin with Daniel Chapman, "The Case for not Going to College," *Look*, Nov. 29, 1966.)

[2] In what I think is a highly perceptive article, John Finley Scott, of the University of Washington, ("Who Marries Whom and Why; Marriage is not a Personal Matter," *The New York Times Magazine*, October 30, 1966) points out that women gain higher status by marrying men who have higher status than themselves. It is the occupation, the

a good person is not sufficient, but it is important to marry into a family of some status and consequence; and the spouse should also be a graduate of a prestige college and working at some glamorous job, so that the combined parents are proud and all others feel outpaced. There is no end.[3]

Also there are sex roles set by our society—equally hard, equally difficult, equally overwhelming. It is expected of a man that he be tall, dark, and handsome; also, physically powerful so that with one blow he can avenge any insult to a woman. He should, like a troubadour of old, enchant women. When married he should play the role of a Don Juan to his wife, keep her perpetually entertained and above all happy; and of course, he should be a generous provider. When he buys his suburban home, as he should,

---

kind of work the husband does, that determines in a large measure the social position of the wife. Of course, a woman can achieve upward mobility by her own work, but it is much easier to obtain it by marriage. Since Jewish men do well in this area, more non-Jewish girls marry Jewish men. Catholic girls on the other hand marry more Protestant men because they either already have higher occupational status or give more promise of moving upward.

About upper class women, he writes: "A well-born woman, if she is to maintain through marriage the status conferred on her by her parents, must marry a man at least equally well-born—but for such men she faces a deadly competition from lower-status female rivals who also regard them as desirable husbands. As a result, low status men are more likely to remain bachelors, and high status women are more likely to remain spinsters. This is the 'Brahmin problem,' so named because it reached its most extreme form among the high castes of Hindu India (but it can be observed among Boston Brahmins as well)."

[3] At a university on Saturday night the women students were in great excitement and expectancy about a possible date. A Hindu woman student was aloof from all this tumult. She was asked by the other students whether she didn't miss the excitement of dating. "Heavens no," she said, "I would dread it—to have to worry whether I will or will not have a date and anxiously to wait for the telephone to ring! My marriage is arranged for me by my family. I don't have to be beautiful, popular or likeable."

he automatically takes on added tasks: he should after coming home at night from his city job help his wife, wash the dishes after supper, help take care of the children, see to the repair of his home. At the same time, he should be a leader of men—in the business world, in society, in the community. He should exemplify all virtues, but most important, he should in all ways be BIG, BIG, and EVEN BIGGER, SUCCESSFUL, SUCCESSFUL, and EVEN MORE MORE SUCCESSFUL.[4]

The role set for the woman is equally frightening. First of all, she should be very beautiful, with a beauty sufficient to inspire poetry and song. She should be smart, sophisticated, fashionable, chic, and withal, be a glamorous career girl. Naturally, she should have been graduated with honors from a prestige college. Her person should at all times be flawless, sanitized to the nth degree. Her home, equally sanitized, should reflect her exquisite taste. When she entertains, she should be a charming hostess, witty, understanding, captivating, so that her husband's business associates and friends are enchanted. As a couple, they both should be popular and sought after for all purposes. She should be a perfect mother, tender, maternal, gentle, know exactly what is the right and proper thing to do for her children under all circumstances. Although feminine, lacy, and frilly, she should be able to fight with the courage of a lion to protect her children from any

---

[4] The story is told of a high school student who applied for admission to a college. That evening his father asked him what he wrote on the application. When his son said that he did not indicate that he was a leader, his father was furious. "You schmo!" he shouted. "Have you no brains at all? Do you think you will ever be admitted to any college if you write so stupidly?" Shortly thereafter, the story goes, a reply came from the college stating that he was accepted. The letter said. "We have had applications for admission from 625 leaders and we are delighted to have one follower."

jeopardy. To her husband her role is equally complex. She should be siren, mistress, wife, mother, companion, lover. And above all she should have intuition. By that is meant, I suppose, she should know what is exactly the right thing to do, the perfect solution for all problems that may arise. If you heed at all television, cinema, popular periodicals, you will know that only woe and tragedy befall any mate who is indifferent, and even worse, goes counter to a woman's intuition. So I suppose by assigning to women this divine intuition, it has placed on her the burden of being all-knowing and wise.

Also from parents, so many of our children do not get unconditional acceptance. So many parents like their children—if. They would like them if they were changed, different; if they were smarter or if they were better behaved, or if, if, if. The offspring of these parents have trouble because they never have had the feeling of acceptance. These parents don't like these children; they would like them if they were like someone else. When you come down to the basic fundamental, the parent feels: "I don't like *this* child, this child before me." I am coming to believe that children brought up by parents who would like them "if" are never quite right. They grow up assuming that their parents are right and that they are wrong; that somehow or other they are at fault; and even worse, very frequently they feel they are stupid, inadequate, inferior. And even more unfortunately, it often happens that as they were done by so they do. Critical, demanding, unaccepting of themselves, they may become critical, demanding and unaccepting of others. Never having known full acceptance, they may never be able to give to others full acceptance.

We do not realize what a demanding culture is this in which we live. J. W. M. Whiting and I. L. Child compared the cultures of forty-seven societies studied by anthropologists as to the severity of parental demands placed on children. They concluded that there were only two more severe with children than our own middle class families.

Dr. Erik E. Erikson of Harvard University in his book *Childhood and Society* reports that native Indian mothers cannot understand why the whites are so cruel to children. Writes Dr. Erikson: "Whites, they thought, want to estrange their children from this world so as to make them pass through the next world with the utmost dispatch. 'They teach their children to cry!' was the indignant remark of an Indian woman when confronted with the sanitary separation of mother and child in the government hospital. . . . Since the earliest contacts between the two races the Indians have considered most repugnant the white habit of slapping or beating children into compliance. . . "[5]

Dr. Erickson recounts how an Indian child of three, sitting on a mother's lap and eating crackers, reached out imperiously for his mother's breast for a sip of her milk. If his own mother were not available, it would have been proper to reach out for the milk of another mother's breast, and it would have been given to him gladly if the mother had a surplus.[6] A white teacher tells of an Indian mother coming to school to nurse her eight-year-old son.[7] There is no schedule for weaning. When the child develops an interest in other foods, he abandons the breast. In toilet

[5] Erik H. Erickson, *Childhood and Society,* p. 107, W. W. Norton & Co.
[6] *Ibid,* p. 136.
[7] *Ibid,* p. 136.

training, too, there is the greatest latitude. A white Indian trader tells of five-year-old children excreting at whatever spot struck their fancy. These indulgent parents have faith in their child, that as he matures he will do what he has to do and what the tribe prescribes.

To the chagrin of their white teachers, these children avoid competitiveness; they avoid doing better than their classmates, for they do not want to shame others; and also they do not want to be shunned for unmannerly behavior.[8] What is admired by the Sioux Indian is generous sharing, not possessions. If luck befalls one—should he be the recipient of a relief check or acquire food on the basis of an old treaty—you will observe relatives from all over the prairie converging on the house, for it would be unthinkable not to share. Nothing make a Sioux Indian so proud as to offer his possessions to his guests at a feast in honor of a relative or friend. Children save up their meager pennies for the joy of giving them away at some ceremonial occasion.[9]

Dr. Erikson writes: "We found among the Sioux little evidence of individual conflict, inner tensions, or of what we call neurosis. . . . Only in a few 'white man's Indians,' usually successfully employed by the government, did we find neurotic tensions, expressed in compulsions, over-conscientiousness, and general rigidity."[10]

Margaret Mead, in *Coming of Age in Samoa*, reports on another culture where neurosis and psychosis are practically non-existent. In this island, the culture is

---

[8] *Ibid* p. 128–129.

[9] This holds true for the Eskimoes. Keeping possessions to oneself and not sharing is regarded as shameful and disreputable, and respectable Eskimoes would not be guilty of such an offense.

[10] *Ibid* pp. 135–136.

placid; here there is no rivalry and no striving for eminence and success. In this culture, the pressure is on conformity, on learning the ways of the people, and doing that which tradition expects of them. Any person who attempts to do things radically different or tries to improve on the accustomed ways is repressed; the person who wants to get ahead or to gain attention by any but the routine, traditional ways is regarded as pushing and aggressive. In this culture, the individual experiences a minimum of failure and frustration; and because of this, we find in this island an almost complete absence of delinquency, neurosis, and psychosis.

Unfortunately—and this is a great tragedy—the human being and the society in which he lives are so constituted that they come to believe that their customs, their traditions, their ways are obviously right and any deviation is obviously wrong. In some cultures, men barter goods for goods; we exchange goods for money. This foreign culture, we say, is primitive. In some cultures, promiscuity is permitted until marriage or till conception takes place. This we say, is immoral. In some cultures man works only to provide for his needs and then he stops all work until new material needs arise. We have created a culture where needs and wants are insatiable and never stop, and thus we keep on working piling up more and more possessions, in many instances much more than any individual could possibly need or use. We call individuals living in these other cultures lazy, good-for-nothings.

Such an attitude is as old as time. In fact, the word barbarian is a Greek word meaning foreigner, a non-Greek, an outsider. In ancient times, the Koreans put up a sign which read: "If you see a stranger, kill him." The

Chinese built a great wall to keep out the uncivilized pagan foreigners. Certain small, primitive tribes simply call themselves, "The Human Beings," "Men," and the member of any other tribe or anyone else is not a man; you have their permission to kill or do anything else you want with such other walking animals. We can say that our own traditions, customs, ways, and mores we come to regard with a reverence akin to holiness; and even to question these ways becomes sacrilegious and heresy. In many, many instances, society has forced the hemlock on a Socrates who had the impudence and the arrogance to question the divinity of these ways.

This is no place to argue the relative merits of different cultures. Sigmund Freud has maintained that suppression is the price of civilization, and our present civilization has brought us many magnificent things. We may suffer from emotional problems, but we live considerably longer than in most other cultures, and we live with considerable ease and luxury; and for the most part our people have an abundance of food and good shelter. We should remember that the two major problems in the United States at present are finding parking places for the automobiles that clog our cities and keeping our waistlines in reasonable proportions because of overeating. We are a society of many achievements, some indeed remarkable. In most other areas of the world, man's crucial problem is to find enough food so that he will not starve. Three-quarters of the human beings in this universe go to sleep at night hungry. So it is a matter of values, choosing what you think is important. But in *humane* values I believe we are paying a terrible price for the vast output of material available to us. Perhaps it may be better and wiser to have less material abundance and softer, kindlier, less competitive, and more loving and lovable people. At least it is something we ought to begin to think about.

I ask: Is our middle class culture geared to rearing good spouses? The solid middle class represent, I believe, the foundation and the strength of our society, but I fear that their very strength—their driving ambition, their desire to achieve and excel—may be doing irreparable damage to their offspring. I further ask: Is our competitive culture destroying our capacity for good, warm, loving relationships? Are our ambitions devouring us? Do parents cast their children into impossible roles so that these children are broken by parental demands, failures even before they start to live? Set almost from infancy in these roles, do they not act thereafter like automatons, machines, seeking to achieve what they themselves would never want and never seek? How many at the end of their life do not know who they are, what they are and what this life was all about. How tragic for the many who even when life is about over cannot find an intelligent answer!

I raise these questions because I have a great fear that our society as at present constituted is not a good breeding place for good husbands and wives. Our very culture destroys them for such roles; it stresses wrong and sick values. John Bowlby has told us how good, kind, humane beings are made. And he has told us what environmental forces create human beings who are hard, unloving, cruel. I have the fear that because of the obsessive need for success, material achievement, fame, middle class parents are doing terrible things to their children, blighting them for soft, loving, sympathetic relationships, the key to a good marriage and to the good human being.

In *Life Is With People,* there is this story:

According to the Talmud, a Roman matron once asked the rabbi, "In how many days did the Holy One, blessed be He, create the universe?"

"In six days," he answered.

"And what has He been doing since then, up to now?"

"He has been arranging marriages."

"Is that His occupation? I, too, could do it. I possess many male and female slaves, and in a very short while I can pair them together."

He said to her, "If it is a simple thing in your eyes, it is as difficult to the Holy One, blessed be He, as dividing the Red Sea."

He then took his departure.

What did she do? She summoned a thousand male slaves and a thousand female slaves, set them in rows, and announced who should marry whom. In a single night she arranged marriages for them all.

The next day they appeared before her, one with a cracked forehead, another with an eye knocked out, and another with a broken leg.

She asked them, "What is the matter with you?"

One female said, "I don't want him."

Another male said, "I don't want her."

She forthwith sent for the rabbi and said to him. "There is no God like your God, and your Torah is true. . ."[11]

There is no royal road to a good marriage. Even at best, it requires a person of some maturity who can cope with frustrations and disappointments, the vicissitudes that enter into any relationship, especially one as complex, neurotic, demanding, and close as in a marriage.

Yes, finding a good spouse is difficult indeed!

---

[11] Mark Zborowski and Elizabeth Herzog, *Life is With People,* p. 269.

31

HOLLYWOOD AND LOVE

PERHAPS IN NO AREA OF LIVING DO SUCH MORONIC AND IM-
becilic notions prevail as about courtship and marriage.
In popular song, to be kissed by one's beloved is equival-
ent to being in ecstasy; to be denied a kiss is to be cast
into a black despair, everlasting. According to the modern
popular troubadour, all one needs for eternal happiness is
to have the right boy or girl to love. A cottage and you
and for what more can one ask and what more is needed?
The kiss of the beloved is sufficient to transport one, to
make one afire with a divine joy. But being disappointed
in love, rejected by the beloved, is catastrophic. The musical wailing of the singer is reminiscent of a person suffering from an incurable disease, and at times even worse,
like one whose life had ceased—forevermore.

Over the radio and television, in story and folklore, in
fiction and in the cinema, our people are bombarded with
a plethora of Cinderella tales, with infantile relationships
that befuddle and debase the thinking of our people, so
that they cannot gain insight into the real meaning and
purpose of marriage; so that they come to their own marriages with lies, with impossible notions, with unrealizable
dreams and fantasies.

In these media, marriage is depicted in the glow of a full moon, pink lights, music, Coney Island, New Orleans Mardi Gras, gondolas, a chimerical never-never-land. Here you will not find any inkling of the ordinary workaday world. In this imaginary world, all needs and all desires center around love and more love. Love is the elixir. All one's problems can be solved by merely finding the right marital partner. Once this partner is found, life thereafter is an eternal holiday.

Since the cinema has been most influential in furthering these marital stereotypes; since the Hollywood portrayal of courtship and marriage is not only typical but also pervasive, it should be discussed. It can be said from the outset that Hollywood emphasizes cheap, physical sexual contacts. Its heroes and heroines kiss ad nauseam, but in this repeated and repeated pressure of lips, there is little, if any, real spiritual exaltation, real affection, nothing of the wonder and awe and the mystery and the beauty of a man and a woman in love; nothing of the trials and the tribulations of two people forging a life together, or rearing a family, of creating a home, of integrating the home into community living, so that it becomes the fulcrum for growth and richness of living—social, moral, communal.

In the Hollywood movie, the physical appearance of the person is all-important. The hero and the heroine have to be good-looking, and the villain evil-looking. It is rare, almost inconceivable, for a sympathetic character to be misshapen, paunchy, bony—in short physically ugly. This notion is really nonsense and it is, I believe, responsible for a great deal of mischief. It distorts an intelligent concept of what is good and worthwhile in man. Ugly, misshapen persons may be good and kind and capable of the warmest, deepest, self-sacrificing relationships. What matters is the character of the person. This has nothing to do with the physical attributes of a person. There are ugly-looking persons—yes, horribly ugly-looking persons—who are wise and good and noble. And there are good-looking persons who are greedy, selfish, mean, contemptible. I believe it is nothing short of tragic that our popular media convey the impression that physical beauty is in any way connected with character. What is crucial in the person is to be beautiful, not outside, but inside.[1]

Its concept of courtship is plain drivel in terms of an intelligent approach to the subject. A boy meets a girl on a bus. The girl has a cute dimple, played up in crescendo fashion by the camera. The boy has a wavy lock of hair, played up in crescendo fashion by the camera. If it is combined with a pleasant smile and with romantic music,

---

[1] Foreign movies do considerably better in this regard. Producers are less apt to confuse physical good looks with virtue. Once upon a time foreign pictures depicted love and marriage—at least the foreign imports that came to America—in a more mature way. In them there was a more honest and truthful presentation of what love is and means and what it can be. In them there was less physical sex and more of an attempt to probe the import of the relationship. Physically, the characters were not Hollywood replicas; they could be old or crochety or ugly or short or tall. What went on between the hero and the heroine, how one affected another, what one meant to the other, how one enriched or demeaned the life of the other—that was the main theme of the plot. The relationships depicted were considerably more mature and honest than in Hollywood films.

But that was once upon a time. Although the relationships probed are still more mature than in Hollywood productions, nearly all the foreign films I have seen of late require an obligatory sex scene where intercourse take place—vividly portrayed. Those deep feelings prompted by love seem to have been blunted and replaced by a passing, physical encounter. I myself feel that this is a most unfortunate turn of events. I am sure that even those film producers concerned only with monetary profit would do better, they would make more money, if they dealt with the mature love of a man and a woman, with all its infinite mystery and wonder. How much more interesting it would be, how much more beautiful, than a meaningless, passing physical encounter!

you may be sure that you have hit paydirt, for that to Hollywood is a sufficient base on which to arrange a successful marriage. Or the romance may take another track. Boy meets girl unconventionally. Boy takes girl to a Greenwich Village restaurant. Our hero knows the proprietor and solicits his aid in the preparation of his special favorite dishes. The dishes are prepared and served with delicacy and flourish. Music plays and the couple look at each other wistfully. Later they may indulge in a little whimsey; throwing a nickel to a squirrel in a park, and, still later, riding home that night in a hansom. By now, it is dawn, and they encounter the milkman, and all three march arm and arm down the street. Rest assured that Hollywood will consummate that marriage, no matter what the obstacles or the false starts; that marriage in Hollywood is impregnable. What a woefully inadequate and asinine base for marriage—a dimple, a shapely ankle, an adolescent, boyish smile, rumpled hair, a bus ride, acquaintance with a restaurant owner; adolescent escapades, such as eating hamburgers in a diner at four in the morning, or making friends with a milkman. Here we find no effort made to appraise a character honestly and intelligently, in terms of his decency, generosity, kindliness; his social and emotional maturity. Here we find no attempt made to come to grips with the wide gamut of marital problems—financial, social, vocational, familial. Here we find none of the storm and stress that inevitably result when two people try to merge their lives.

If Hollywood motion pictures were regarded as a fantastic make-believe world, a fairy tale to escape reality, its harm would not be so damaging. Unfortunately, Hollywood's approach to marriage is widely accepted as truth and fact, and it is reechoed, reaffirmed and reasserted in popular song, in fiction, in radio, in television, in newspapers, in the folklore of large segments of our population. The women in American motion pictures are something apart, expensive functioning creatures that must be maintained in idleness, in luxury and comfort. Occasionally, a heroine is a salesgirl, working in a department store. But you will not find her living in a shabby back hall bedroom or wearing the inexpensive clothes that a girl in her position can afford. At night, while keeping her tryst with her hero, you will see her in glamorous evening clothes, surrounded by the appurtenances of wealth. If a woman allows the wear and tear of raising a family and sharing a husband's problems to make wrinkles in her face, or to compel her to wear simple household clothes, or to find pleasure in doing household tasks, Hollywood will consider her as a hopeless failure. To Hollywood, she is no longer of any interest or moment and can only serve as a prop from which to further the action of the more important and exciting characters in the story.

Seldom will you find a woman depicted as a mature contributing adult, working hard and sharing in common sacrifices. Although physically mature (especially sexually), these women have all the attributes of children. They have never grown up, psychologically or emotionally. This infantile behavior becomes especially noticeable when the hero is being attacked by the villain. Any mature person under such circumstances would pick up a chair or any heavy object and clout the villain on the head, as he richly deserves. Not the Hollywood heroine. Her role is to whimper like a child. At times, the heroine is confronted with a real marital dilemma. Her suitor has a slight blemish. He may be an alcoholic or a gambler or a thief or a shiftless, irresponsible good-for-nothing. Any-

one who has the slightest knowledge of marriage knows
that such people make poor marital risks. They are emotionally disturbed people, often neurotics with deep-seated
difficulties.

In the movies, the situation presents no real problem,
at least, not one that cannot be solved. The thief is saved
for conventional society by rescuing a child at great risk
from a burning building; whereupon, his whole past is
automatically forgiven; and it is inferred that thereby he
has overcome his anti-social tendencies. One bright day
the alcoholic, with a brave flourish of music, passes by
his favorite saloon and every good movie habituee knows
that another wayfarer has been saved for the good life and
that the marriage may now be consummated with success.
The shiftless shirker finally accepts a job offered him by
his father. A close-up of our hero reveals a clenched fist
and a determined look and these are sure signs that henceforth there will be no backsliding.

What poppycock and nonsense! What tragic notions
are spread by such fabrications and dishonesties!

In a special dispatch from Rome, the *New York Times*
reported on an address by Clark W. Blackburn of the
Family Service Association. Parts of the dispatch follow:

Teen-age marriages in the United States, contracted
under the romantic-erotic stimuli of movies, television and
advertising, are foundering in increasing numbers on dirty
dishes in the sink and end-of-the-month bills. . . .

The epidemic of under-age marriages in the United
States, he said, has produced such phenomena as the
drawing up by high school principals of codes for married
students—including school-leaving schedules for pregnant

teen-age wives—and 70,000 divorces or separations among such couples in 1961.

Between 1951 and 1960, he reported, marriages by American girls under 20 years of age rose from 21 to 30 per cent. This, he said, was almost twice the rate in France, for example, five times that in Ireland or Germany.

"An essential factor (in teen-age marriage problems) is the romantic idea of matrimony that appears dominant in America today," Mr. Blackburn said. "They marry for love, often without understanding the real meaning of love. The themes that appear in the magazines, the movies, on television, in advertising do not represent love but rather eroticism, whether presented openly or covertly."

This "ideal" of marriage obscures the material difficulties of money, children and the necessity for personal maturity, he said, producing profound discontent among young couples.

"We have the duty as professions, to improve the preparation of the young so that they approach the realities of matrimony better prepared," Mr. Blackburn said.[2]

How sad!

---

[2] Robert C. Coty, "Experts Told to Prepare Teen-Agers for Marriage," *New York Times*, July 7, 1965. Report of an address by Clark W. Blackburn before The International Union of Family Organizations.

32

GIFTS IN MARRIAGE

Insist on yourself; never imitate. Your own gift you can present every moment with the cumulative force of a whole life's cultivation; but of the adopted talent of another you have only an extemporaneous half possession.

RALPH WALDO EMERSON

I ENCOUNTERED THIS AD IN THE *New York Times* OF A FIFTH Avenue jeweler: "Guaranteed to surprise her. . . . Kashmir sapphire and diamond pin, may also be worn as a pendant. One-hundred and twenty-two thousand dollars."

In our culture when we think of gifts to women, the feeling is that they ought to be expensive and because of their costliness, the lady fair should become meltingly oozy; and this should bring out all her affection, all her love; and if the cost is truly overwhelming, then her love should match the cost and also be overwhelming.

I realize that this is a "thing" society, a society that finds respect and repute by what Veblen calls "conspicuous consumption." Ah, for a mink coat, a Cadillac, diamonds, a manorial house, big and resplendent! Oh, these beautiful "things!" Such giving of things reminds me of Goethe who spoke of the person who "had every other thing and wanted love."

I believe that the giving of things to overwhelm has nothing to do with marriage. They are extraneous to it. If one partner judges a token of regard and affection by the monetary price of the thing, then I would suspect that partner; the thought would occur to me that the partner is exploiting the other, using the other. I know of a wife who is the possessor of three mink coats. They were obtained in this way: one was given to her by her husband after the death of her child during birth, the second when she caught her husband in adultery, the third when she recovered from an operation. I know of instances where women allowed their husbands to have sex with them on payment. Their argument was that if the husband went to a prostitute, there would be a cost; and certainly when provided by a woman of virtue, the cost ought to be considerably higher. For most persons, this attitude is repugnant; it is outside the conventions. Gifts—I mean these costly, overwhelming gifts—represent for me for the most part an ugly approach to a relationship. Some of them are not even gifts; they smack of payment in kind, and even worse, bribes. "Rich gifts wax poor, when givers prove unkind," said Shakespeare.

But gifts do have a place in a marital relationship—when they show regard, concern, affection, understanding. Especially understanding. It is not easy to give the right gift; it is indeed difficult. The right gift depends on understanding the person, the kind of person he is, what he appreciates, what he values, what he needs, and what he will not buy for himself.[1] Such a gift may not involve money at all; or if money is involved, a very inconsequential amount. But always a gift involves understanding. When a man or woman provides a gift to a spouse and it isn't used or appreciated, it seems to me that the fault lies not with the recipient but the giver who knew so little of the person. Only an intimate knowledge of the person can make possible the perfect gift. Most gifts are waste because they are given by persons who do not really know, deeply know, the person to whom they are making the gift.

I know that in a relationship between a man and a woman, there is strongly rooted in our culture the notion that the man gives the woman gifts. So strong is this feeling that I find it hard to write sentences where this arrangement does not hold. Quite rightly Emerson said. "The gift, to be true, must be the flowing of the giver unto me, corresponding to my flowing unto him." Each in a marriage ought to give to the other, in every way, with their whole being, fully, every part of him involved; and each should take delight in the delight of the other. I say down with expensive gifts! Long life to thoughtful gifts that have no relationship with money but have a great deal of meaning in sensitive knowledge of the mar-

---

[1] A famed tycoon, whose philanthropies ran into the millions, bathed in the old bathtub of his mansion. He detested the bathtub and liked a shower but he was reluctant to make the expenditure for the alteration. The wife of a Harvard University professor, who occupied the professorial seat endowed by this philanthropist, knew of his dislike and threatened to install a shower herself if he didn't; and then he did. How often does a person refrain from buying what he really wants and yet unhesitatingly makes greater expenditures for what he doesn't need or want nearly so much. It takes an understanding friend to know what these things are and give them to him as a gift.

ital partner, for such can touch a person to the quick. I believe strongly in little gifts given many times a day. "Married people can give to each other a thousand times a day without talking," says a proverb.

I shall set down below what I have in mind. They are only suggestive. Each marital pair, I know, find their own unique gifts, dependent on the ingenuity of the pair, their creativeness. What I have set down are humdrum things, nothing breathtaking, nothing overwhelming, and for you who read this perhaps they may sound silly. But for the pair involved these simple things engender vast good feeling for they know the act represents a wish to please, or to show concern, or affection, or regard.

. . . . .

The husband is hard-working and his work makes him tense. There is a favorite program of his which seems to relax him. When he comes home at night, he can be certain that his wife will have his meal prepared, and she will fight savagely to make sure that he is undisturbed while he listens to the program.

The wife is alert to the telephone. Her husband receives many telephone calls, and when she thinks he has had more than his share, she is there to intercept them and save her husband, especially when she knows they might be unpleasant calls.

Knowing how his wife appreciates a day in town, the husband at odd intervals takes off an afternoon from work and then they make a day of it—eating out, going to the theatre or a museum, or doing whatever the mood suggests.

One single American beauty rose, and what it has meant to this couple! In their courting days, they had had a quarrel, and he came to her home one day holding before her a flower. "This is the sign of my surrender," he said. And the rose still plays this function in their marriage and they still make a great fuss about what to someone else may be nothing. "You don't know how queasy I get inside when John holds up that lovely red rose," the wife said to me. "All my anger leaves me and I'm ready to eat him up."

How many are the gifts, infinite in variety, one can give another: a nod of encouragement to a nervous spouse at a party; buying little knicknacks that one knows the other wants and would not buy for herself; reframing an old picture which has special meaning for the spouse or the marriage; the wife changing a typewriter ribbon for the husband who is a writer; finding a story, a poem, a piece of gossip to share; going for a walk in the park, taking a ferry ride, going picnicking, etc., etc. No one thing especially momentous in itself but how heartwarming in a relationship.

Here are two instances which show the concern for the other which I think is valuable in a marriage: one involved several electric bulbs and the other several safety pins.

The husband was an omnivorous reader and they had planned to stay at a resort hotel for a number of days. As so often happens, the illumination of their room was abominable. His wife knew of her husband's discomfort and was upset. All her efforts with the management did not succeed in changing the situation. An idea occurred to her during the night and the next morning she bought several bright electric bulbs which she replaced for the dingy ones. Several days of misery for her husband became several days of delight.

Safety pins: You wouldn't think that such bitsy things, negligible in cost, could mean so much. The couple travel a great deal and the husband cannot stand the woolen blanket next to his skin. When the wool touches his skin, the husband fidgets about and cannot sleep. Knowing of her husband's discomfort, the wife makes sure to carry safety pins with her. As soon as they check into the room, the wife takes a margin of linen from under the blanket and arranges a generous overlap over the blanket and then securely fastens the overlap with safety pins.

I suppose the act itself—what the husband avoided in discomfort and what the wife experienced in added pleasure—made each of them feel good, but I am pretty sure that in both instances there was more involved: the knowledge that in their wives they had sympathetic, concerned persons to whom their comfort meant a great deal. The two foregoing incidents show feeling for, awareness of, the sense of vicarious suffering with, being in and understanding the world of the other. A better gift than that bauble—selling for $122,000—which overwhelms! The money gift shows enormous wealth and extravagant use of money. There is nothing against buying a Cadillac or even a Rolls Royce, and I suppose it means something —and indeed it is overwhelming—to think that anyone is willing to spend all that money for you.

A gift, as I view it, need not be a material thing at all; it may be a touch of the hand, a loving glance, an appreciative word. These tokens of affection touch the deepest self in man and it is these moments that stay with him and give him a lasting sense of gratitude and joy.

Sometimes a gift may involve money. It may be a trip to Europe that both had planned, wanted and saved for; a mink coat that represents a kind of achievement privately shared by both; and there may be even a place for a Cadillac. But a good gift should not represent penance but sensitive thoughfulness. I know that some marital pairs celebrate certain occasions, birthdays, wedding anniversaries, etc. For me, they have in them a sense of duty. Said J. R. Lowell:

> He gives only the worthless gold
> Who gives from a sense of duty.

In a good marriage, gifts are given to each other every moment of the day, never-ending, a constant stream of them, flowing like an open faucet, each delighting the other; for in their love and understanding of each other, they have acquired the capacity to be so sensitive to the other that they know what deeply pleases the other. And they are so concerned about the other that they want above all else to please, and by pleasing they are doubly pleased—pleased that their beloved is pleased, and pleased that they are able to give their beloved pleasure.

But the greatest gift of all is to make your beloved feel good and noble and beautiful. Wisely, William Congreve said: "Beauty is the lover's gift."

33

WINSTON'S CLEMENTINE

COUPLES WHO CONSULT THERAPISTS COME WITH BAD MAR-
riages; there would be no sense otherwise; and hence, in
this book flaws and faults in marital relationships are cited.
I should not want these marriages to be regarded as typical My hope is that from a study of the irritants in mar-
miages, what makes marriages dull or imperfect or bad,
may come insights and understandings which will make
it possible to create better, more satisfying, more fulfilling
marriages.

There is one marriage, however, that I should like to
cite which seems to carry out many of the precepts of
what comprises a good marriage. It concerns the marriage
of Winston Churchill, who said of it: "I married and lived
happily ever afterwards." I never had the good fortune
to know this remarkable man, although much would I
have given for the privilege. Through the modern miracle
of television and the cinema, it was given to us to acquire
in a very slight, in a very faint way, some awareness of
this mighty person.

I should confess that Churchill, this man who will in-
trigue man's mind for centuries, has been a man of enor-

mous interest for me. When I watched him on television or in the cinema, which I did whenever possible, what struck me was Clementine, his wife, who was nearly always by his side. While Sir Winston addressed distinguished audiences, accepted high honors, met great personages, mixed with the populace, nearly always she was there—by his side—with her eyes only for him, her whole person, her whole concern concentrated on him; all the others seemed to matter little, so great was her pride and concern.

Particularly do I remember the television broadcast at Westminister, Missouri, at Fulton College, where he first used that famed phrase, "the iron curtain," referring to the Russian government and its satellites. While the applause from the audience was still going full blast, Churchill went over to his wife who was seated in the front row with eyes riveted on him, uplifted to him, her pride and concern patently visible. If my memory serves me, even before the applause had died down, he turned away from the audience and went up to his wife and tenderly kissed her. As I saw this scene enacted, I remember thinking: "Here is the very thing that I think is good in a marriage, the sense of closeness, affection, admiration—all the healthy, beautiful attributes that bodes such good for both the giver and the taker. How lucky is he who has such a marital partner and has the opportunity of building a life with such a one!"

This prompted me to dip into the book *My Darling Clementine*, by Jack Fishman[1] and there I found ample evidence to corroborate my hunch. It is true that Mrs. Churchill was by his side—always there while he con-

---

[1] Jack Fishman, *My Darling Clementine*, David McKay Co., 1963.

ducted political campaigns, made important addresses, met important personages, always there, giving him courage, support, admiration. She protected him from annoyances, helped him entertain, saw that he had and protected him while he was taking his afternoon nap which he relished, attended to his papers and his books; and in all ways she was sensitive to him, his needs and his wants, and was there by his side at pivotal moments. She arranged her schedule to suit his needs, not her own. In return she had an adoring husband. He described her as "my devoted aide." "I could never have succeeded without her." "My marriage was the most fortunate and joyous event which happened to me in the whole of my life, for what can be more glorious than to be united in one's walk through life with a being incapable of an ignoble thought." As she made a slave of herself to him, he made a slave of himself to her.

"Whenever he made an important speech in Parliament, as he rose to speak, he never failed to look to the gallery where Clementine sat, and she would acknowledge his gaze with a little encouraging wave," writes Jack Fishman.[2] "Then, when he had finished and before resuming his seat, he would look again to her for the smile of approval. That is the way it had always been, and always will be as long as the M. P. for Woodford serves his country." Concerning the closeness of the two, Colonel Barlow Wheeler said: "I have noticed time and time again at social gatherings that if he speaks she is looking at him, taking in every word he is saying. And when she speaks, he is looking at her and taking in every word. They might almost be a young, newly-married couple, completely absorbed in each other."[3]

[2] *Ibid*, p. 323.
[3] *Ibid*, p. 353.

She protected him in all ways. When she entertained, and she did frequently with groups of seventy and eighty, she saw that her husband was not monopolized or held up by bores. In fact, she perfected a method by which she would hurry large groups past Winston and then allow him to go off by himself, to do what he liked. She would take over for him. Before any address, she saw that none disturbed him, for she knew that he wanted the time for quiet reflection. In all ways, she served him, intelligently, sensitively, wisely.

She knew when to be forceful. Winston could not abide fools easily, and he had a protective device, his poor hearing. Once seated next to a person of great importance, Winston chose to be particularly difficult, and ignored his table companion. Mrs. Churchill, with her eagle eyes, observed this, and told him forcefully to get his hearing aid and use it. He said that he didn't need a hearing aid; and that he could hear perfectly. "Then hear me," she said. Whereupon she lambasted him for not being more attentive to his important table companion.

She was, however, protective when a bore cornered him in the quiet seclusion he sought; and she would lead the intruder off to see the goldfish or the paintings or anything.

I cannot refrain from recounting another incident which indicates how solicitous and thoughtful she was of her husband. After winning a war for Great Britain, he was repudiated at the elections that followed the conclusion. Winston Churchill was making his comeback; and he was engaged in a vigorous campaign. Now an old man, he was in the thick of the difficult and enervating process of electioneering. His wife, Clementine was by his side, campaigning with him. Let Mrs. Doris Moss continue: "They had been on a non-stop tour of committee rooms in the

constituency and our place was the last stop. When they
came into the room, he looked exhausted—he wasn't a
young man then, and although he has remarkable powers
of relaxation, he takes so much out of himself. As soon
as they walked in, Mrs. Chlurchill came over to us and
said, 'You know, Winston's tired. Do you think he could
have a real rest for a few minutes?'

"She made him comfortable in a large chair; he closed
his eyes, and was asleep in a few minutes—being able to
go off like that is a gift he had. She went on chatting with
us, keeping everything around her going in the extra-
ordinary way she does while, at the same time, diverting
attention from him awhile.

"After about 10 minutes she went over to him, and it
was just like a mother waking a baby. She roused him
gently and said softly—'Winston—time to go now.' He
opened his eyes, and the smile that passed between them
was something to see."[4]

Is it surprising that about her, Winston said: "She has
been the companion and prop of all my life in so many ups
and downs and stresses, long and hard"?[5] And that he
turned to her "in moments of world tragedy, and in personal political defeat, he had literally run to his Clemmie,
calling for her, seeking solace in her smile, and in her
words."[6]

On the occasion of their golden wedding anniversary
the *Sunday Times* said: "It has cynically been said that
happy marriages are not news; it is those who have failed
that make the headlines but here, to confound the cynics,
is a marriage the success of which has never been in doubt

---

4 *Ibid.* pp. 366–367.
5 *Ibid.* p. 363.
6 *Ibid.* p. 368.

which has always been news; for all the civilized world has known that 50 long years besides the fighting, turbulent personality that has evolved into the much-loved world figure of today has been the serene and strengthening companionship of his wife, comforting and supporting him in good days and bad.[7]

"It is a tremendous tribute to Lady Churchill that, never seeking the limelight of public life herself, though always engaged in good works, she should have impressed herself on the public mind by her perfect share in one of the most felicitious partnerships of our time."

The book *My Darling Clementine* is a mine of what is desirable in a marriage; how a wife can give support and comfort to her husband; what it means to be sensitive and generous and kind; how pivotal two persons can come to be to each other; what a good life this can make for the two, as they become intertwined, each giving the other the strength to grow and to find fulfillment.

---

[7] Apparently, David Ben-Gurion, for many years the Israeli Prime Minister, was lucky enough to have the same kind of wife. In an obituary in the New York Times,[1] it tells how Mrs. Paula Ben-Gurion, when she would be congratulated by her old friends on marrying a prime minister, answered: "A Prime Minister's wife? That's nothing. Being Ben-Gurion's wife, that's important. Ben-Gurion was a great man when I married him." If she were entertained and she thought a cake served to her would please her husband, she would say: "Ben-Gurion would like that. Have one baked for me to take to him." When he was ill, she would invade the Knesset (the Israeli Parliament) against protocol to bring him whatever she thought might help him to overcome some indisposition. (She was trained and worked as a nurse in America.) Also against protocol, she would hide in the recesses of the Knesset to glower at opponents of her husband. Eventually, she was assigned a place behind Knesset curtains so that she could follow the proceedings. It is this involvement, concern and regard that make for a good marriage.[1]

[1] Paula Ben-Gurion Dead at 76; Wife of Israel's Former Leader, N. Y. Times, January 29, 1968.

34

MARRIAGE, GROWTH AND CREATIVITY

THERE IS NO FINALITY TO MARRIAGE. IF IT IS A GOOD MAR-
riage, in it there is a constant ferment, a constant growing,
an ever-expanding creativity. Walter Lippmann in his
book *A Preface to Morals* said: "Lovers who have nothing
to do but love each other are not really to be envied; love
and nothing else very soon is nothing else. The emotion
of love, in spite of the romantics, is not self-sustaining; it
endures only when the lovers love many things together,
and not merely each other. It is this understanding that
love cannot be isolated from the business of living which
is the enduring wisdom of the institution of marriage."[1]

How much superior is this concept of marriage to the
folklore of eternal love, namely, once a man or woman
has found a good spouse, all thereafter is eternal bliss and
divine contentment. "It does not occur to anyone," said
Rainer Maria Rilke, "to expect a single person to be 'happy'
—but if he marries, people are much surprised if he isn't."

Marriage doesn't do anything but bring two people together; it is what they do with the marriage that matters.
Certainly marriage cannot make anyone happy; it can only

---

[1] Walter Lippman, *A Preface to Morals,* New York: The MacMillan Co.,
1967.

create a relationship that has the potential to promote and facilitate the growth of the person, and in the growing and in the unfolding of the person lies happiness.

When past seventy, Bernard Shaw was asked what constitutes happiness. He said in effect that he didn't know; that he had been so busy working that he did not have time for such nonsense. Happiness, he said, was not something that one sought like a lost cuff link, for that was the best way to miss it. "The secret of being miserable is to have leisure to bother about whether you are happy or not," wrote Shaw. "The cure for it is occupation, because occupation means pre-occupation, and the preoccupied person is neither happy nor unhappy, but simply active and alive, which is pleasanter than any happiness until you are tired of it. That is why it is necessary to happiness that one should be tired. Music after dinner is pleasant, music before breakfast is so unpleasant as to be clearly unnatural. To people who are not overworked holidays are a nuisance. To people who are, and can afford them, they are a troublesome necessity. A perpetual holiday is a good working definition of hell."[2]

When Vincent Van Gogh was confined in a mental institution, the doctors were loath to encourage him to seek solace in his paintings; they thought the excitement of working would retard his recovery. But he had better insight about his needs than his doctors. "Dr. Peyron," he said, "my work is necessary for me to recover. If you make me sit around in idleness like those madmen, I shall become one of them."[3] As soon as Van Gogh began to work, his improvement was marked and rapid.

---

[2] Hesketh Pearson, *G.B.S.: A Full Length Portrait*, pp. 112–113, New York: Garden City Publishing Co., 1946.
[3] Irving Stone, *Lust for Life*, p. 433, N. Y.: Pocket Books, 1946.

What appeals to me is the thought expressed by Antoine de Saint-Exupery: "Love does not consist in gazing at each other but in looking outward toward the same direction."

Each of us is an unique being, never duplicated before, never to be again. Said Martin Buber:

"Every person born into this world represents something new, something that never existed before, something original and unique. It is the duty of every person to know . . . that there has never been anyone like him in the world, for if there had been someone like him, there would have been no need for him to be in the world. Every single man is a new thing in the world and is called upon to fulfill his particularity in this world."[4]

Each man has to actualize his potential, to become what he was made to become. Each man has to form his person, create his being. No one can live a meaningless life. Each of us must have a bright beckoning beacon, a dream, a lovely bell that tinkles for him in the distance. As his main and primary task, each is mandated to form his person, to carve out a meaningful life for himself. Each is mandated so to do on penalty of finding his days long and weary and tedious, and his life empty and meaningless and nothing. In life below man, each creature evolves essentially according to a pre-set plan, and his movements and behavior are essentially fixed by what can be described mostly by instinct; there is little leeway and freedom. A bird raised by another species will build his nest, which it has never seen, and sing the song, which it has never heard, similar to that of his own species. His freedom of action and power of thought is small indeed. But man has

---

[4] M. Buber, *Hasidism and Modern Man*, p. 136 Translated and edited by M. Friedman: New York, Horizon Press, 1958.

enormous freedom—of thinking, of action, of behavior. There appears to be no limit to his potential. When he is born, he is mostly head, larger in proportion to that of any other living organism. Man has to create a life for himself; he cannot live by instinct. His infancy is so prolonged that we do not know at what point he is child and at what point he is man. This plasticity allows man his long infantile state and gives him his vast learning potential. His ability to learn means the capacity to change and alter himself and his environment and this gives him boundless power. Man is now traversing outer space. What new wondrous things will he do tomorrow? Because man has to form his being, to create himself, a brand, new unique self for each person, because he cannot, like other life in the universe, operate mostly by instinct, he is confronted by crucial tasks, frightening in their import. The stakes are high: life itself. "Man's unhappiness," said Carlyle, "comes out of his Greatness; it is because there is an Infinite in him, which with all his cunning he cannot bring under the Finite." This is his greatness and his tragedy. The wonder of man is his infinitude and his glory that he can strive. The ideal human life, wrote George Santayana, is an "evolution of a given seed toward its perfect manifestation."

Wrote the poet W. H. Auden:

> God may reduce you
> on Judgment Day
>   to tears of shame,
> reciting by heart
>   the poems you would
> have written, had
>   your life been good.

Said Thomas Wolfe: "If a man has a talent and cannot use it he has failed. If he has a talent and uses only half of it, he has partly failed. If he has a talent and learns somehow to use the whole of it, he has gloriously succeeded and won a satisfaction and a triumph few men ever know."

For this kind of life there can be no completion, no end, only growth and more growth, never ending. Growth should lead to further growth. "Man is never complete; his existence lies in becoming," wrote Van Herder. Harvey Cushing, the famed brain surgeon said: "The only way to endure life is to have a task to complete." The late psychiatrist, Dr. William C. Menninger, said that the way to improve the state of one's mind is: "Find a mission in life and take it seriously."

I have had patients who feared the day; it hung too heavy on them and it was too long to endure. They counted the slowly passing minutes and the slower torturesome hours; they could not fill the void of an unending day. Some of them lay in bed till four or five in the afternoon. They would explain: "I have nothing to get up for." Others said: "The day is too frightening for me." It is mandated for each of us to create a life for oneself. If one doesn't, then one is doomed to suffer long, long stretches of suffocating boredom and nothingness. "Imagine yourself alone in the midst of nothingness," suggested A. S. Eddington, "and then tell me how large you are."

"In this world," said Oscar Wilde, "there are only two tragedies. One is not getting what one wants, and the other is getting it. The last is much the worse: the last is the real tragedy." John Dewey said: "If it is better to travel than to arrive, it is because traveling is a constant arriving, while arrival that precludes traveling is most easily attained by going to sleep and dying."

Says Frankl: "Everyone has his own specific vocation or mission in life; everyone must carry out a concrete assignment that demands fulfillment. Therein he cannot be replaced nor can his life be repeated. Thus, everyone's task is as unique as is his specific opportunity to implement it. As each situation in life represents a challenge to man and presents a problem to him to solve, the question of the meaning of life may actually be reversed. Ultimately, man should not ask what the meaning of his life is, but rather must recognize that it is *he* who is asked. In a word, each man is questioned by life; and he can only answer to life by *answering for* his own life; to life he can only respond by being responsible."[5]

Even if theoretically the two in the marriage were perfect and right and complete, what would be there to hope for, to strive for, to fantasize about and dream about? What would one say to the other? What a horribly dull union! I like better Goethe's concept of *der strebende mensch,* the striving man. It is the growing that gives interest and zest to life; and this is never-ending; and it goes on, if life proceeds well, until death. I once asked William Heard Kilpatrick, the educatonal philosopher: "If you were to die tomorrow, what would you do?" He said: "If I were to die tomorrow, I would try to do a little better what I did yesterday." The good life represents it seems to me, this constant striving, this constant growing. Perfection is not for man. Man is fallible, mortal and weak; God is said to be perfect, infallible and immortal. Anyone who attempts to be God is in a bad way,

5 Viktor E. Frankl, *Man's Search for Meaning,* p. 172, N. Y. Washington Square Press.

and his life would be hard and impossible and very, very sick.

To become what one was meant to is a solemn task that requires all the courage that man possesses. In our alienated society, where man is so apart from his fellows, in a society as complex as ours, man is threatened by non-being, literally he is threatened by the danger of becoming a nothing. When through fear, through lack of courage, the person adopts defenses, subterfuges, avoidances, deep down he knows it and he experiences a sense of emptiness and nothingness. And this sense of emptiness and nothingness and meaninglessness leads to anxiety and to guilt—guilt that this, one's life, one's very being, is passing away, unfulfilled, wasted, in nothingness.

"Man," says Paul Tillich, "literally is required to answer, if he is asked, what he has made of himself. He who asks him is his judge, namely he himself, who, at the same time, stands against him. The situation produces the anxiety which, in relative terms, is the anxiety of guilt; in absolute terms, the anxiety of self-rejection or condemnation . . . the anxiety of guilt lies in the background and breaks again and again into the open, producing the extreme situation of moral despair."[6]

Fortunately, there is evidence to indicate that a person gravitates to health and to meaning if at all possible. In this connection, Kurt Goldstein writes:

"We can say an organism is governed by the tendency to actualize, as much as possible, its individual capacities, its 'nature' in the world. . . . This tendency to actualize its nature, to actualize 'itself,' is the basic drive, the only drive

---

[6] Paul Tillich, *The Courage to Be*, pp. 51–53, New Haven, Yale University Press, 1952.

by which the life of the organism is determined. Normal
behavior corresponds to a continual change in tension, of
such a kind that over and over again that state of tension
is reached which enables and impels the organism to
actualize itself in further activities, according to its
nature."[7]

Said Nietzche: "He who has a WHY to live for can sur-
mount any how."

Since I regard marriage as a relationship where each
gives to the other, supporting the other, this struggle for
each to live a rich, creative life becomes the center of the
marriage. I am convinced that there is nothing like another person to give one courage and strength to persevere
and to be. Nothing has the like capacity to reach a person
in his inmost, central self as another human being. We
know human beings who have made us feel small, weak,
inadequate; who have made us feel depressed, so black
in heart and spirit that we could scarcely live. And we
have known other human beings who have made us feel
as big as a mountain, as mighty as a steel pillar, and as
vast as an ocean; who have made us feel confident and
powerful so that we dared and ventured. "Ideas are born
in the arms of a sympathetic friend," said the Swiss his-
torian, I. Muller. "Man's best possession is a sympathetic
wife," said Euripides and I would add also a sympathetic
husband.

Like all human relationships, marriage is a living entity;
in it there are all the elements of life—love, hate, growth,
regression, the whole gamut of human emotions, enormous
warmth and admiration and the opposite, suspicion, jeal-

[7] Kurt Goldstein, *The Organism*, pp. 196–197, New York, American
Book Co., 1939. © Beacon Press.

ousy, hostility, irritation; a rankling sense of injustice, gratefulness beyond words, enormous need for the other, and also an equally enormous need to separate. It is a refuge and an arbor and also a fearsome, unendurable hell. It is never quiescent; like life, it is always in upheaval. It is as complex as man and what is more complex?

Marriage is an art, a high art. Since each person is unique and special, so each marriage is unique and special. Hence, there can be no rules for it, other than what Havelock Ellis calls the "golden rule," which he says is "always to give and never to demand." Even this rule—wise as all that Havelock Ellis says generally is—is not simple. How much and to what extent, I ask, should one give when one does not receive and there is no possibility of ever receiving?

Each couple must create its own marriage to meet its own unique life needs. A marriage ceremony does not make a marriage; it only gives legality and solemnity to the official start of a relationship. Sex in and of itself is not sufficient to bind two people for a lifetime. Even if it were at the beginning, which I doubt, we know that sex powers wane; and now with man living longer than ever, much beyond his most active sexual period, it requires much more to create a viable marriage. Marriage is a test of character. It is a task requiring all the ingenuity, the creativity, and patience of man. It is built, as Herman Keyserling so brilliantly pointed out, on pain, suffering, and disillusionment. It is the pain, the suffering, the self-sacrifice, Keyserling maintains, that forges the human being, brings out the best in him, makes him the good man. Further, the very nature of the relationship keeps the two taut and tense, highly sensitive to the other, and this sensitive intimacy only exacerbates all the imperfections in man, exacerbates his demands and disillusionment. If the marital relationship were flaccid and calm, it would lose all its heightened zest and excitement and make the relationship an ordinary one, not nearly resembling the permeating, mutual, powerful awareness. The suffering indigenous to marriage is necessary to make man kind and good.

Wrote Havelock Ellis:

Marriage, he [Keyserling] asserts, is really and properly a tragic affair. There is, in other words, a state of tension. That is its value. That is the way in which it brings us into touch with the world and initiates us into the mystery of life. If we may compare the union of two people in marriage, as is often done, to playing on a musical instrument, then it must always be remembered that there is no playing save on tightened strings.

The ideal of marriage presented by Keyserling may seem of rather an arduous and heroic character. But for how many people marriage is now arduous and heroic! All the while they are ostentatiously protesting how easy it is, how comfortable, how "happy." In time, perhaps, they will learn to be honest, and not always be pretending, even to themselves, that marriage is what it is not and never can be.[8]

Discussing Keyserling's contention that the "discipline of marriage," is "in it's very nature difficult, painful, even tragic," Havelock Ellis says:

When the marital bond was a rigid framework, not easy and sometimes impossible to break, the conjugal partners within it might flaunt their revolts and persecute each other in private with full confidence that they were running no risks of serious damage. Their discipline was imposed from without;

---

[8] Havelock Ellis, *Sex and Marriage*, p. 87, Pyramid Books Edition, 1957. © Random House.

but now it is imposed from within, by themselves, and that involves the assumption of much responsibility and the exercise of much art. It is not less binding because it is free. Most wholesomely constituted people desire, and will continue to desire, to have children; and they go on feeling that the best guardians of children are their parents living together in a permanent union. And when we put aside the question of children—for marriage nowadays does not rest merely on the fact of procreation—and consider only the facts of personality, a permanent union is still required for development. In a series of transitory unions no two people can really ever know each other and the possibilities each holds; they only take the first step on a road which beyond all others leads to the heart of life. To the career of Don Juan no goal of achievement is placed. And on the other hand, all development involves difficulty and pain. The ideal of an easy and comfortable existence of marital bliss, the "happy marriage" of which so much has been heard and so little has been known, even if it were possible (save for those simple folk who live in a kind of spiritual sty), would be a false ideal. It would not even be true to human nature, wherein indeed its chief falsity lies. Difficulty and pain, at least as much as ease and pleasure, are demanded by human instincts. Life has been full of difficulty and pain from the first; it has become organized for meeting difficulty and pain and in so doing to achieve its sublime conquests. When it ceases to do so, its function is gone and the stream of life ebbs away. So it is that in order to avoid the dangers of ease and comfort, it becomes necessary, when all other means fail, to climb the Himalayas and discover the Poles, to conquer the air and navigate the depths of the sea. Man thus achieves, beyond happiness, a further happiness which embraces suffering and gratifies his deepest instincts.[9]

It is indeed a horrible delusion that is popularly fed the public, namely, that marriage is a perpetual honeymoon. This fiction leads to horrible disillusionment. It is my belief that more harm has been done to even good marriages

---

[9] *Ibid,* pp. 86–87.

by the long honeymoon, where comparatively two strangers have to abide each other in idleness, feeding on themselves and boredom, day after day.[10]

Marriage is an achievement. The ceremony and the vows do not make a marriage. When two people enter on marriage, and there is nothing between them, then the relationship is nothing, whether with or without a ceremony. It is what happens in the relationship that matters. If the relationship enhances and enriches life, then the marriage has meaning and significance. Marriage, it cannot be repeated often enough, is an art and it requires patience, ingenuity, creativeness and a high form of emotional maturity for it to develop and to grow. It comes slowly and is built slowly over the years.

Nothing is so difficult as a human being, so hard to live with. Man gives to man his greatest misery and pain. The maintenance of marital love and deep involvement is no mean task and requires constant and persevering effort. But a good marriage is a magnificent achievement.[11] It is

---

[10] In *Sex and Marriage,* Havelock Ellis relates the story as told in "Les Amants de Toledo." After Torquemada, the Grand Inquisitor, has performed the marriage services for a young, devoted couple, he placed them as his gift into the Chamber of Happiness; and there after unclothing them, he strapped them together—of course, "by bands of perfumed leather"—for twenty-four hours. As they lay on their nuptial bed, they were at the beginning in great joy, grateful to their benefactor. When Torquemada, the Grand Inquisitor, came to release them, there emerged from the chamber two dejected and saddened youths. What was the outcome? Horrible! Thereafter for their entire married life, the story goes, they shied from any embrace for fear it would be as long-lasting. pp. 111–112, *Sex and Marriage.*

[11] Concerning his own marriage, D. H. Lawrence wrote to a friend: "For ourselves, Frieda and I have struggled through some bad times into a wonderful naked intimacy, all kindled with warmth, that I know at last is love. I think I ought not to blame women, as I have done, but myself, for taking my love to the wrong woman, before now. Let every man find, keep on trying till he finds, the woman who can take him and whose love he can take, then who will grumble about men or about

the very hardship of marriage, the demands that one learns to comply with, the self-sacrifice that is involved, willing but nevertheless there, that is, I believe, essential for the formation of the good person. That is why I believe that in this culture one cannot live a full life outside of marriage. Outside of marriage, it is hard, if not impossible, to become a good person. The bachelor is a marginal person. Every datum concerning the bachelor establishes this. He has a higher mortality rate, a higher criminal rate, a higher suicide rate, a higher rate of admittance into mental institutions. As a group, bachelors appear to be inferior in all ways. It might very well be because he has not been forged and molded by the stresses of marriage. Or it might very well be that from the first he realized his incapacity to cope with the difficult demands of a marriage.[12]

This view of marriage, as one which embraces pain and suffering, is set forth in an interesting manner by Oswald Schwartz. He writes:

Loving is a creative act, as we have seen, and therefore it holds all the bliss and all the suffering every productive man knows so well. Hardly ever, if at all, is the created work an adequate presentation of its idea. Similarly, love is a yearning which cannot be satiated because it is an everlasting desire. This sense of inadequacy, this despair of one's ability, is the cause, or at least one cause, of the suffering which seems to be inherent in true love. For this we have the testimony of a few women who ought to know. Thus Mademoiselle de

women. But the thing must be two-sided. At any rate, and whatever happens, I do love, and I am loved. I have given and I have taken—and that is eternal. Oh, if only people could marry properly; I believe in marriage." D. H. Lawrence, *Selected Letters*, p. 42, Penguin Books, 1954.

[12] I have deliberately omitted spinsters. In our culture, nearly every man who wishes can marry, women, unfortunately, cannot.

Lespinasse wrote to a friend: "I love you as one ought to love —in despair." And Mariana Alcoforado, the famous Portuguese nun and one of the greatest of lovers, wrote to her lover: "I thank you from the bottom of my heart for the despair into which you have thrown me. Farewell: love me and make me suffer still more." But there is still another aspect of this problem: not, as the theologians and philosophers maintain, the purpose of suffering, but its actual effect, is a great opening-up of our spiritual and emotional sensitiveness, an unlocking of hitherto inaccessible spheres of life. In Kierkegaard's words: "Despair is one of the maladies of which it can be said that it is the greatest misfortune not to have known it," because "the awareness of the spirit can never be achieved but through despair." . . . Love and despair, joy and pain, are co-ordinated experiences, and both of them enhance our personality—if there is a personality capable of being enhanced—and not a lack of personality which only makes for bitterness and resentment.[13]

When Oliver Wendell Holmes was appointed justice of the Supreme Court, President Theodore Roosevelt asked Mrs. Holmes what she thought of the people she was meeting in Washington. She said in effect: "I see here successful people who had married wives when they were not successful."

I have stressed the need in a marriage for sharing and giving, and it might be inferred that I seek the merging of two persons into a sort of a glorified combined single *one*. That would be farthest from my thought. It is mandated for each of us to form his own person and to find his own meaning and purpose in life. Each person is an end in himself and should never be used for purposes other than his own. When a person is used as a means, no matter how laudable, then his own life is diminished, and

---

[13] Oswald Schwartz, *The Psychology of Sex*, pp. 106–107, Penguin Books, 1958.

he is prevented from fulfilling himself. Says Oswald Schwartz: ". . . by belonging to someone else we belong to the world at large, far from losing individuality we find it for the first time. For 'whoever will save his life must lose it'."[14]

Erich Fromm puts it this way: "In contrast to symbiotic union, mature *love is union under the condition of preserving one's integrity,* one's individuality. *Love is an active power in man;* a power which breaks through the wall which separates man from his fellow men, which unites him with others; love makes him overcome the sense of isolation and separateness, yet it permits him to be himself, to retain his integrity. In love the paradox occurs that two beings become one and yet remain two."[15] At another point, he says: "In this act of loving, of giving myself, in the act of penetrating the other person, I find myself, I discover myself, I discover us both, I discover man."[16]

Frustrated people, unhappy people are permeated with bitterness and hostility; they need giving to and cannot give. Marriages proceed best when there is giving and taking by equals, by peers, and for that you need good, strong actualizing people; the healthier and the stronger they are, the more richly and sensitively they can give. From this standpoint, there is never possession, but peers giving from independent choice and decision.

It is the giving in the sense described by Fromm:

"Some make a virtue out of giving in the sense of sacrifice. They feel that just because it is painful to give, one *should* give; the virtue of giving to them lies in the very

14 *Ibid*, p. 80.
15 Erich Fromm, *The Art of Loving*, pp. 20–21, N. Y. Harper & Row, 1962.
16 *Ibid*, p. 31.

act of acceptance of the sacrifice. For them, the norm that it is better to give than to receive means that it is better to suffer deprivation than to experience joy. For the productive character, giving has an entirely different meaning. Giving is the highest expression of potency. In the very act of giving, I experience my strength, my wealth, my power. This experience of heightened vitality and potency fills me with joy. I experience myself as over-flowing, spending, alive, hence as joyous. Giving is more joyous than receiving, not because it is a deprivation, but because in the act of giving lies the expression of my aliveness."[17]

The fawning, weak, dependent person becomes a nuisance. The more the person becomes a self-actualizing, fulfilled person the better he can relate to another person, and the richer and the more meaningful and growing can the relationship become. It is through such a relationship that we achieve best our own person.

Marriage as here conceived is a high art, a grand adventure; the stakes are high, the good life itself. Marriage is not an easy task. It is an achievement. In the good marriage, there is no placidity, but a ferment, an unsatiated need, as deep and cavernous and unsatisfied as man himself. If it is a good relationship, it is taut, never still, demanding—as nothing else in life—the whole person. It is never static. The relationship goes forward or backward. It cannot be taken for granted. It demands the best there is in a human being. And because it demands so much it brings forth from the human being so much. In it, there is no finality, no end, and if it is a good marriage, there is a sense of continuous growth and development of the person and deepening of the relationship.

---

[17] Erick Fromm, *The Art of Loving*, p. 23, N. Y., Harper & Row, 1962.

You may say, "I want happiness, not a task." But where in life is there happiness to be found and once found forever had? Man finds happiness not in self but outside of self, as a concomitant of rich, creative living. The surest way to lose happiness is to seek it directly. It is a byproduct. The pain and the agony of living cannot be bypassed by man. But in the pain and the agony man forges his life and his happiness. So it is in marriage. Marriage represents the most profound and stirring form of living, the most intimate and the most trying. And from it we acquire the byproduct, if lucky, of happiness.

Man is bottomless. No one can plumb his full depths. He is that profound, mysterious, intricate. Getting to know oneself is a life-long task. Each act, each expression of thought, is revealing of the person. In a good marriage, where there is increased understanding, each of the other, where there is increased sensitivity, each of the other, this knowledge becomes cumulative; and this growing awareness and sensitivity goes on unendingly, till death, for man can never be fully plumbed.

How can such a relationship become stale and boring? In such a relationship, there is the grand adventure of ever growing, of ever becoming, of ever further discovery of the "I" in the presence of an appreciative and sympathetic "thou." The story is told of Michelangelo, nearly ninety, blind and frail, who begged to be led to pieces of sculpture, and as he caressed the work with his sensitive fingers, he said: "I still learn! I still learn!" So in a good marriage one ever learns.

There was a young man, it is said, who kept pestering John Dewey, asking: "What is the purpose of your philosophy?"

The young man persisted in asking and, finally, Dewey

told the young man to sit down and when he did, he said: "The purpose of my philosophy is to climb a mountain."

"To climb a mountain?" questioned the young man, somewhat surprised.

"Yes, to climb a mountain."

"And when you get to the top?"

"You'll see another mountain," said Dewey.

"And then?"

"You'll climb that," said Dewey.

"And then?"

"You'll see another mountain," said Dewey.

"And then?"

"You'll climb that," said John Dewey.

"And what will happen when there will be no more mountains?"

"When you see no more mountains," said John Dewey, "it will be time to die!"

The hope is that the married couple will climb many mountains together, and from the new vantage ground, they will see new views, new vistas and new mountains, ever and always.

35

SEX WITHOUT A PERSONAL RELATIONSHIP

EARLY IN MY CLINICAL PRACTICE I LEARNED WHAT LITTLE meaning there was in the sex act if in it there was not an emotional, interpersonal involvement. How often have patients come to me after a loveless sexual experience and said, to me, disappointed, befuddled: "Is that all there is to it?" Or "It was disgusting and I couldn't get away fast enough." Or "I was so ashamed of myself." I have recounted how a patient proposed to his wife. He had picked up a girl and was having sex with her, and in the midst of coitus, he got out of bed, phoned her, and proposed marriage to her.

There is no society other than ours, I believe, where there is so much talk of sex, where it permeates the society, saturates it, where soap, cigarettes, automobiles, and toothpaste are sold through sex, and yet where there is so little understanding of what sex is and what it can mean. "I find that Venus, after all," said Montaigne, "is nothing more than the pleasure of discharging our vessels, just as nature renders pleasurable the discharge from other parts." I know when necessary urination and defecation give relief but certainly it does not exalt.

322

If the sexual act is purely a physical act of relief, then it is a pretty nothing thing. If in the sex act there is no love or caring, it depletes the person and drains him. After physical satisfaction, there is generally such a let down, such a sense of depression and disgust, that the two cannot separate fast enough.

I do know there are those who will contradict and say otherwise. I suppose there are crude animal-like men—I use the word generically—who have sex like an animal. After they are through, they walk away and have no further need for the partner, no need for personal involvement. There are such, I suppose, but I don't believe there are many such.

To the extent that sex represents involvement and affection for another it has meaning. If any rule holds true in sex, it is only by giving that we receive. It is the lover who gives sexual pleasure to his beloved who experiences the most satisfying and deepest satisfaction. The taking is in the giving. One-sided, selfish sex, impersonal and without attachment, is drab and dreary.

Even in the animal world, it is believed there is a sense of let-down and depression after the completion of sexual intercourse. Dr. Eustace Chesser maintains that all animals after coitus become sad (*post coitus omne animal triste*).[1] From my clinical experience, I would say that what appears to happen to animals also happens to many human beings when the sexual act represents merely physical relief, not a caring personal relationship. Under such circumstances, the desire for separation from and leaving the partner may become so pressing that one can scarcely make a polite exit. "In true love," said Stendhal, "it is

---

[1] Eustace Chesser, p. xvi, in foreword to "Eros at Bay," by Charlotte Köhn-Behrens, London: Putnam, 1962.

the soul that enfolds the body." When there is no love, merely a body enfolds another body.

How an affectionate relationship can vitalize a person and give his life meaning and ennoble him, even under the most degrading circumstances, comes from a strange source—Dr. Viktor E. Frankl, an Austrian psychiatrist, who spent three years in Auschwitz and other concentration camps. To retell the horror of Nazi concentration camps is to go over familiar ground, but yet how else can one appreciate the uplift and strength that reside in the spiritual union of a marital pair unless, in this instance, it is seen in juxaposition to the depraved, sadistic environment in which it took place? In recounting his experiences, Dr. Frankl tells how in his camp the dying prison inmate, even while his body was still warm, was denuded by other inmates of clothes, shoes, other possessions, and how his watery bowl of soup was eagerly gobbled by one lucky enough to seize it; how servile, fawning inmates ingratiated themselves with their persecutors and became brutal and bullying, in many instances worse than their overseers; how he and the other inmates slept on tiers of boards, six and a half to eight feet, nine men to a board, with one blanket normally meant for two among them; how they would sleep squeezed together on one side, close fitting like tightly packed sardines; and if one coughed or snored, there was no way for any to wiggle around for comfort or relief; how they were flogged; and when they fell, stood up and were flogged some more.

In this degrading environment, Dr. Frankl was able to sustain himself, his sense of worth and dignity, by the memory of another human being, his wife. In poetic language, he relates how the thought of her filled him with a sense of beauty, peace and goodness; how it gave strength and meaning to his life. I set this down to suggest how uplifting and beneficent a relationship can be if it reflects profound affection and spiritual union.

I am quoting below two passages from Dr. Frankl's book, *Man's Search for Meaning.*

"Can't you hurry up, you pigs?" Soon we had resumed the previous day's positions in the ditch. The frozen ground cracked under the point of the pickaxes and sparks flew. . . . The men were silent, their brains numb.

My mind still clung to the image of my wife. A thought crossed my mind: I didn't even know if she were still alive. I knew only one thing—which I have learned well by now: Love goes very far beyond the physical person of the beloved. It finds its deepest meaning in his spiritual being, his inner self. Whether or not he is actually present, whether or not he is still alive at all, ceases somehow to be of importance.

I did not know whether my wife was alive, and I had no means of finding out . . . (during all my prison life there was no outgoing or incoming mail); but at that moment it ceased to matter. There was no need for me to know; nothing could touch the strength of my love, my thoughts, and the image of my beloved. Had I known then that my wife was dead, I thought that I would still have given myself, undisturbed by that knowledge, to the contemplation of her image, and that my mental conversation with her would have been just as vivid and just as satisfying. "Set me like a seal upon thy heart, love is as strong as death."[2]

Here is the second passage:

Another time we were at work in a trench. The dawn was gray around us; gray was the sky above; gray the snow in the pale light of dawn; gray the rags in which my fellow prisoners were clad, and gray their faces. I was again con-

---

[2] Viktor E. Frankl, *Man's Search for Meaning,* pp. 61–62, N. Y. Washington Square Press, 1964.

versing silently with my wife, or perhaps I was struggling to
find the *reason* for my suffering, my slow dying. In a last
violent protest against hopelessness of imminent death, I
sensed my spirit piercing through the enveloping gloom. I
felt it transcend that hopeless, meaningless world, and from
somewhere I head the victorious "Yes" in answer to my question of the existence of an ultimate purpose. At that moment
a light was lit in a distant farmhouse, which stood on the
horizon as if painted, there. . . . For hours I stood hacking at
the icy ground. The guard passed by, insulting me, and once
again I communed with my beloved. More and more I felt
that she was present, that she was with me. I had the feeling
that I was able to touch her, able to stretch out my hand and
grasp hers. The feeling was very strong; she was there. Then
at that very moment, a bird flew down silently and perched
just in front of me, on the heap of soil which I had dug up
from the ditch, and looked steadily at me.[3]

❋   ❋   ❋

The lowest form of sex, in terms of a human relationship, is that rendered by a prostitute, who feigns passion.
Sex is her business and even in far earlier times, a more
dreary kind of sex is hard to envisage. Ferrante Pallavicino,
a Venetian, in the 1630's advised prostitutes as follows:

Let her go along with the humor of these people, and speak
as they wish, even though she holds them in scorn. Let her
expression be in general common ones, as my dear, my own
heart, my soul, I am dying, let us die together, and such like,
which will show a feigned sentiment, if not a true one. Let her
add panting and sighing, and the interrupting of her own
words, and other such gallantries, which will give her out to
be melting, to be swooning, to be totally consumed, whereas
in fact she is not even moved, but more as if she were made
of wood or of marble than of flesh. It is certain that the whore
cannot take pleasure in all comers. . . . She must nevertheless

---

[3] *Ibid,* pp. 63–64.

give pleasure through her words, if not her deeds, and let her put into operaton what she can, authenticating her words by closing her eyes, by abandoning herself as if lifeless, and by then rising up again in full strength with a vehement sigh as if she were panting in the oppression of extreme joy, though in fact she is reduced and languid. These lies can be singularly useful, although they are discredited by too common feigning, and often obtain little credence.[4]

Here is a London prostitute talking "shop," and her "shop talk" has all the earmarks of authenticity. It deals with how best to conduct her business.

There's some of them lies still as stones, they think it's more ladylike or something, but I say they don't know which side their bread's buttered. Listen, if you lie still the bloke may take half the night sweating away. But if you bash it about a bit he'll come all the quicker and get out and away and leave you in peace. Stupid to spin it out longer than you need, isn't it? I learned that from Margaret. Wonderful actress, that girl. . . . It was her I learned to grunt and groan from.

And another thing: when I'm with a client I always put the rubber on him very gentle, you know, stroking him and spinning it out as long as I can. "You ought to have been a nurse," they say. That's always what it makes them think of. And then with a bit of luck they come before they even get into me. When they do I look ever so loving and gentle and say "Traitor!" Well, I'm not paid just to be a bag, am I? I am paid to make them feel good. It's easy for me, so why not? That's how I see it.[5]

No great passion here. No deep personal involvement in such fraudulent sex.

---

[4] Wayland Young, *Eros Denied*, p. 127, quoted. N. Y., Grove Press, 1964.

[5] Wayland Young, *Eros Denied*, p. 128, N. Y. Grove Press, 1964.

Now we come to the floozie, the easy pick up, the bar habitute, the school "sex pot." They are not prostitutes. Sexual accommodation is not a business with them. They use sex as a bribe for a date; and they eternally hope for marriage. In their sex there is a kind of relationship, true, minimal, surface, of the moment, but still a relationship. In a brilliant, unique book, Dr. Lester A. Kirkendall describes such encounters. Wherever the letter "M" is mentioned it means Male and whenever the letter F is mentioned, it means female.

A professional football player is talking of "easy-to-be-had" female "camp followers." He judges that for the most part the girls are from 17 to 20 years old, of low intelligence, trying to break away from their homes. Let Dr. Kirkendall continue:

They (the girls) would ordinarily work, then get an apartment of their own and begin inviting men to come to their apartment. "They seemed to think it a big deal, but in terms of what they want it is actually getting them nowhere." M feels they are wanting an experience with a man which will lead him into marriage. They are using "sex as a bribe." However, men who meet women under these circumstances are interested in sex—not marriage. "Even sex every night gets old. You sort of get tired of that sort of thing." M thinks that "practically every woman has marriage in the back of her mind. You can't meet a woman like that who isn't trying to get married."

In one of the communities in which M's team played there was a large apartment house for girls, with two or three girls to each apartment. The existence of an apartment like this was well-known, and fellows exchanged information readily about their experiences there. As many fellows as girls would get together in one apartment. The girls would get dinner, they would spend the evening and later have intercourse. Nobody ever paid any attention to the use of contraceptives.

"There were so many guys going in and out of the apartments that they couldn't prove anything on you.[6]

Here are other cases of casual sex contacts as described by Dr. Kirkendall:

"F was a girl who was starved for affection if I ever saw one." M thinks this was what she was seeking in the relationship. She indicated as much while M was trying to talk her into intercourse. She wanted him to promise, if she agreed to go ahead, to return to see her, and M had to do this before he was able to secure her consent to intercourse.[7]

In the same vein, Dr. Kirkendall reports other such relationships:

M and a boy friend picked up two girls who were "just pigs" at a football game. "Both of them had put out before and everyone knew it. Both of them were doers." F "was the kind of a girl I'd be ashamed to be seen with in public."

The sexual experience was so poor that "it wasn't worth trying to take her out again." F, however, did try to be friendly with M by speaking to him on different occasions at school. One time she asked him if he would be her date at a girl-ask-boy dance. M refused. During her senior year she got to the point where "she would hardly speak to me, which was okay with me."

M had only one sexual relation with F. After this she wrote him several letters, and for a couple of months thereafter called his home on week ends to see if he was there. M asked his parents to tell her when she called that he would not be home that week end. M heard later that she was sent to the State School for delinquent girls, and that she also had an illegitimate child.

Though F was a girl who lived in the neighborhood, M

---

[6] Lester A. Kirkendall, *Premarital Intercourse and Interpersonal Relations,"* pp. 62–63, New York: Matrix Press, 1966.
[7] *Ibid.*

never attempted to see her again. This was probably because
he felt a little ashamed of his relationship with her. Also,
because "she was no raving beauty. She just didn't appeal to
me at all." As soon as M had finished intercourse with her,
"I wanted to get out of the room as soon as possible. I didn't
want to have anything to do with her." However, as he has
seen her afterward, "I have kind of nodded to her."[8]

Certainly no strong bond in this kind of sex to create
a lasting, permanent relationship of dignity. Instead what
emerges from Dr. Kirkendall's sketches is a sorry spectacle,
not at all glamorous or attractive. It is sad, shabby, and
depressing. We do not find in this promiscuity any evidence of carefree adventure. As a group these promiscuous girls feel unattractive and inferior, and they use sex
in payment for a date. Some, to preserve a shred of respectability, will beg a young man to say "I love you"
before they surrender. More pathetic is the girl who will
beg the boy: "Promise to see me again." For the most
part, such girls come from unloving homes, and they try to
snatch moments of false and fraudulent affection in brief
sexual encounters. What a sad and sorry lot! Summarizing studies made of sexually loose girls, Lawrence F.
Frank writes:

From clinical records there are indications that some of the
young girls who are involved in sex delinquencies and who
have venereal infections are individuals who have never accepted, indeed have rejected, the female and feminine role.
They are likely to be daughters from families where the mother
has been of little importance, receiving little or no respect
from her husband, often a cowed, submissive wife; moreover,
these girls have never enjoyed approval or admiration from
their fathers and so have never developed any feeling of being

---

[8] *Ibid*, pp. 64–65.

a woman with a sense of their own dignity or worth as a woman. Consequently they have no difficulty in playing the role of sex object, offering themselves freely to any casual male, calculatingly cool and deliberate. They have little sex interest and are passive if not frigid. To speak of them as victims of passion, or weak-willed individuals who could not resist sex temptation, is to misunderstand completely their conduct and their feelings. By exercising power over men, some are getting revenge for the years of humiliation they have suffered as girls under dominant fathers and contemptuous brothers.[9]

I remember a patient, a rather good-looking girl of twenty-two, who may be typical of such girls in many respects. Her sex life started with the abuse by a relative when she was about five or six, and then by her brother when she was older, and then by many others. In payment for a date, she would sleep with a man. There was one man who actually showed kindness to her; he was tender and showed an affection which she had never before experienced, and with him she insisted that they have a baby. As she said, "I never had anyone love me." She did have a baby, but marriage was impossible. The man was already married and had three children. She bore the illegitimate child alone and tried to rear him alone, but now her lot was worse. She was ostracized by the family. When she first entered therapy, she described herself as being "from the bottom of the barrel." She could not imagine that any man would want her for herself. In therapy, she began to perceive herself differently. She developed a measure of self-regard and self-respect. As a result of these changes, she wanted more from the sexual

---

[9] Frank, Lawrence K., *The Adolescent and the Family*, in National Society for the Study of Education, 43 Yearbook, Part I, Adolescence pp. 244–245.

relationship. She wanted sex to be an outgrowth of a worthy relationship. She objected to being used as a sex object to satisfy a male's needs. As a result, her phone was quiet; she had few dates and her life was lonely. One day she came to me irate and bitter. "Before I at least had sex and company but now I have nothing." My heart went out to her. How sad and hard life was for her!

Below you will find two aging bachelors talking, both in their forties. Both have "chased" around considerably; and both once regarded sleeping with as many women as possible as the main interest of their lives. At this point they are both lonely, frightened, scared of the future and of their atomistic living.

Let us start with Bachelor One, still handsome, but his hair has begun to gray. I do not notice his graying hair, but he is acutely and sensitively aware of it. When alone at night, he is in despair because, he says, it means the end of things. Dates are more difficult to get, and he fears his "dates" are less enamoured of him. "I still have sixteen women I can call," he says, "I do call them but this one is busy and the other one is busy. Then I begin to feel low that at my age I have to resort to such things. I can't make out with any of those I call. I go back to a woman I've seen off and on for about five years. Many times I have left her house saying I'll never see her again. We haven't seen each other for a long time. But tonight I'm desperate and I'm frightened. I pace the apartment like a caged lion. Finally, I call. She berates me, but I act my nicest. I convince her. I drive out and I practically force her into bed against her wishes. You can't imagine how cheap and low I feel afterwards. I wish she'd kick me out as she ought to. Once she threw a shoe at me. Why doesn't she do it now? I am ashamed—forcing sex on her. I'm not an animal. Oh, God, what has happened to me! At my age . . . chasing like this!

"Once I thought it was great. I'd look at a girl and then I'd wonder how long it would take me to get her to bed with me. It was wonderful then. But now! At my age! Gods! My mother has gone away on a vacation, and my friends invited me to their houses. They think I'm a gay bachelor and live a gay life. It is to laugh. I was very lonely one night and went for supper to a family I have known for years. It was a good meal and there were people there and there was good conversation. They have three bright children, one going to college. But the evening came to an end, and I left and I entered my dark, empty apartment and I was alone again. I couldn't sleep all night. That family has a life. What have I? What am I? A carbuncle."

"The wives of the families I know still try to match me up and they give me addresses. So I ask, 'How old is she?' and they tell me they're wonderful girls—teachers, social workers—they make good money. So I think, 'If they're so wonderful how come they're not married?' Oh, God, what will happen to me and where will it all end? I'm not young anymore. I'll soon be old and die.

"Not being tied up used to be wonderful once. The whole world was my oyster. I was smarter than they. I wouldn't be caught like the other guys, not me. I wouldn't be stuck with a woman and then have to support her and a family. I wanted a woman to have a good time with and then to lay her. But you know it's all different now.

"The other day my cousin invited me over for supper. They have a fine house and beautiful children. I'm the bachelor cousin. I myself could have children going to college. I spent a good evening with them. When I left that house and I drove from the suburbs back home again —again to that damn, lousy, empty house, and afterwards I had to lay in that damned bed alone, I got scared and frightened. You know, doctor, I was sweating all night. What's going to happen to me? The next morning I was so sick and nervous that I couldn't trust driving my car into the city to go to work. I'm frightened. What a low level of crap I have become! I'm just scared. All the others envy me. They think I live a gay, abandoned life." He laughed harshly and bitterly. In the laughter was grief, self-disgust, and despair. "You know, doctor, of all the sixteen names in my book there isn't one I'd be willing to marry."

Here is Bachelor Two, also in his forties. His adult life has been a series of affairs, one following another. Like all such vehicles for sexual outlets, they are precarious, and he had been without sex for eight months. At the moment, he was like an unsatisfied animal, sniffing around to satisfy his needs. Last night he had induced a woman to sleep with him and he was now in my office feeling sad and depressed.

"I wasn't attracted to the woman. She wasn't my kind and normally I wouldn't associate with her. But I've been so lonely lately that anyone would do. And she was there. I tried to make conversation but I wanted her in bed; I practically forced her into bed. We ate supper out and then I insisted that she come to my apartment. She wouldn't come, but I wouldn't have no for an answer. I was that insistent. In my apartment, I practically had to rape her. When I was through, I was ashamed. She wasn't a bad sort of girl but she wasn't for me. I'm ashamed. Now I feel worse than ever."

When he is not carrying on an affair, he is even worse off. Feeling weirdly alone in his shut in apartment, he experiences a ravenous need for sex, a terrible sense of being rejected by the world, of being inadequate and inferior, of life ebbing away into nothingness. When he is invited for an evening to a home, the end is invariably the same—he comes back to a dark and empty apartment, empty as he himself feels. It is true he has a book of addresses, but every single one of them has proved unsatisfactory in the crucial human need for an intimate relationship. Every single name in this book has had a past history, starting with high hopes and then disillusionment. When not in the midst of an active affair, in desperation, when terribly lonely at night, he turns the pages of his address book, embarrassed by his need, feeling cheap and tawdry; he starts calling up names for a date, getting one excuse, then another. If he makes no successful strike, the long, desolate evening faces him, as aimless and pointless as his life. If he obtains a date, he discovers anew what he already has learned: this girl, with or without sex, is not for him, and that it was an unpleasant evening, altogether unsatisfactory.

The older unmarried male is faced with the horrible existential confrontation: his aging, his isolation, his disintegration. In my experience, I have never found an older unmarried male who ever succeeded in carving out a meaningful life for himself beyond a preoccupation with sexual conquests. And the pursuit becomes and looks ever more ugly. The chase of sex objects in the elderly takes on a different hue than that of the young. The young person has time to squander and dreams to buoy him up. How cruel time is to all of us; how it takes time to prove that we are made of common clay and that we are weak and full of grief, and that we need succor and support merely to have the strength to live.

You may ask: Why don't they marry? None of the

patients I had—although they were lonely, miserable, admitting how aimless the whole "chase" is, although they spoke of wanting to marry—not a single one ever did. I believe one of the principal reasons is their inability to form a warm, giving, mature relationship. They want to be loved but they cannot love. They may have the capacity for a one-night, one-stand relationship, or a temporary affair, limited and restricted. But when it comes to a life-long commitment, the capacity to give without demanding, the devotion of the whole self, total and dedicated, with no escape clauses—that is not for them.

From all I have seen of bachelors, I find nothing to envy. The Bible tells us that "It is not good that the man be alone." How the legend arose that bachelors' lives are carefree and gay I cannot conceive. "A man may be cheerful and content in celibacy," said Southey, "but he should not think he can ever be happy; it is an unnatural state, and the best feelings of his nature are never called into play." The unmarried male is a marginal person, in all ways inferior to the married male. Wrote André Maurois: "Small groups of men and women have attempted to achieve happiness by means of promiscuous indulgence. . . . The mechanical repetition of sexual indulgence may help him momentarily to forget his despair, as does opium and whiskey, but he cuts himself off from all vivid sensation, perhaps the horror of life and approaching death, which so often goes with loose living. The libertine of the eighteenth century was bored by their feasts of sensuality and they made the sentimental Heloise their favorite reading."

Speaking of bachelors Thackery wrote: "It is better for you to pass an evening . . . in a lady's drawing room, even though the conversation is rather slow and you know the girl's songs by heart than in a club, tavern, or smoking room, or a pit of a theatre. All amusements of youth to which virtuous girls are not admitted, are, rely on it, deleterious in nature. All men who avoid female society have dull perceptions and are stupid, or have gross taste or revolt against what is pure. Your clubswaggerers who are sucking the butts of billiard cues all night call female society insipid. Sir, poetry is insipid to a yokel; beauty has no charms for a blind man; music does not please an unfortunate brute who does not know one tune from another.

"Our education makes us eminently selfish men in the world. We fight for ourselves, we push for ourselves, we cut the best slice of the joint at club dinners for ourselves; we yawn for ourselves and light our pipes, and say we won't go out: we prefer ourselves and our ease—and the great good that comes from a woman's society is, that he has to think of somebody besides himself—somebody to whom he is bound to be constantly attentive and respecful."

In nearly every measurable respect, the married man and woman stand out as more wholesome and better adjusted persons. For one, they live longer. Even widowers have a shorter life expectancy than those men who have wives who remain alive. The mortality figures are indeed striking: for bachelors, the rate is approximately 1,218 per 100,000 as against 875 for the married.[10] According to Thomas C. Desmond, the bachelor has a greater chance of ending his days in the poorhouse. He cites a study of inmates of old age homes and country poorhouses, and in them resided 23,000 married men and 82,000 unmarried men.

[10] Thomas C. Desmond, "The Plight of the Unmarried," *The American Mercury*, May, 1948.

Comparing the married and the unmarried in other respects, Desmond says: "For every married man in a mental institution, there are three bachelors, according to the U. S. Census Bureau tabulations. For every two married women in mental institutions, there are three spinsters. Government statisticians find that bachelors have a suicide rate 66 per cent higher than that for married females. A check of the inmates in our federal and state jails uncovers the fact that there are 67,000 bachelors behind bars, compared to only 18,000 married men. Unmarried women in prison outnumber married females 11,000 to 3,400."[11]

In all measurable ways the unmarried are inferior to the married.[12]

----

[11] *Ibid.*

[12] In an article, appearing in *Time* (September 15, 1967). "The Pleasures and Pain of the Single Life," the following passage is included:

. . . the unmarried in America are in many respects at a clear disadvantage. The single male who goes to the hospital stays there an average nine days longer than the married man—presumably because there is no one at home to take care of him during convalescence. The married man gets more out of life—in years, that is—because the single man tends to die earlier. A study at the Mental Research Institute of Berkeley, Calif., of men and women, nearly all of whom were 23 years old or more, found that the single male ranks highest in severe neurotic symptoms. Whether he is neurotic because he is single, or single because he is neurotic, is not clear. The study did find that the least unhappy person is the married person.

For business careers, singlehood has its liabilities. As Vance Packard reports in "The Pyramid Climbers:" "In general the bachelor is viewed with circumspection, especially if he is not well known to the people appraising him." If he is still in his 20s, the personnel manager worries whether he is too busy with his love life to devote full attention to his job. "The worst status of all is that of a bachelor beyond the age of 36. The investigators wonder why he isn't married. Is it because he isn't virile? Is he old-maidish? Can't he get along with people?" Maybe he can't. "Failure to marry in either sex is the consequence of a fear of it," says Psychiatrist Irving Bieber. "There is increasing recognition that bachelorhood is symptomatic of psychopathology and that even though women may yearn for a husband, home and family they withdraw from

I do not speak in the same vein of the spinster. Her problem is quite different. For the most part, she is willing to get married; many are worthy of marriage, and if married would make good wives. In a culture committed to a family life based on monogamy, there can be at the optimum only one marriage for each male. If there are 90 marriageable males and 100 marriageable females, 10 females can never achieve in our society their own husbands or their own families, no matter how worthy they may be.

During our colonial period, when there were many men and few women, marriage presented no problem for the woman; she was valuable, sought out and sought after. In new, unsettled areas of the world, males still predominate and women are esteemed and at a premium due to the fact that males are more daring and venture first. Under such conditions a woman can award her favor to the lucky competing male who succeeds in winning her consent to marriage.

For the same reason until recently the United States was a haven for unmarried women. Young, adventuresome males in great migration waves set out for these shores, leaving the womenfolk behind in the old world. As emigrants left Europe, making the lot of the native women

---

fulfilling their wishes because the anxiety they associate with marrying is more powerful than their desire for it.

In speaking of the loneliness of the single state, an unmarried woman writes in the same article:

The lack a single person feels most acutely is when he leaves his group to go off somewhere on a trip. It can occur in front of a castle, on the quiet deck of a boat going up the Rhine, or on any overlook anywhere, looking at a sunset. Faced with such a sight, the natural tendency is to want to turn to someone to say, "Isn't that beautiful!" and to enjoy it together. And when you turn, there isn't anyone there. ("The Pleasures and Pain of the Single Life," *Time*, September 15, 1967.)

more difficult maritally, the lot of the American woman correlatively improved. This imbalance of the sexes, where there were more males than females, was largely responsible for the enviable position held by women, for their being placed on a pedestal, for their being revered.

All this is a story of yesterday. The situation in the United States has radically changed. No longer are young males admitted to our shores with the old liberality. Between 1820 and 1920, about 40 million immigrants settled here; between 1931 and 1947, only a negligible dribble of about 900,000 entered. Our young women can no longer wait for an importuning male to plead for her hand; she now has to compete for a husband in the same fashion as the European woman.

The fact is that women are the hardier of the species and because of this there are normally more females than males. It is true that more males are born, but since males are the weaker sex, and they die off more rapidly, by age twenty both sexes are about equal, and then the imbalance begins, with males becoming fewer than females. Further, women suffer from another disadvantage. About 10 per cent of the males choose to remain single. This only aggravates an existing bad condition.[13]

Even though in many instances no fault of theirs, studies indicate that single women are not nearly as happy as those who are married. As a group, they are more neurotic; they have more problems; they are beset with

---

13 To illustrate the marked difference of the death rate between the sexes, the U. S. Census Bureau provides these figures: In 1940, 63,557 infant boys died as compared with 47,424 infant girls. In that year, the death rate for men was 12.5 per 1,000 as compared with 8.6 for women. In April, 1951, there were, according to preliminary report of the U. S. Census Bureau, 53,420,000 males and 57,354,000 females who were fourteen years of age and older.

difficulties. Our hostesses plan in terms of paired couples; our society is geared to the married couple. Despite its appearance of instability, the family and the home are still the base of our culture and mores; they are still the most fundamental and cherished of our institutions.

Any woman who does not marry cannot help but feel that she has failed in a most important aspect of living. She cannot help but feel that she is inadequate in some way; that she does not measure up; that no man has wanted her. Even if these feelings are not justified, the consciousness of failure clouds her life. Since the pressure of our society is such, it is inconceivable to me how any woman in our society and in our time can possibly manage to forge a full and adequate life outside of marriage.

The moral is simple: It is bad for a man to live without a woman; and also bad for a woman to live without a man. They were meant for each other—paired.

PART II

Observations About Sex

36

SEX AS COMMUNICATION

AS IS SPEECH, SEX IS A FORM OF COMMUNICATION. IT IS A bodily form of communication. When there is quarreling and bickering, we know that the sex of the couple is impaired. A male patient said to me: "I was all ready for sex, eager, and I could hardly wait to get to bed when that bitch of a wife starts an argument and gets me so angry that I was ready to puke at the thought of having to sleep next to her all night." A female patient, also commenting on a domestic argument, said: "He began to appear so mean that he became horribly repulsive. If he tried to touch me I would scream."

Warm, affectionate verbal communication is the best prelude to good sex. The sex act itself is the tenderest kind of communication known to man. When between the two there is verbal closeness, desire mounts. When there is verbal hostility, the two bodies want to draw apart. Sex is the consummation of the Greek myth, the two wanting to become one and reach a healing completeness. When communication stops, when hostility enters into the relationship, then the body cannot transmit love and affection. The whole person experiences sex, not the sex organs;

345

the latter are minor to the act. Impotence has many of the aspects of a stuttering person; one who out of fear or whatever else feels he cannot communicate successfully and then can't. If one feels that his partner is condemnatory, rejecting, making demands which he cannot fulfill, then the bodily communication, the sex of the pair, is impaired.

The best preparation for good sex is warm, close discourse. The worst preparation for the sex act is hostile discourse. In another context I have said that the most passionate love-making may result as the aftermath of a quarrel. This holds true when one or both of the participants experience a sense of guilt, for hostile man has a way of inflicting hurt even on those he cherishes and loves, and through the sex act he wants to show repentance and ask for absolution.

Because sex is a form of communication, it is altogether different in spirit and substance than a physical act; it has no connection with defecation and urination, purely physical acts. Sex is a human act, involving two communing people; and because it is a human and spiritual act, it is anything but simple. Since man himself is so mysterious and unplumbed, the act that brings two people so intimately and passionately together need never become routine or ordinary or mechanical. If the two involved are creative, ever growing, then the sex between them, too, penetrates ever deeper layers of feeling, understanding, and spiritual communion.

The tragedy is that for so many marriage represents completion and end, rather than the beginning of a novel, dual adventure. If there is dullness in the living, and life becomes repetitive and trivial, then sex, too, becomes that. Trivial, vapid living and communication makes for trivial, vapid sex. It is my belief that rich, creative growth can go on indefinitely, unendingly, so that the two in the marriage can become ever renewed and ever refreshed, ever more able to give each other strength. If the two in the marriage never stop growing, the married couple have variety in themselves, as endless, as mysterious, as fathomless as man himself.

37

GOOD AND BAD SEXUAL COMMUNICATION

DR. JOHN E. EICHENLAUB, IN HIS BOOK *The Marriage Art*, suggests that the sexual act is the result of the accumulation of good feelings and kindly deeds that a couple stores up preceding coitus. Every time, Dr. Eichenlaub says, that there is thoughtfulness—one to the other—sexual feelings are engendered, and eventually, when there is a sufficiency of it, it bursts out in the passionate act of sex. The sexual act, he suggests, it not something that occurs out of nothing; it occurs out of the accumulation of affection and marital concern.

When feelings that are communicated are hostile, denigrating, the sex of the marital pair becomes distorted, twisted and, yes, even destroyed.

I asked a patient: "When did you first become impotent?" His marriage had been deteriorating, and there had developed a great deal of hostility between the pair. "I was having intercourse with my wife," he said, "and I thought of an argument I had with her and I became angry and I couldn't complete the act. I hated her. And I have been frightened ever since." That was his first sexual impotency and it happened again and then **again**; and now he had a frightening problem.

As the stammerer lives in agony, so does the impotent male. Impotence comes in the main, I believe, from the terrible demands that the male places on himself to please the woman. You have to be close to an impotent male, listen to him, hear his agony and despair, feel his loss of self-esteem to appreciate what it means. If he has an irritable, demanding wife sleeping next to him, he—always conscious of his impotency and simultaneously wanting to please her—finds his agony mounting and his fears mounting, so that his very desire to please makes it impossible for him. *Fear of impotence is the principal cause of impotence.*

Dr. William Farber, a urologist, states it well: "What happens above a man's neck is vastly more important than what happens below the belt. The overriding difficulty with male sexual problems is that they tend to become self-perpetuating. The more a man frets about his capability, the more he cripples it. That's how 98% of all cases of impotence originate—in the mind."

Fear is debilitating. The fear of not being able to talk creates the stammerer. Try to become conscious of your breathing, the blinking of your eyes, your speech and then see in what trouble you are. In this connection, the story of the centipede comes to mind.

An onlooker engaged a centipede in conversation. "It is simply marvelous how you manage those feet of yours! The grace, the beauty, the rhythm!"

"I," said the centipede, not comprehending.

"The way those feet of yours undulate in such unison, such beauty! It is truly beautiful!"

"I," said the centipede in astonishment.

"How gracefully you sway those feet!"

"I," said the centipede, never realizing that his feet were moving in any particular way.

When the stranger departed, what happened to the poor centipede? His feet got tangled up, going this way and that way, and the poor centipede was immobilized; he remained in a heap, unable to move an inch.

This is very much the story of the great majority of impotent males.

To illustrate the importance of the relationship in the matter of sexual potency I shall cite three instances.

The marriage had gone bad. "When I am waiting for him in bed," his wife complained, "he is viewing television. When he is sure I am asleep, he joins me. He avoids me as if I had a disease." He is now talking: "I have no pleasure in sex. I work hard at it and I'm never able to satisfy my wife. She always makes me feel like a failure." When confronted with this statement, the wife said: "I never remember having an orgasm. I'm still young and I feel that my life is slipping away."

For the last two years, he had been impotent, or so he thought. In therapy, when the marital relationship improved and the wife became less demanding, in fact, made no demands, and became more appreciative of him sexually, he became potent.

This patient was deeply in love with his wife, but unfortunately it was one-sided. She did not love him. He told me how terrified he was at going any place with her. She would dance wildly and attract men and then get lost. When reunited, he would try to have passionate sex with her. She laughed at him and he failed, and the failure only added to his low self-esteem, his sense of misery.

He told how they were one night in a restaurant and she had been drinking heavily. She taunted him: "Oh, for a man! How I need a real man!" That night when they prepared for bed, he remained in the bathroom, fearful of approaching her, crying all night. Eventually, he was lucky enough to muster the strength to divorce her. After the divorce, unable to approach women he respected, in desperation he sought out prostitutes and with them, he was potent. That did not dissipate his fears about his impotency. "They're whores," he said. "Anyone can sleep with them." Two years after his divorce he fell in love with a woman he respected. They were in bed together naked but he did not attempt sex with her. "I was too frightened," he said. He eventually developed a sort of liaison with a loose woman, not exactly a prostitute but one who was free in granting her favors. She was divorced and had two children and she was much older than he. He resented her way of life; she was slovenly and a horrible housekeeper. With her he was potent. He even contemplated marrying her. "She's very good to me," he says. "I feel like a man with her. I can fuck her without any trouble." He described how after sex she kissed his genitals out of gratitude and how excited he became. "She's wonderful." He would have preferred the woman he admired, but he was scared of her and fearful that with her he would be impotent.

An actor was certain he was a homosexual. He did not like to be one. He had taken out several girls in the chorus and had been impotent with them. It got bruited about and this made him shy away from dating women or mixing with them. He met an older woman, a social worker; she was kind and admiring of him, and then this miracle happened to him. He attempted sex with her and was potent. He was so happy, so overjoyed that he married her. He thought she was the only woman in the world with whom he could have successful sex; that she represented his only chance of being a sexually adequate male. I wish I could report that the marriage proved a good one. It didn't. The marriage ended in divorce. In one respect it served its purpose; he overcame his impotence and his fear of impotence. When he became a patient of mine, he was nearly fifty. The presenting problem was not impotency. He was depressed, fearful of becoming an old, lonely, isolated man. He had had one affair after another, all unappetizing and pointless. His problem was centered around his inability to develop a deeply meaningful relationship.

Some of you may have seen *Tea and Sympathy*. As I remember the play, a young student at a prep school, to prove his virility, tried to have sex with a brash, hard local waitress and didn't succeed. His fellow students taunted and ridiculed him in a cruel way. His father, who had always wanted an athletic, robust son, came for a visit and aggravated the problem by showing his disgust of his shy, sensitive son. The young man was almost destroyed by the hostile and critical forces surrounding him. The master's wife felt kindly toward the young man and perhaps was drawn to him. There is a scene where the master's wife comes to the young man's room, where he had been isolating himself, and approaches him gently and lovingly. There the play ends, but the implications are that she allowed him to have successful sex with her. Whether the part left to inference was enacted on the stage or not, the belief that he probably could have successful sex with her is justified.

38

PLEASING ONE ANOTHER

THERE ARE NO RULES ABOUT SEX EXCEPT THIS: ONE PARTNER should try to give the maximum pleasure to the other. There is no right or wrong, only that both in the relationship should find it pleasurable, and that no harm is done to either of them or to anyone else. There was once a time when I believed that the sex act should end with the penis inside the vagina. I no longer believe it. If pregnancy is desired, then it becomes a practical matter, not a moral one. Whatever pleases and does no harm is right. If the man finds fellatio (the use of the mouth to the penis) stimulating and pleasurable, then it is right. If the woman finds cunnilinctus (the use of the mouth to the female genital organs) pleasurable, then it is right.

If there is love present—the desire to please the other and to give to the other the maximum pleasure—I can scarcely conceive under such circumstances how the act can become immoral. If there is no love present, if the partner becomes a sex object for selfish pleasure, I cannot conceive a sex act that is good. Again, we should remember that in the sex act there is nothing to offend the partner, so that it becomes for one a disgusting experience. I had a patient who could not tolerate the demand for fellatio on the part of her husband. "It disgusts me," she said. The marriage eventually dissolved. She later took up with a man and became his mistress. Interestingly enough, her new partner also demanded fellatio from her; and although it still disgusted her, she pleased him. If the two love one another, there is scarcely anything in the sex act that appears to be wrong.

Even an elementary knowledge of anthropology indicates that there is no right or wrong in the kind of sexual technique that two lovers use to satisfy each other. This is well illustrated by Julius Fast, who in his book *What You Should Know About Human Sexual Response*, writes succinctly but excellently as follows:

Masturbation, in both boys and girls, is allowed by Hottentot people in Africa, and by Polynesian island people. Polynesian islanders pay attention to little boys' genitalia, praising them, caressing them, and in general making the boys aware and proud of them.

Heterosexual play between children is permitted in some primitive cultures. The Carib Indians in South America, the Ainu people in Japan, the Arunta in Australia, the Masai in Africa, and in Polynesia and Trobrianders, all encourage sex play between boys and girls, even to the extent of sexual intercourse. Sometimes they invent ways that make conception unlikely, but not always. Indeed in some cultures a teen-age girl who has had a baby has an exceptionally good prospect for marriage. The would-be husband knows she can bear children. He's not taking a chance on a possibly infertile wife.

Even the manner in which sexual intercourse takes place is different in different cultures. Men and women in some cultures kiss, in other societies they find kissing distasteful. Some cultures are involved with elaborate foreplay including manipulation of the breasts which seem to be erogenous zones for them. In the Polynesian Islands, however, before the Europeans came women went with uncovered breasts as a matter of course. There was no mystery about the breasts,[1] and they were not involved in love-making. The Polynesian women experienced no erotic arousal from manipulation of this area, and they were amused by the European sailor's preoccupation with breasts.

Even in the position of love-making there is tremendous variation. The Trobianders of the Pacific Islands have intercourse with the man squatting. In Tikopia, some islands away, the man lies on top of the woman. Other Pacific Island people have intercourse in a standing position when it is inconvenient for them to lie down. Being "stood" in a tenement hallway when there is no other place available is not uncommon among teen-agers in our society. In some cultures the man and woman lie side by side. In one Australian primitive community the man customarily approaches the woman from behind.

Which of these positions is natural? Which did nature intend man to assume? Is there a natural way, a right or a wrong way?

In all probability there isn't. What nature may have intended has been so thoroughly influenced and changed by any particular civilization man finds himself in, that there is no "natural" outlet for sex, any more than there is a natural method for achieving the release of sexual tension, whether that method is masturbation, heterosexual coitus, or homosexual union.[2]

There is no right or wrong in any sexual technique outside of the moral demand that neither the participants nor anyone else is injured. Each should try to please the other; that should be the sole and only objective. In this way sex becomes a spiritual act.

---

[1] Pearl Buck in one of her books expressed surprise that the breast should prove such a sexual fetish in our society. In China, where she was reared, it had no sexual meaning at all.

[2] Julius Fast, *What You Should Know About Human Sexual Response*, pp. 10–12, N. Y.: Berkley Publishing Co., 1966.

It is not necessary that there be this number or that number of copulations a week. The important thing is that both are satisfied. I have had couples—very much in love, and both in the prime of life—who have had sex infrequently, perhaps not more than once in several months; and they both were content. It is when there is uneven demand in sex that trouble arises.

A couple, very much in love, still in their twenties, both in excellent health, had sex rarely—about twice a year. This bothered the wife very much. "When he touches me, I am all ready for him. I feel like a whore." Although there was this great disparity in sex needs, they carried on the greatest love affair I have ever witnessed. He was a mechanic, rather gruff, not polished, but when he saw his wife, he acted coy, shy and blushed, although they had been married twelve years and had three children. "Whenever my wife is any place, I see only her, no matter what other women are in the room. And I think: 'How lucky I am to have such a lovely and pretty wife'." She would listen, blushing like an adolescent, shy and worshipful in his presence. She would touch his hand gently as he spoke and say nothing. But to me she would say: "I'm so ashamed that I can't resist him when he touches me. I wish I could be shyer."

Although they had many troubles their marriage was healthy and strong and a powerful support to both of them.

Contrary to the nature of the male who needs an erect penis which cannot come at demand, the woman by her nature can always accommodate her husband. Writes Dr. Stafford-Clark:

Owing to the very nature of her anatomy, a woman can

permit intercouse even though she is in no way inclined for it, and not in the least interested in it. She can permit it physically while she is worrying about housekeeping or about children, or thinking of other things or even another person, with her mind perhaps loaded with anxious or even guilty preoccupations of which her husband or lover may know nothing. On the other hand, a man is very rarely able to do anything like this. He cannot command his own erection; it is something which happens to him when he is in a certain emotional frame of mind. Anything which prevents that frame of mind possessing him may prevent his erection. . . . Therefore in one sense the man is, so to speak, on trial in a sexual situation. It may be no good his protesting sincerely that he loves or desires his partner if he cannot produce the physical evidence by his condition. Yet the more he worries about a possible difficulty, the more likely it becomes that this difficulty will arise. And once it has arisen, the effect both upon him and his partner in terms of further guilt, anxiety and discouragement, may well reinforce the already unhappy situation which precipitated it."[3]

There are peculiar notions held by woman, I believe, more so than by men, about the proper place and time. There is no such thing. There is no reason why sex should be confined to the night. If it serves neurotic needs, it may take place before breakfast, after breakfast, and during lunch. But the wife ought to be ready to make her husband feel wanted. Unfortunately he cannot reciprocate because he cannot will an erect penis.

[3] David Stafford-Clark, "The Etiology and Treatment of Impotence," in the "The Practitioner," April, 1954, quoted in "Sex and Society" by Kenneth Walker and Peter Fletcher, p. 172, Penguin Books, 1958.

39

SEX AND SOCIETY

YOU WOULD THINK THAT THE TECHNIQUES OF THE SEX ACT
would come naturally and spontaneously. It doesn't at all.
In the lower animals sex does appear to come instinctively.
In the higher animals, among the primates, sexual techniques are not instinctive and they have to be learned.
Man, apes, monkeys reach success in the sex act after trial
and error, and it requires a high form of cooperation of
the mating pair. It is anything but a natural process. Professor Harlow's monkeys raised in isolation haven't the
faintest notion of how to go about cooperating in copulation and many have never succeeded in mating successfully.

In other societies where there is more frankness, openness, less restrictions and secrecy about sex, the learn-
ings necessary for the sex act come earlier and more
naturally. In some societies parents play with children's
genitals, examine and praise them and masturbate infants
to keep them pleasantly content. Samoa adolescents are
encouraged to mix heterosexually and to have intercourse.
In the small huts of some native villages children watch
their parents during coitus.

Margaret Mead, the anthropologist, tells of ". . . the Maori father who has offered his daughter to an honoured guest, only to have her churlishly refuse the guest her favours. The guest is then entitled by custom to fasten a log by a long vine, and, naming the log after the ungracious girl, to drag it about his host's village, heaping the most definite and vigorous abuse upon this dummy. Such a father, although his daughter's virginity may be preserved, will bow his head in shame."[1]

It was the custom in Teutonic countries at one time for marriageable girls to have trial nights when young men would call on her and then sleep with her. If the two were not amiable, they would separate and the girl would accept another night suitor. When asked by a fellow townsman about his daughter, the father proudly announced that she had begun to have trial nights. If pregnancy resulted, it was the automatic obligation of the child's father to marry the mother. To refuse would be unthinkable. The man would be ostracized by the townspeople, and if he persisted in refusing to marry the girl, he would be railroaded out of town.

Here are two native customs described, hardly conceivable in our culture. The one below is told by Captain James Cook, who witnessed the ceremony on the invitation of the Queen of Tahiti.

"A young man, nearly six feet high, performed the rites of Venus with a little girl about 11 or 12 years of age, before several of our people and a great number of natives, without the least sense of its being indecent or improper, but, as appeared, in perfect conformity to the custom of

---

[1] Margaret Mead, "Jealousy; Primitive and Civilized." In *Woman's Coming of Age: A Symposium,* Samuel Schmalhausen and V. F. Calverton, eds. New York: Liveright, 1931, p. 38.

the place. Among the spectators were several women of superior rank, who may properly be said to have assisted the ceremony; for they gave instructions to the girl how to perform her part, which, young as she was, she did not seem much to stand in need of."[2]

Here is an account of a marriage custom in the Marquesas Islands as described by L. F. Tautain, the French anthropologist:

"At a sign from the bridegroom, all the men present assembled, forming a queue, and each in turn passed before the bride, who, lying in a corner of the *paepae,* with her head on the bridegroom's knee received them all as husbands. The procession was headed by the oldest man and those of lowest birth, then came the great chiefs, and last of all the husband. . . . A newly married woman was sometimes half dead and obliged to keep to her bed for several days afterwards." What was the test of her desirability? This: ". . . the more men a bride had satisfied, the prouder she was."[3]

In societies where there is such openness about sex, the techniques of the act are learned early and naturally. But that is not to advocate the practice. It is only to explain why we have the problem. In nearly every society we know about, the illegitimate child is a cursed child; he bears a stigma; and he is denied what every child needs: full acceptance. If the illegitimate child is not born inferior, he becomes inferior because he bears the heavy burdens that go with illegitimacy.

Bronislaw Malinowski, the great anthropologist, writing about illegitimacy in various societies says:

---

2 Ruth and Edward Brecher, *An Analysis of Human Sexual Responses,* quoted, p. 49, N. Y.: The New American Library, 1966.
3 *Ibid.*

"In all human societies—however they might differ in the patterns of sexual morality, in the knowledge of embryology, and in their types of courtship—there is universally found what might be called the rule of legitimacy. By this I mean that in all human societies a girl is bidden to be married before she becomes pregnant. Pregnancy and childbirth on the part of an unmarried young woman are invariably regarded as a disgrace. Such is the case in all human societies concerning which we have any information. I know of no single instance in anthropological literature of a community where illegitimate children, that is children of unmarried girls, would enjoy the same social treatment and have the same social status as legitimate ones."[4]

So parents in our culture keep their daughter close, carefully guard her, caution her about men, how evil they can be and are; and consciously or unconsciously, the little girl and later the woman begins to think of the world as populated by horrible, evil men, ready to prey upon her if she does not exercise the greatest caution. We may regard this as old fashioned and silly, but even the sophisticated know that it is the woman who bears the child and on her rests the responsibility of rearing the child. In our culture, two parents, bound together in a permanent, stable relationship, living together in a strong, safe, secure home, are needed to rear a healthy child and a good person.

Sexual promiscuity, I am sure, is not the answer to our problem. I believe with Freud that suppression is the price

---

[4] Bronislaw Malinowski, "From Instinct to Sentiment," pp. 25–26, in *The Anatomy of Love,* ed. by A. M. Kirch, N. Y., Dell Publishing Co., 1960.

of civilization, at least our kind of civilization. Wrote Freud:

The injurious results of the deprivation of sexual enjoyment at the beginning manifest themselves in lack of full satisfaction when sexual desire is later given free rein in marriage. But, on the other hand, unrestrained sexual liberty from the beginning leads to no better results. It is easy to show that the value the mind sets on erotic needs instantly sinks as soon as satisfaction becomes readily obtainable. Some obstacle is necessary to swell the tide of the libido to its height; and at all periods of history, wherever natural barriers in the way of satisfaction have not sufficed, mankind has erected conventional ones in order to be able to enjoy love. This is true both of individuals and of nations. In times during which no obstacles to sexual satisfaction existed, such as, may be, during the decline of the civilizations of antiquity, love became worthless, life became empty, and strong reaction-formations were necessary before the indispensable emotional value of love could be recovered. In this context it may be stated that the ascetic tendency of Christianity had the effect of raising the psychical value of love in a way that heathen antiquity could never achieve; it developed greatest significance in the lives of ascetic monks, which were almost entirely occupied with struggles against libidinous temptation."[5]

Freud maintains that this suppression is essential if we are to maintain a civilization in which there is high striving and great achievement. He says:

So perhaps we must make up our minds to the idea that altogether it is not possible for the claims of the sexual instinct to be reconciled with the demands of culture, that in consequence of his cultural development renunciation and

[5] Freud, Sigmund, *Collected Papers, Volume IV* quoted in *The Anatomy of Love,* compiled by Aron Krich, Dell Publishing Co., 1960, pp. 160–161.

suffering, as well as the danger of his extinction at some far future time, are not to be eluded by the race of man. This gloomy prognosis rests, it is true, on the single conjecture that the lack of satisfaction accompanying culture is the necessary consequence of certain peculiarities developed by the sexual instinct under the pressure of culture. This very incapacity in the sexual instinct to yield full satisfaction as soon as it submits to the first demands of culture becomes the source, however, of the grandest cultural achievements, which are brought to birth by ever greater sublimation of the components of the sexual instinct. For what motive would induce man to put his sexual energy to other uses if by any disposal of it he could obtain fully satisfying pleasure? He would never let go of this pleasure and would make no further progress. It seems, therefore, that the irreconcilable antagonism between the demands of the two instincts—the sexual and the egoistic—have made man capable of ever greater achievements, though, it is true, under the continual menace of danger, such as that of the neuroses to which at the present time the weaker are succumbing.[6]

The mess we are in about sex, according to Freud, is inevitable; and there can be no way out if we want our civilization to continue to bring forth its wonders and triumphs. Although it may be inevitable, that does not minimize the problem. It presses on us and makes life hard.

[6] *Ibid*, p. 163.

40

SCARED OF SEX

THERE ARE MANY, MANY MEN AND MANY, MANY WOMEN who are frightened and scared of the sex act. Sexual frankness and spontaneity are fiercely suppressed in our society and the ignorance of even the simple mechanics of the act is widespread; and this is responsible for unbelievable mischief.

I have had patients describe their first night of marriage as one of disillusionment, tension, and sometimes horror. One told me of being in her negligee which she had so carefully bought for this occasion, wearing her most expensive perfume, and waiting in bed for her husband to join her, which he never did. He remained in the bathroom all night. I have had patients tell me of nightmarish experiences while their husbands tried to have sex with them and failed. In the early hours of the night a bride called me from her hotel room screaming hysterically that her husband was trying to attack her. A bridegroom, also on his so-called honeymoon, phoned in equal despair, saying he was frightened of intercourse.

A highly intelligent couple, both high school teachers, the wife a teacher of biology, came to a gynocologist very much worried since they had no children after four years of marriage. The examination revealed that the woman's hymen had not been broken and that during their entire married life, they could not have had any real, satisfying sexual relationship.

Drs. Hannah and Abraham Stone cite a similar instance. A couple had been married eleven months and they had been unsuccessful in completing the sexual act. This had created a great deal of irritations between them and they decided to seek professional help. "An examination disclosed that entry had not taken place and the wife was still a virgin. The difficulty was found to be due simply to a lack of understanding of the mechanics of sex intercourse. Neither of them had any knowledge, for example, of the positions to be assumed during the sex relation. When they attempted coitus, the wife would remain rigid and tense and lie with her thighs and legs fully extended, a position in which entry is hardly possible. She had no idea that it was necessary to bend or draw up and separate her knees. An explanation of the cause of their difficulty, and some instruction in sex anatomy and technique, helped solve their problem in a short time."[1]

What continually amazes me is the amount of male impotence I encounter in my practice. I am not talking of elderly people, who you might expect would have difficulty in this area, but of young, healthy, vigorous men, in the prime of life, young men in their twenties and their thirties. I would hazard the guess that in no species outside of man are so many healthy specimens so incapacitated for the sexual act. It is also amazing how vast is the ignorance in this area.

[1] Hannah and Abraham Stone, *A Marriage Manual*, p. 197, N. Y.: Simon & Schuster, 1952.

To be sexually potent all that is required, according to Dr. Kinsey, is an erect penis for a minute or two, for that is the time necessary once penetration is achieved to complete the act of coitus. Stekel maintained that few are able to go beyond five minutes; and no study that I know maintains that the act can be prolonged beyond 15 to 20 minutes at the most.

In what other species of life is there so much travail about sex? Even the supposed experts in the field are of little help. Dr. Harold Lief of the Tulane University Medical School made a study of medical students and interns, and he concluded that "physicians are more often inhibited about sex than others in the same social order," and that they shy away from discussing sex, marriage, and family. Admittedly an extreme instance, Dr. Lief cited two medical interns planning to marry, who declared that they had no notion of how to "proceed with the sex act."[2]

Sex permeates our society; it saturates it; we are obsessed with it, yet our ignorance concerning sex is truly beyond belief. In this repressed, restrained, secretive, sin-and-guilt-ridden sexual environment, it should not really surprise us that persons who talk so much about sex are ignorant of even the simple techniques of coitus. Our society is still weighed down, no matter how it professes otherwise, by Victorian attitudes toward sex, which regarded it as some base, vile, animal need. Decent people would have none of it; and since women are decent, they naturally would be repelled by it. William Action, an English physician and an authority on sex, less than a century ago, viewed any imputation that a decent woman would or could enjoy sex as a "vile aspersion" on her

---

[2] Leonard Gross, "Sex Differences Come of Age," *Look,* March 8, 1966.

character. Another medical authority insisted that if it does occur, it happens only "to lascivious women."[3] Since there were "vile men" who had the capacity to enjoy sex, women had to assume this awful burden, this self-abasement to appease the brutal animal in man.

Our girls are guarded and sheltered and cautioned against men. This is understandable. The illegitimate child, as we have noted, bears horrible scars and so does his mother. And it is the women who bear the children and who are left with them. After marriage, however, sexual prohibition is not necessary; it becomes a detriment. Unfortunately, the early attitudes of caution and fear of sex may stay on and the bride cannot cast out what has been implanted in her. Such a woman comes to the marriage bed with crippling sexual attitudes, so that she is ashamed of her sexual feelings and she cannot unashamedly abandon herself completely with full joy to her passion. If our society were not so reticent, did not surround sex with so much mystery, so much sin and guilt and shame, our people through open discussion could develop more intelligent attitudes to sex and what it fully implies.

I do not know whether our homes reflect the societal attitudes of secrecy, mystery, and shame, or whether they create these attitudes. The child learns to look sheepish when sex is mentioned at home. He learns his lesson early and well. One doesn't talk about such things or even appear to know about them. One learns about such things on the street and what one learns about such things on the street only confirms that sex is filthy and sinful. Also, unfortunately, what one learns on the street amounts to abysmal ignorance of the real meaning of sex.

---

[3] Havelock Ellis, *Psychology of Sex,* p. 75.

The problem originates from the shame taught, fostered, and developed in the home. It is essentially a grown-up problem, not a child or a youth problem. If the elders were honest and open, our youth and our adults would be able to come to more intelligent grips with the problem. I have faith in the human mind. By thinking, discussion, study, I have faith that we could reach solutions that would be wiser and more intelligent than our prevailing practices. By avoidance, by suppressing, we can never hope to come to grips with the reality that confronts us. Our only hope is to confront the situation realistically and intelligently. The suppression, the guilt, the shame attached to this healthy and desirable appetite, which is the source of life—the source of you, mother, father, sister, brother, aunt and uncle, cousin and niece, husband, wife, son, daughter and friend, the source of home and family—is not only indefensible but prevents the use of our intelligence to find wiser and better ways to manage this powerful and magnificent life force.

41

SEX AND THE FIRST YEARS OF MARRIAGE

UNFORTUNATELY, THERE HAS BEEN SO MUCH MISEDUCATION, so much unnecessary reticence and shyness, that couples, even those who are mature and intelligent, will suffer sexual distress and tensions for years and years of married life and not come to intelligent grips with the problem. In this regard, there is a great deal of ignorance as to the psychological and emotional nature of the act, and also a cultural reticence about learning sexual techniques.

The technique of sexual intercourse is a learned act, and if there is good will and frankness and openness of discussion the problem generally will be overcome. The misfortune, I believe, is the many legends that have been formed around the honeymoon period, and the effort of the newlyweds to meet this expectation. Sexual compatibility does not come naturally; it is learned by trial and error and by talking about the problem, not in accusation, but in love and sympathy. Even in the animal world, sex is a cooperative task for two. It may take as much as five years to reach a satisfactory sexual relationship.

A couple should not despair when they find little pleasure and much blundering during the early days of their marriage. At times, the hymen of the woman may be so strong that the male cannot penetrate. This is perfectly normal and natural. If the situation continues, professional help may be advisable. There is this danger: Because of a bad experience—the lack of love-making, or kindliness, or gentleness—the woman might thereafter regard sex as something ugly, something which offers her no pleasure, only pain. Patience, understanding, great affection, unselfishness—these are the traits on which to build a good sexual adjustment.

There have been instances where a marriage has been ruined because the man was impetuous and callous in his approach to his wife on the first night. "I felt as if I had been raped," one woman declared, in recounting her first night's experience. Runs a proverb. "The married woman is like a cake; woe to the glutton who wants to eat his cake at once."

Said Hawthorne: "Caresses, expression of one sort or another, are necessary to the life of the affection as leaves to the life of a tree. If they are wholly restrained, love will die at the roots." With all that, the sex act requires techniques that must be learned. Under the best of circumstances, trial and experimentation, aided by intelligence, honest and frank discussion, are necessary. It does not come about automatically. If after nine months or a year, a couple has not learned how to adjust sexually, they should not feel bitter and frustrated, but they should seek professional help.

If one is mature and intelligent and is willing to learn and experiment in working out the problem in a mutually satisfactory manner, one should not worry unnecessarily about the sexual aspects of marriage. But the problem should be faced, not ignored. "The art of love," said Havelock Ellis, "is the most neglected aspect of human life; man has not nearly developed the potential pleasures that can be obtained from it." And this striving of the couple to develop for themselves the richest and most satisfying kind of sex life should be a continuous process, and it should be the subject of frank and open discussions. The couple should overcome any notion that sex is sinful, neither should they be shy and reticent about it. It is a healthy, normal appetite, one that enriches life, and gives it zest and beauty.

As in other forms of personal relationships, sex proceeds best when there is the fullest communication. During the sex act, express your appreciation. "What a good lover you are!" "You are better than ever tonight." "Your skin is like silk." "From the moment I saw you I loved you and now I love you even more." "How kind you are to me!" "What enormous pleasure you give me!" Talk of your love. Communicate to your spouse what excites you sexually, what disgusts you, but always be appreciative of any kindness shown. Make your beloved feel strong and adequate as a lover. Unfortunately, there is so much reticence about sex that even those with good marital relationships avoid honest communication.

I have a feeling that because of our unhealthy attitudes toward sex we have not begun to exhaust its full potential for pleasure. In food, we are not content merely to satisfy our appetites. We do not crudely gobble up food. We are continually fussing with new recipes; we try out new dishes; we aim at a pretty setting; we seek an inviting background, with lovely dishes, music, beautiful table settings. All this adds to the joy and the delight of living.

What can be done with food can be done with sex, only

much more so. We are not nearly creative enough in sex. A couple should try to make their sex life an adventure. They should experiment and not permit the act to become stale from unimaginative repetition. How much more can be done to further the excitement of life when the couple become gourmets in sex! And why not? Is this not a legitimate appetite? And how powerful it is! If in speech one confined oneself to shibboleths and conventionalities, how dull would be the communication! Do not settle for the piddling in sex, try to seek new experiences. There are many books dealing with the subject, and I see no reason why they should not be read.

Try out new sexual approaches, tell each other what pleases, what doesn't. Adding to your sexual skills ought to be as pleasant and as satisfying as discovering a new food recipe that delights the palette. One has to be a clinical psychologist to know the ingrained reticence, the vast silences that prevail, even among couples having a good marriage, when it comes to a matter of frank sexual discussion. After a lifetime, few husbands and wives know or ever will know to what extent each has pleased the other; how each felt about the other as a sexual partner; to what extent they were pleased by their sexual life.

Don't settle in sex for mediocrity and unimaginative repetitiveness. One should seek to grow in the sexual capacity to delight and be delighted. There is much in this appetite that can delight.

And yet it cannot be repeated often enough that sex is a byproduct of the living personality, and that, by and large, two mature persons will manage to work out the problem in a mutually satisfactory manner. As the mature person can give maturely in other relationships, he can give maturely in the sexual relationship. Sex is the man. The considerate, sensitive man has kind, considerate, sensitive sex. The uncouth, crude, selfish man has uncouth, crude, selfish sex.

Dr. Donald Laird sent out a questionnaire to married persons listed in *Who's Who* asking about their marriages. Of those who appeared to have discord in their marriage, the problem of sexual adjustment was way down the list as the cause. Professor Terman in his study on marriage also found that there was a low correlation between the frequency of copulation and marital compatibility. It seems that unsatisfactory sex relations are most frequently the result of a bad marriage and not the cause of it. If the couple is happy, their sexual relations generally will be satisfactory; if their marriage is not satisfactory, then their sexual relations generally aren't. Professor Terman states it this way: ". . . there is ground for believing that the sex satisfactions are less the cause of happiness than its results. Couples who are psychologically well-mated show a surprising tolerance for the things that are not entirely satisfactory in their sexual relationships. The psychologically ill-mated show no such tolerance but are prone to exaggerate the amount of sexual incompatibility that may be present. Analysis of the sexual complaints expressed by the less-selected group of 792 couples points clearly to the conclusion that sexual complaints are often just a convenient peg on which to hang the psychological discontent."[1]

This study confirms the position so strongly insisted upon by Alfred Adler. Although couples seeking divorce will emphasize sexual incompatibility, this is only the surface manifestation of deeper difficulties. Write Ogburn

---

[1] L. M. Terman and Melita Oden *The Gifted Child Grows Up*, p. 251.

and Nimkoff: "Sexual maladjustments of an organic nature are rare. Burgess and Cottrell report that 'with the majority of couples, sexual adjustment in marriage appears to be a resultant not so much of biological factors as of psychogenetic development and of cultural conditioning of attitudes toward sex.' A somewhat similar position is taken by Levy and by Harriet Mowrer, who see the sexual side of marriage as largely a matter of personality adjustment between two individuals. According to his view, personality is regarded as generally the most crucial single factor in marital adjustment."[2]

[2] William F. Ogburn and Meyer F. Nimkoff, *Sociology*, p. 723–724, N. Y.: Houghton Mifflin Co., 1940.

PART III

The Family as an Institution

The Family as an Institution

I don't know whether this portion belongs in the book. It discusses home and family as an institution. It takes us somewhat afield. It is an intellectual discussion, that is, it comes from the mind. In the main, hitherto, I have tried to convey my feelings about human beings in a marriage. What follows will not be in the same vein. Yet somehow— I do not know precisely how and why—I believe it does belong. The kind of marriage as I have envisioned it is democratic, equalitarian, companionate, based primarily on affection of the two. It is a brand new kind of marriage, never experienced before in the world.

In the familiar, traditional marriage of old, each married person entered a manufacturing household. He or she was valued as to how he or she was able to produce in the household; how he or she contributed to the economy of the household. In the household, cloth was woven, clothing sewed, soap made, wheat grown, flour ground, bread baked, leather treated, fuel gathered, heat maintained, food grown, cattle raised, the home built, defects repaired, furniture made, the sick members nursed with home remedies.

It was also a social and entertaining unit—for young, for old, for the neighborhood. There were no restaurants, no phonographs, no records, no movies, no radios, no television sets, no automobiles, no professional sports, no canned foods, no prepared foods, no surplus money for vacations, or trips abroad, no traveling for pleasure. The home was the center of life and living; within it life was created, within it one grew, within it one found and did his work, within it one entertained each other, friends, the neighborhood, within it one found a meaning and a philosophy of life. The home was the fount of life and living. Marriage of old was meant for this life.

We have become an urban people. Although the substance is no longer there, many of the forms and the attributes of this old kind of marriage linger on as vestigal remains, although meant for other times, other purposes and another kind of life, never to return. Our marriages in outlook, philosophy, and purpose have to change to accommodate to the life of an urban society.

Change always come hard, and at times this shift from the old to the new appears chaotic. "When external authority is rejected," said John Dewey, "that does not follow that all authority should be rejected, but that there is a need to search for a more effective source of authority." In the interim, while new and better ways are groped for, there is tension and difficulty and cries of despair.

Our marital institution is undergoing a transition, a period of profound change in philosophy and attitude that is so far-reaching and fundamental that the old forms and the old ways no longer suffice to hold the institution firm and solid. While this new form of marriage is emerging, the old kind of marriage seems unstable and chaotic; but one should not be fooled by this outward appearance. Marriage, it should be reiterated, is fundamental to the human species; it is omnipresent; it will not die out. While new conventions and new ways take form to build the modern marriage, it is inevitable that there should be groping, false moves, some chaos; but we can rest assured that the new form of marriage, more in conformity with our needs and with the changes that have occurred in our industrial and social life, will emerge and bring about better marriages, for it will serve man better and it will be more in conformity with reality. Because the old concept of marriage has been so firmly rooted, and because it had in it so many traditions and customs and taboos, the shaking loose of this institution from old, moribund ways is responsible for the appearance of upheaval and collapse.

The new kind of marriage that will eventually emerge will be stronger and better. It will be more in conformity with reality and the world that is, not yesterday's world, and not a world that exists in fiction and in legend. Such a new kind of relationship, rooted in current living, will represent the best adjustment in terms of our present knowledge, our present insights, our present morality. This is a rapidly changing, dynamic world, and these changes affect everyone in his way of life. To meet these changes, institutions, if they are to serve the people, must

*also change; and the institution of marriage must also
change, and it is now in the process of change.*

We can say that the fairly stabilized marriage took form
about 10,000 years ago when man learned how to domesti-
cate animals and how to plant food for his needs.[1] This
made it possible for him to live in a fairly fixed abode. In
our own colonial period, the household was a manufacturing and farming unit; it made its own clothes, grew its
own food, raised its own cattle or hunted for its meat, built
its own home. The word economy originally applied to the
family household. In such a household economy, a husband and a wife were a necessary and essential pair; each
was essential to the well-being of the other; they supple-
mented one another and they strengthened one another.
The Book of Proverbs describes the ideal wife, and in the
agricultural household of old for what better wifely virtues
can one ask?

Who can find a virtuous woman? for her price is far above
rubies. . .
She seeketh wool, and flax, and worketh willingly with her
hands.
She is like the merchants' ships; she bringeth her food from
afar.
She riseth also while it is yet night, and giveth meat to her
household, and a portion to her maidens.
She considereth a field, and buyeth it: with the fruit of her
hands she planteth a vineyard.
She girdeth her loins with strength, and strengtheneth her
arms.
She perceiveth that her merchandise is good: her candle
goeth not out by night.

---

[1] The Annals of the American Academy of Political and Social Science,
November, 1950, footnote 53.

She layeth her hands to the spindle, and her hands hold the distaff.

She stretcheth out her hand to the poor; yea, she reacheth forth her hands to the needy.

She is not afraid of the snow for her household: for all her household are clothed with scarlet.

She maketh herself coverings of tapestry; her clothing is silk and purple.

Her husband is known at the gates, when he sitteth among the elders of the land.

She maketh fine linen and selleth it; and delivereth girdles unto the merchant.

Strength and honor are her clothing; and she shall rejoice in time to come.

She openeth her mouth with wisdom; and in her tongue is the law of kindness.

She looketh well to the ways of her household, and eateth not the bread of idleness.

Her children arise up, and call her blessed; her husband also, and he praiseth her. . .[2]

The children in the household were also assets; they contributed their work, and there were never-ending tasks to do. The needs of life created its own natural cohesive forces; the family stayed together through necessity and need; they were an integrated unit, and it was a calamity for this natural unit to drift apart. This domestic economy produced strong and stable marriages.

Along came industrialization, and with it factories and urban living. Urban living weakens the family. Even at present, the divorce rate is considerably higher in urban areas than in rural areas. With industrialization and specialization, the home takes on a different character. The husband works away from home, and increasingly so the

---

[2] *Sociology*, Ogburn, William F. and Nimkoff, Meyer F., pp. 711–12, Houghton Mifflin Co. 1940.

wives. Each person becomes an individual entity. In the modern city apartment, the home is no longer a manufacturing or even a social unit. Impersonal forces supply the needs of the individual. Food is brought from the grocery, bread from the baker, clothes from a store. The home is rented, and the care and the repair of the home are the responsibility of the landlord. Even amusement is bought, whether in the form of professional theatricals or athletic spectacles or in the form of gadgets, radio, television, and the like.

Furthermore, even the large social group has no fixed cohesion, for urban areas are characterized by constant shift and movement, so that neighbor does not know neighbor. This too has a disintegrating effort on the family. When conscious that their neighbors' eyes are upon them, the husband and the wife and even the children are more circumspect in their behavior; they are ashamed to do things which they would normally do if assured anonymity. One should not underestimate the power exercised by neighbors who peep behind curtains to check up on what is going on in making us do what is conventionally fitting and proper.

This commercial, money-centered urban living creates what sociologists call "atomistic" families; each individual is an end in himself; even the children go out and make their own friends and find their pleasures outside the family circle. Hence, the forces of urban life tend to draw the family apart. The emphasis centers on material things and pleasures. Each of the members of the household is bombarded with a plethora of things to buy, all sorts and every conceivable kind of gadget. And, unfortunately, the very prestige of the household and of the individual members of the family are tied up with the costliness and the luxuriousness of these gadgets. Hence, it should not surprise us that money becomes an important factor in the marital happiness of a family. It has been estimated that about forty per cent of the divorces have been caused by financial discord. In fact, many urban marriages are contracted not because of love or affection but because of prestige, whether in terms of money or family or position. Along with the emphasis on "conspicuous consumption," urban life creates financial uncertainty and instability. The costliness of city apartments, added to the fact that children become a luxury and a responsibility, causes urban birth rates to drop markedly. In fact, a city could not survive by its own birth rate, if it did not draw on an agricultural hinterland, where the birth rate is high enough to provide a surplus.

Although it is highly questionable whether childless marriages are as happy and satisfactory (Professor Donald Laird maintained that the greater the number of children, the less the real happiness of the parents), the fact that more childless couples end up in divorce courts is not subject to dispute. In 1945, for instance, 71 per cent of childless marriages ended in divorce, against 8 per cent for couples with children. Furthermore, the city creates a hedonistic attitude toward life. It tends to make people less religious; it tends to make people seek individual pleasures; it tends to make them think in terms of self-interest. And since the city sets the style, this attitude tends to spread even into the rural areas. And the United States is increasingly an urban society, with the majority of its people living in cities, and the trend is still strongly upward. In an urban society, the stress is on individualism. Since the women are increasingly gaining economic emancipation, they no longer need to tolerate what they feel to be unfair and unjust treatment. Also, the city creates tensions of its own; people have to live closer together, they are more crowded; because of anonymity, immorality and anti-social conduct can thrive.

But perhaps even more important is the lessening of the religious hold on people generally, and the emphasis on individualism and personal satisfaction. Both the man and the woman demand that from the marital relationship they obtain personal satisfaction and pleasure. This is a comparatively new thing in our civilization. In India, the girl is married by her parents before she is even conscious of her own sexual and social needs and wishes. It is done deliberately, for to Hindus, any marriage based on passion or personal pleasure is wicked and sinful. The purpose of marriage is to create children and to perpetuate male offspring; and in this family, several generations may live together as one. For here, the emphasis is on the family and the bearing and rearing of children to perpetuate this institution. Here the emphasis is not on personal pleasure, but on duty and service to the family. The wife looks up to and respects her husband because he is a *husband,* she respects his role.[3] Several extracts will be quoted from Tagore to illustrate this attitude.

"There is a particular age," points out Tagore, "at which this attraction between the sexes reaches its height; so if marriage is to be regulated according to the social will, it must be finished with before such age. Hence the Indian custom of early marriage.[4] ". . . Scientific feeding with specially cultivated fodder-crops only could yield the best

[3] Rabindranath Tagore, in *The Book of Marriage,* pp. 98–122, edited by Count Hermann Keyserling, New York, copyright, 1926 by Harcourt, Brace & Co.
[4] *Ibid.,* p. 112.

results. This must have been the lines of argument, in regard to married love, pursued in our country. For the purpose of marriage, spontaneous love is unreliable; its proper cultivation should yield the best results—such was the conclusion—and this cultivation should begin before marriage. Therefore, from their earliest years, the husband as an ideal is held up before our girls, in verse and story, through ceremonials and worship. When at length they get their husband, he is to them not a person but a principle, like loyalty, patriotism, or such other abstractions which owe their strength to the fact that the best part of them is our own creation and therefore part of our inner being."[5]

In pre-revolutionary China, essentially the same attitudes toward marriage prevailed. It was the household that was important. And the household was part of the religious structure of the nation. The wife left her home, completely severing herself from it, and worshipped at the shrine of her husband's male ancestors. Several generations lived in the same household, and the wife and her children, as well as her husband, became part of this tribal unit. Each had a function and a place in the hierarchy of things.

Says Richard Wilhelm: ". . . marriage (in China) does not lead to a separate family being set up. The woman becomes a member of her husband's family, and it is her duty to maintain, tend, and see to its continuance. She takes part in the filial duties of her husband. As son, he has in the first place to serve his father, while she as daughter-in-law has to serve her mother-in-law. She becomes a member of the clan's household, and her relationship to her mother-in-law is much more important than that to her husband. If she bears sons, she has fulfilled her

_____
[5] *Ibid.*, p. 113.

principal duty and attains a position of esteem. Barrenness is the main reason for divorce, i.e., for returning her to her family. In wealthy families, this expedient is seldom resorted to, if the relationship is otherwise happy, for it is the woman's prerogative to give her husband one or more female servants, whose children then look up to her, his principal wife, as mother."[6]

Our own customs and traditions about marriage have come down to us mainly from the Roman patriarchial system. It was the old virile Roman family, before its decadence, that the Christian church sought, with modifications, to set up as an ideal. The Roman law regarded the family as a unit, and its power was lodged completely and absolutely in the male head. His authority over his wife and children was unlimited; and it was sanctioned almost by divine authority, granted to him by his household Gods and his ancestors. For misdeeds, he could banish his children, sell them into slavery, sign them over for adoption in another family, and even put them to death. All their earnings belonged to him; he had complete power to choose their mates, and in this respect rank and property were the most important considerations, not romance or affection. As for his wife, here too his control was absolute. He could divorce her at will or sell her into slavery. This absolute power ceased only with his death, and then the sons inherited it; and they could then, as the head of their own households, carry on in the same tradition.[7] The daughters always occupied a lowly and

---

[6] Richard Wilhelm, "The Chinese Conception of Marriage," p. 127, in *The Book of Marriage,* edited by Count Herman Keyserling, © Harcourt, Brace & Co.

[7] Hutton Webster, *Early European History,* pp. 144–145, New York: D. C. Heath and Co., 1917.

servile position, and nothing could emancipate them from that role. The emphasis was on obedience and subservience to the lord of the household.

With the growth of Christianity, the old form of patriarchal marriage was stressed, only the position of the woman was glorified and elevated. However, the power of the head of the household was still regarded as considerable and formidable. It was this type of family relationship that held sway until the advent of the industrial revolution, say 200 years ago.

A passage written by a clergyman, cited in an article, "The Concept of Family Stability," by Ray H. Abrams, protrayed the role of the ideal wife.

"The family is ordained by God, and organized much on the plan of divine government . . . the ordained head of the house is responsible for the exercise of authority which God has invested in him. In a certain sense he represents God there. . . . A prevailing sentiment may revolt against it, but it stands in the Scriptures as an injunction of God—'Wives, submit yourselves to your own husbands in the Lord,' 'be in subjection, be obedient to your own husbands.' . . . The true wife, the Christian wife will not rebel against the unqualified utterance of the injunction, when she thinks of the submission of the Church to Christ, of which her submission to her husband was designed to be a type—not a slavish or reluctant submission, but a cheerful obedience, which is the highest expression of love."[8]

In the spirit of Roman marital tradition, the New York State marriage certificate of 1848 contained this injunction: "Wives submit yourself unto your own husband as

---

[8] Passage quoted in "The Concept of Family Stability," by Ray H. Abrams, *The Annals of the American Academy of Political and Social Science*, November, 1950.

unto the Lord." In Russia, it was a custom for the bride during the marriage ceremony to kiss her husband's feet. The French achieved this symbolic obeisance more delicately. The bride dropped her marriage ring and then fell to her knees to retrieve it.

How different is our present concept of marriage. Here the emphasis has turned from duty to personal happiness. The members are bound, not primarily by economic necessity or by religious mandate, but because it is better that man and woman should live together; it is better for them in marriage to bear and to rear children. The emphasis is on affection, on mutual respect, on the give and the take of living. Our present marriage stresses individualism, individual well-being, individual happiness, individual affections. There has been a marked drift away from the semi-patriarchal relationship that stressed duty, religious sanction, personal denial, and female subservience. It is a democratic relationship, with the stress on respect for personality and the equality of the sexes. It is a relationship that not only elevates the woman but also elevates the man. By enthroning the personality of each of the partners, by recognizing the sanctity of each person, the modern marriage when successful is an exciting adventure. For here two human beings can help and support one another in the normal trials and vicissitudes of life; and can become entwined and cemented in an unsurpassed amalgam of love and respect. "We know," said John Milton, "that it is not the joining of another human body which will prevent loneliness but the uniting of another compatible mind."

This modern companionable, democratic marriage presents problems. It is new and untried. Each marriage be-

comes an adventure of two human beings trying to forge
a good life for themselves. Because of its novelty, because
it stresses affection and companionship, not duty and
tradition and custom, it must inevitably have in it a large
measure of groping and experimentation. Each couple
must find their satisfaction in their own way, depending
on their interests, their values, and their demands from
life. It is a marriage based on activity and on living; and
on a man and woman both facing the world together,
working together, playing together, entertaining together,
taking counsel one from the other. For here, it cannot be
repeated sufficiently, each person is enthroned; and they
both are joined in common partnership, not out of duty,
religion or economic necessity, but out of affection and
mutual respect. Each experience becomes a common bond
to strengthen the marriage, and to provide a rich store of
memories.

Because companionable, democratic marriage enthrones
the individual and personal happiness, because it is not
moored as strongly as the old to custom and tradition, it
is inevitable that many men and women should expect
and demand and want from marriage things that cannot
be possibly gotten from marriage; it is inevitable that
many, not held in leash by the old conventions, will floun-
der and make spectacles of themselves with the new. As
John Dewey so frequently pointed out, when the log-jam
of old traditions begins to break, there occurs a chaotic
period when the old controls do not operate and the new
ones are not yet strong enough to hold. Said Professor
Ellwood: "The problem before our civilization is whether
such a democratic ethical type of family can become
generalized and offer a stable family life to our whole
population. It is evident that in order to do this there must

be a considerable development, not only of the spirit of equality, but even more, a considerable development of social intelligence and ethical character in the minds of the people. To construct a stable family life of this character, however, which is apparently the only type which will meet the demands of modern civilization—is not an impossibility, but is a delicate and difficult task which will require all the resources of the state, the school, and the church. There is, however, no ground as yet for pessimism regarding the future of our family life; rather all its instability and demoralization of the present are simply incidents, we must believe, to the achievement of a higher type of the family than the world has yet seen. Such a higher type, however, will not come without thought and effort or without wise social leadership."[9]

Both man and woman need each other; they supplement each other; and they were made for each other. The present travail and the disorganization of marriage are only the birth pangs of something new and better. How can we have anything but faith and confidence that the union of man and woman, socially and sexually, is permanent and lasting and will remain, and that whatever problems this union may face will be worked out, and that in the end there will emerge a form of marriage more in conformity with reality and a changing world?

Statistically, our marital institution gives every appearance of cracking up. Never a nation that has been noted for its enduring marriages, the United States as far back as 1885 had the questionable distinction of having more divorces than the total of all the rest of the Christian

---

[9] Charles E. Ellwood, *Sociology and Modern Social Problems*, p. 48. New York: American Book Co., 1919.

nations in the world.[10] Between the years 1940–1948, about 3,620,000 divorces were granted—equal to the number granted in the previous eighteen years. Commenting on this situation, John McPartland writes: "Our country . . . has a much higher divorce rate than similar cultures. Before the war, we had about twelve times as high a divorce rate as Great Britain, more than twice as much as Canada, three times higher than that of France. The war multiplied divorces in every country involved, but we increased our relative lead. We do not have the highest divorce rate in the world—the Levantine countries (Egypt, Palestine) have that distinction."[11] At present we have the highest divorce rate in the Western world. Professor Carle C. Zimmerman of Harvard University envisions the gloomiest prospects. ". . . unless some unforeseen renaissance occurs," he says, "the family system will continue headlong its present trend toward nihilism."[12] Maintaining that the health of the family is an index of the health of Western civilization, Professor Zimmerman compares our present marital impasse with that of ancient Greece and Rome. The western family, he declares, collapsed once in Greece in 300 B.C. and another time in Rome in 300 A.D., and in both instances, the civilization of the two countries simultaneously collapsed with it. In Rome, during its decline, marriage became a temporary and transitory affair. Divorce was a simple matter and could be obtained for trivial reasons. "Among certain classes in Roman society," writes Professor Ellwood, "the instability of the family became so great that we find Seneca saying

---

10 *Ibid*, p. 48.
11 John McPartland, *Sex in Our Changing World*, p. 99.
12 Carle C. Zimmerman, *Family and Civilization*, p. 808, N. Y.: Harper & Bros., 1947.

that there were women who reckoned their years by their husbands, and Juvenal recording one woman as having eight husbands in five years.[13]

Although the outward façade of the marital structure may look wobbly, on closer study the institution is sounder and healthier than its appearance. Our people are marrying in larger proportions and at earlier ages. In nearly all cultures studied by anthropologists, no matter how primitive and no matter where found on this globe, marriage is regarded as a fundamental, crucial, and pivotal institution. Commenting on marriage in other cultures, Dr. George P. Murdock, professor of anthropology at Yale University, says: "Nearly as universal are prohibitions of adultery. A very large majority of all known societies permit relatively free sexual experimentation before marriage in their youth of both sexes, but this license is withdrawn when they enter into matrimony. In a world-wide sample of 250 societies, only five—a mere 2 per cent of the total—were found to condone adulterous extramarital liaisons. In many of the remaining 98 per cent, to be sure, the ideal of marital fidelity is more honored in the breach than in the observance."[14]

Sexual monogamy after marriage—although not before—is still the prevailing pattern of family life among the majority of the peoples that inhabit our universe. The late Professor Ellwood regarded monogamy as the normal sexual relationship of the human species. The monogamous family, he argued, has been better able to take care of its youth, better able to preserve and feed them; and hence, in the process of survival, the monogamous strains have

[13] Ellwood, p. 138.
[14] George Peter Murdock, "Family Stability in Non-European Cultures," *The Annals of the American Academy of Political and Social Science,* November, 1950, Volume 272.

flourished, increased and conquered promiscuous or polygamous tribes.

Furthermore, he pointed out, the sexes are about evenly balanced, and hence, if the human species preferred polygamy, there would not have been sufficient females to make this arrangement widespread. Even in the few areas where polygamy has social and religious sanction, only a small proportion maintain more than one wife, since the cost is prohibitive. ". . . consider," says Dr. Ellwood, "the family life of the anthropoid or manlike apes—man's nearest cousins in the animal world. All of those apes, of which the chief representatives are the gorilla, orangutang, and the chimpanzee, live in relatively permanent family groups, usually monogamous. These family groups are quite human in many of their characteristics, such as the care which the male parent gives to the mother and her offspring, and the seeming affection which exists between all members of the group. Such a group of parents and offspring among the higher apes is, moreover, a relatively permanent affair, children of different ages being frequently found along with their parents in such groups. So far as the evidence of animals next to man, therefore, goes, there is no reason for supposing that the human family life sprang from confused or promiscuous sex relations in which no permanent union between male and female parent existed. On the contrary, there is every reason to believe, as Westermarck says, that human family life is an inheritance from man's apelike progenitor."[16]

Despite travail that the institution is undergoing, surveys indicate that from 75 to 85 per cent of the marriages are good. Dr. Katherine B. Davis asked this question, in

---

[16] Charles A. Ellwood, *op. cit.*, p. 100.

the course of her study on "Factors in the Sex Life of 2,200 Women": "Is your married life a happy one?" The answer: 872 out of 988 women answered unequivocally in the affirmative; and only 116 qualified their answers, saying that it was partially or totally unhappy. Dr. G. V. Hamilton made a study of the marriages of 100 married men and 100 married women. Of them, he asked: "Do you wish to go on living with your (spouse) because you love him (or her)?" Here too the response was overwhelmingly favorable, 78 men and 75 women answered "Yes" or "That is the only reason," and only 11 men and 16 women answered with an unequivocal "No," while the others qualified their answers. He asked another question: "If by some miracle you could press a button and find that you had never been married to your husband (or wife) would you press that button?" Seventy-four men (8 qualified) and 72 women (8 qualified) answered that they would not press the button; 18 men (3 qualified) and 14 women (2 qualified) answered that they would. He asked still another question, a rather pivotal one. "Knowing what you now know, would you wish to marry if you were unmarried?" The response was "yes" from 82 men (5 qualified) and 84 women (10 qualified); while 11 men (4 qualified) and 8 women (2 qualified) answered negatively.[17]

Lewis Terman and Melita Oden asked this question of 800 persons selected for their high intelligence. "If you had your life to live over again, would you marry the same person?" Answering yes were 82.7 per cent of the husbands and 86.1 per cent of the wives; 10.1 per cent of the

---

17 Studies summarized in *The Sexual Side of Marriage*, by M. J. Exner, pp. 3–4. New York: Pocket Books, 1948.

husbands and 3.5 per cent of the wives said they would
not marry at all.[18] In another study of 526 couples by
Burgess and Cottrell, 74 per cent described themselves
as "very happy" or "happy" with their marriage, and 8
per cent described themselves as "very unhappy" and 14
per cent as "unhappy," while 4 per cent had middling or
"average" feelings about their marriage.[19] Dr. Lester
Kirkendall, professor of family life, Oregon State University, a student of the subject for about forty years,
maintains that at any given moment, 75 per cent of married people would say they are happy with their marriage.

A recent survey, conducted under the supervision of
Elmo Roper, roughly confirmed this percentage. "Over
half of the married Americans—52% of them—say that they
are 'very happy' in their marriages, and another 25% say
that they are 'moderately happy.' Only 5% say they are
'not very happy.' "[20]

The evidence indicates that in no other relationship but
marriage can two human beings live together so closely,
so intimately, and for so long—and so well.

Marriage has its troubles and its woes, more sometimes
than man can bear. Wrote Robert Bridges:

When first we met we did not guess
  That Love would prove so hard a master.

[18] L. M. Terman and Melita Oden, *The Gifted Child Grows Up*, pp.
243–244.
[19] Ernest W. Burgess and Leonard S. Cottrell, Jr., *Predicting Success
or Failure in Marriage*, p. 34. New York: Prentice-Hall, 1939. In their
study of marital happiness, the only child seemed to have the most
trouble in their marriages. Alfred Adler has contended that the pampered
child would be more apt to have marital difficulty, and the study appears to corroborate Adler.
[20] Sandford Brown, "May I Ask You a Few Questions About Love?",
Post Dec. 31, 1966–January 7, 1967.

In his play, *The Days Between,* Robert Anderson makes his character, Ted Sears, speak of his marriage:

> Eight, nine years ago, Meg and I stood at opposite ends of a room and screamed at each other, yelled at each other our misery, our disillusion . . . cried like children for our lost world. But for us . . . there was no meddling visitor out over the barn . . . and in time, thank God, we managed to . . . crawl to each other. What you saw was not our marriage, but a kind of re-marriage out of the ashes of our illusions . . . I take you for what you are. I will cherish you for what you are, your complexity . . . excluding nothing this time, ugliness, meanness, hate. . . . We could even say, when she knew she was going to die . . . she could even say, "I hate you because you are going on living." And I could say, "I hate you because you are dying and leaving me alone."

Marriage—and the things that go with marriage—are strong and sturdy institutions. Wherever man is, no matter what period of time or what part of the universe, if man is there, then he will marry and form his family and they will live together for better and for worse. Said Frost: "Home is the place where, when you have to go there, they have to take you in." Man needs such a refuge, a place where he can go, and where he has to be taken in. "In the last Götterdämmerung which science and over-foolish statesmanship are preparing for us," said Ralph Linton, "the last man will spend his last hours searching for his wife and child."

NAME INDEX

398   *Name Index*

Duke of Windsor, 139
Duncan, Isadora, 66
Duse, Eleanora, 66

Eastman, Max, 179, 180
Eddington, A. A., 308
Eichenlaub, John E., 348, 349
Ellis, Havelock, 17, 61, 153, 312,
    313, 314, 315, 367, 371
Ellwood, Charles, 388, 389, 390,
    391, 392
Emerson, Ralph Waldo, 62, 167,
    179, 291
Erickson, Erik H., 177, 278, 279
Euripides, 311
Exner, M. J., 393

Farber, William, 349, 350
Fast, Julius, 354, 355
Fine, Benjamin, 257, 258
Fishman, Jack, 9, 298, 299, 300,
    301, 302, 303
Fitzgerald, Scott, 239
Fletcher, Peter, 36, 48, 357
Foote, Arthur, 180
France, Anatole, 19
Frank, Lawrence, F., 330, 331
Frankl, Viktor E., 10, 309, 324,
    325, 326
Franklin, Benjamin, 7
Freud, Sigmund, 83, 135, 143, 153,
    158, 281, 362, 363
Fromm, Ehrich, 21, 83, 172, 318,
    319
Fromme, Allan, 251, 252
Frost, 395
Fry, Margery, 143

Galileo, 172
Gaub, Jerome, 131
Gide, Andre, 172
Goethe, 292, 309
Goldstein, Kurt, 10, 310
Goodman, Philip, 239
Griffin, Jane, 274
Gross, Leonard, 253, 254, 255,
    256, 366

Hamilton, G. V., 393
Hammarskjold, Dag, 25
Hansell, 140
Harlow, Harry F., 146, 147
Haveman, Ernest, 9, 52, 53
Hawthorne, Nathaniel, 370
Hazlitt, William, 108
Hegel, 40
Heloise, 336
Helps, Arthur, 265
Hemingway, Ernest, 165, 239
Herzog, Elizabeth, 9, 17, 111, 112,
    283
Hitler, Adolph, 176
Holmes, Oliver Wendell, 317
Holmes (Mrs.), 317
Horney, Karen, 59
Hunt, Morton M., 9, 40
Huxley, Julian, 9, 152

Jaffe, Jerome H., 184
James, William, 99, 130, 133
Jelliffee, 257
Johnson, Samuel, 166
Johnson, Virginia E., 148, 149
Joyce, James, 239

Kanin, Garson, 134
Keyserling, Hermann, 43, 312,
    313, 383
Khyyam, Omar, 172
Kierkegaard, 317
Kilpatrick, William Heard, 21, 309
King Louis XV, 34
Kinsey, Dr. Alfred, 51, 250, 251,
    366
Kirkendall, Lester A., 328, 329,
    330, 394
Kohn-Behrens, Charlotte, 323

Laird, Donald, 373, 382
Lawrence, D. H., 10, 123, 124,
    125, 179, 315, 316
Lawrence, Frieda, 10, 315, 316
Levy, 374
Lewin, 100
Lewis, Sinclair, 238, 239

SUBJECT INDEX

Kinsey study, 250–251

Listening in marriage, 193–195
and Mabel Dodge Luhan, 179–180
and marriage, 158–159, 162–163, 185–187
and self-development, 177–178
and students, 159–162
and therapeutic effects of, 160, 171–174
and the therapist, 178–179
and understanding, 185–187
Loneliness and man, 19
and our society, 21–25
Love and happiness, 304–306, 313, 316–317, 320
Lovers, 25
and closeness, 38–40
and D. H. Lawrence, 123–125
and self-absorption, 120–121

Man's need for man, 20–26
Marital relationships
and Rogers, 8
and the middle class, 5–7
and the Talmud, 35
destruction of, 5–7
in bad marriages, 28–30
in good marriages, 30–34
Marriage
and Adler, 74, 44–47
and ambition and beauty, 63–67
and bad marriage, 68–69, 131
and children, 94–96
and closeness, 38–40
and communication, 231–232, 236
and coping with differences, 207–236
and desire to maintain, 5, 70, 158, 162–163
and disturbed priorities, 101–107
and divorce, 247–248, 250, 256
and emotional maturity, 257–272

and family, 94–97
and free, open communication, 199–206
and growth and creativity, 304
and individual differences, 152–157
and infantilism, 81–88
and isolation, 21–22
and lack of communication, 231–232
and learning to accommodate to differences, 197–206
and listening, 172–177
and not listening, 188–196
and middle class, 6, 7
and reform of the spouse, 54–57
and romance, 58–59, 272
and social class, 75
and spouses' parents, 96–98
and teen-age marriages, 251–256
and variations in degree of acceptance, 156–167
as seen in fiction, 51–52
as test of character, 313–317, 395
as therapy, 20, 25–26, 68–70, 185–187
Carl Rogers and, 117–120
characteristics of good, 20
communication, 112–126
communication of feelings in, 55
comparison—Greek and American, 21–22
compatibility and sex, 373–374
competitiveness in, 23–24
degree of apparent success in, 393–394
democratic relationship, 387–389
denigration in, 31–33
deteriorating, 121–126
difficulties — illustrations, 217–223
disagreements in, 50
disastrous outcomes of reform in, 54–55

Not taken out